WHEN CHRISTIANS WERE JEWS

Also by Paula Fredriksen

Augustine on Romans: Propositions from the Epistle to the Romans, Unfinished Commentary on the Epistle to the Romans (1982)

From Jesus to Christ: The Origins of the New Testament Images of Jesus (1988; second edition, 2000)

Jesus of Nazareth, King of the Jews: A Jewish Life and the Emergence of Christianity (1999)

Augustine and the Jews: A Christian Defense of Jews and Judaism (2010)

Sin: The Early History of an Idea (2012)

Paul: The Pagans' Apostle (2017)

Edited Volumes

Jesus, Judaism, and Christian Anti-Judaism: Reading the New Testament after the Holocaust, with Adele Reinhartz (2002)

On "The Passion of the Christ": Exploring the Issues Raised by the Controversial Movie (2004)

Krister among the Jews and Gentiles: An Appreciation of the Life and Work of Krister Stendahl, with Jesper Svartvik (2018)

When Christians Were Jews

The First Generation

Paula Fredriksen

Yale
UNIVERSITY
PRESS
New Haven & London

Published with assistance from the Louis Stern Memorial Fund.

Set in Electra type by IDS Infotech, Ltd.
Printed in the United States of America.

Library of Congress Control Number: 2018937826
ISBN 978-0-300-19051-9 (hardcover : alk. paper)

A catalogue record for this book is available from the British Library.

This paper meets the requirements of ANSI/NISO Z39.48-1992 (Permanence of Paper).

10 9 8 7 6 5 4 3 2 1

For Yishai and Lulu,
for Shayna and Leah—
the next generation.

Pray for the peace of Jerusalem
May those who love you prosper
Peace be within your walls

Psalm 122.6–7

CONTENTS

PROLOGUE

Peter, James, and John. Paul and his missionary companion, Barnabas. All of these men were Jews, though we identify them with "the origins of Christianity." This is because we know that their efforts would eventually lead to the formation of that later—and predominantly gentile—religious community. But they did not know this. Committed to their movement's core prophecy—"The times are fulfilled, and the Kingdom of God is at hand! Repent, and trust in the good news!"—they foresaw no extended future. They passionately believed that God was about to fulfill his ancient promises to Israel: to redeem history, to defeat evil, to raise the dead, and to establish a universal reign of justice and peace.[1]

Their immediate source for this good news had been the prophecy of Jesus himself. And in their visions of Jesus raised, his followers' hopes were confirmed: Jesus' own resurrection could only mean that the general resurrection—thus, the coming of God's Kingdom—truly was at hand. Now linking the Kingdom's imminent arrival to the victorious return of their messiah, these followers raced to proclaim the good news in what they were sure was a brief wrinkle in time, the Spirit-charged gap between the raising of Jesus and his glorious second coming. They would continue the mission of Jesus by spreading the message of the coming Kingdom in the unpredictably short period between "now" and "soon."

How can we reconstruct the supreme confidence and the compelling convictions of this generation—especially when we know that history did not, in fact, end in the way that they so fervently believed it would? Fortunately, a voice remains from this moment of the movement: the voice of the apostle Paul.

From his earliest letter to his last, Paul affirms the nearness of the End. Sometime in the late 40s C.E., Paul asserts that he expects both himself and his community in Thessalonika to be alive when Jesus comes back to raise the dead and to gather his elect. "The Lord is near," he later tells his assembly in Philippi. To the Corinthians he confides that the period between "now" and the end of time has already been "shortened": the "ends of the ages" have already arrived. "Now is the acceptable time," he exhorts them; "Behold, now is the day of salvation!" And some time in the late 50s C.E., just as he is slipping from our view, Paul in his final letter, to the Romans, confidently announces that "salvation is even nearer to us than when we first became convinced. The night is far gone. The day"—that is, the Last Day, the day of Jesus' return and of the establishment of God's Kingdom—"is at hand."[2]

Paul is our earliest witness to what would eventually become Christianity. Although he never knew Jesus of Nazareth, and although his letters mention very few of Jesus' teachings, on this point, Jesus and he were agreed: God's Kingdom would dawn in their own day.

Paul never met Jesus. But he did know—and had complicated relationships with—some of the men in the original circle around him: Peter (whom he calls "Cephas"), John (the son of Zebedee?), James the brother of Jesus, and perhaps as well some of those whom Paul eventually distained as "false brothers." From his own account, we see that Paul went up to confer with the Jerusalem leaders at least twice. Presumably, he was attempting to coordinate his own message and mission with theirs. Insisting that his ex-pagan pagans in the Diaspora contribute to his fund drive for "the saints at Jerusalem" in order to provide them with much needed financial support, Paul always maintained contact with this original community. Through him, we still—however distantly—hear them.[3]

Other sources, some familiar and others not, also aid us in this effort. Beyond the New Testament's collection of Paul's letters, we also have the canonical gospels. Mark, Matthew, and Luke are called the "synoptic" or "seen-together" gospels, because they are all somehow related to each other, and tell different versions of what is recognizably the same story. And we have in addition the theologically laden (and intriguingly different) fourth gospel, the gospel of John. Crucially, we can also avail ourselves of "part 2" of Luke's gospel, namely the Acts of the Apostles.

And we can nest these texts within a considerable collection of other less familiar ones. We have the works of Paul's elder contemporary, the Alexandrian Jewish intellectual Philo. We have the rich library of the Dead Sea Scrolls. We can turn to a wealth of Jewish inscriptions from the western, Greek-speaking Diaspora, especially from those Jewish communities settled in Asia Minor, modern-day Turkey. Various Jewish revelations—both biblical texts, like the prophecies of Daniel, and now extrabiblical ones, like *Jubilees*, a rewritten version of Genesis—likewise help us to fill in our picture. Paul does not stand alone.

Framing all of these writings, however, and helping us to read them critically and carefully, we have the works of a singular author, who serves us as an indispensable source. Priest, Pharisee, prophet, military leader, war captive, historian: Josephus. Josephus aids us, in crucial ways, in our quest for the assembly of Jesus' earliest followers in Jerusalem. Indeed, for almost three decades, in this holy city, he and they would have been neighbors.

Yosef ben Mattityahu was born into an aristocratic priestly family in Jerusalem only a few years after Jesus had died there. His father would have served in the temple under Caiaphas, the high priest in office when Jesus was crucified. As a young man, Josephus likewise served in the temple. He was acquainted with those various "sects" or "schools" that shaped late Second Temple Judaism: Sadducees, Pharisees, Essenes, Zealots. He knew or knew of charismatic ascetics, wandering prophets, and various wonder workers. Among these he numbered John the Baptizer and Jesus of Nazareth. He also knew about the community that had formed around Jesus' message and memory after his death. And Josephus played a major role in the catastrophe that brought about the end of that community and of the city and the temple that he had loved: Josephus fought in and lived through his people's war against Rome, which led to the destruction of Jerusalem.

It is thanks to his survival that we have those writings that give us such unparalleled access to this period: the Jewish War (hereafter abbreviated *BJ*, for *Bellum Judaicum*), a history of the conflict, composed shortly after the event; and the *Antiquities of the Jews* (hereafter *AJ*), a much larger and more ambitious history that begins with Genesis and ends with Josephus' own day. The former general, war captive and slave passed the second half of his life in Rome as Flavius Josephus, allied to and supported by the household of the very same imperial family that had led the Roman siege of Jerusalem. Whatever he says about his own people in the period leading up to the War, and just like (as we shall see) the New Testament's evangelists, who were his contemporaries, Josephus says from his postwar perspective.[4]

Josephus helps us to understand the context of this conflict, and the role played by the prophecy that led up to it. He orients us in the War's prehistory. He lets us see the centuries of stable government that developed in Jerusalem after the Babylonian captivity (586–533 B.C.E.), once the exiles returned to the city and aristocratic priests coordinated with imperial governors to rule Judea. He leads us through the clashes between Alexander the Great's successors, the Ptolemies in Egypt and the Seleucids in Syria, and their messy and conflicting alliances with Jerusalem's priestly rulers (after 323 B.C.E.). His account augments the stories in the books of the Maccabees, when the Hasmonean family attained Jewish independence, eventually serving both as high priests and, later, as kings (167–140 B.C.E.). He narrates both the tyranny and the towering achievements of Herod the Great, King of the Jews (who ruled from 37 to 4 B.C.E.).[5]

But most importantly for us, Josephus traces the uneasy relationships, post-Herod, between Jerusalem's chief priests and Rome. He recounts the fatal clashes of Roman prefects and procurators with popular Jewish prophets and militants. He describes the vibrant instability of the city, swollen with pilgrims during the Jewish high holidays, "when sedition is most likely to break out." And finally, he points out the key role played by a messianic prophecy—"their chief inducement for going to war," as he says of his countrymen—in the outbreak of the conflict. Among those Jews holding such hopes, awaiting the establishment of God's Kingdom, expecting the glorious second coming of their messiah, were the men and women of Jesus' community gathered in Jerusalem.[6]

When Christians Were Jews tells the story of that community. It will be, of necessity, a tale of two cities, Jerusalem and Rome. Long before Jewish rebels incited the War, Rome had maintained a strong presence in Judea: had things been otherwise, Jesus of Nazareth would not have died by crucifixion. During Jesus' lifetime and for the four decades thereafter—for the entire lifetime, that is, of this messianic assembly in Jerusalem—Roman power politics and popular prophetic movements made for a combustible mix. Jesus' cross was literally only one of thousands that marked the path to the final Roman siege.

But with the bad came the good: Rome also built great highways and policed the seas, thereby ensuring travelers' safe passage. This combination of imperial power and imposed peace may have brought about Jesus' execution, but it also enabled the message of the crucified, risen, and returning messiah to spread out from Jerusalem to the wider Mediterranean world—indeed, as Paul's letters attest, within twenty-five years to reach Rome itself.

During these same decades, the Jesus movement vigorously grew, and was surprised—indeed, caught off guard—by its own successes. Pressing questions arose about authority, activity, and organization. What should the original community in Jerusalem do while it awaited the return of the messiah? Did it have a message to spread—and if it did, then how, and to whom? How should it relate to its satellite assemblies in the Diaspora, and to the wider world of diaspora synagogue communities? To what ends should it direct its missions? How should it incorporate those ex-pagan gentiles that the mission itself—again, to its evident surprise—started to yield? And the most fundamental question of all: how could this movement stabilize as a community when its very existence was posited upon the conviction that the world hovered at the edge of the end of time?

When Christians Were Jews considers all of these questions. But before we can attend to them, a prior one looms: what was the earliest community even doing in Jerusalem, given that its founding leader, Jesus of Nazareth, had brutally died there, crucified as "King of the Jews"?

ONE

Up to Jerusalem

Sometime in the early 30s of the first century, Jesus and his followers went up to Jerusalem for the feast of Passover. It was probably the largest and the most beautiful city that any of them had ever seen. Indeed, it was perhaps the *only* city that many of them had ever seen.[1]

Built up by David and Solomon, destroyed by the Babylonians, restored by returning Judeans under Persia, Hellenized in the period after Alexander the Great: Jerusalem had swum or been swamped in the tides of power as various empires came and went. The Persian period, beginning in the 530s B.C.E., saw the creation of the city's most long-lived and stable form of government, one that persisted for almost half a millennium. Judea was ruled from Jerusalem by the high priest. This man was thought to be a descendent of Zadok, the priest named in the Bible who had anointed David's son Solomon as king. Under Persian dominion, the high priest was particularly charged with supervising the temple's operations. But he was also responsible to the governor, the imperial ruler's local representative. His office combined what we would distinguish as political and religious functions. Together, the high priest with the imperial governor insured that tribute or taxes were duly collected, and that quiet prevailed.[2]

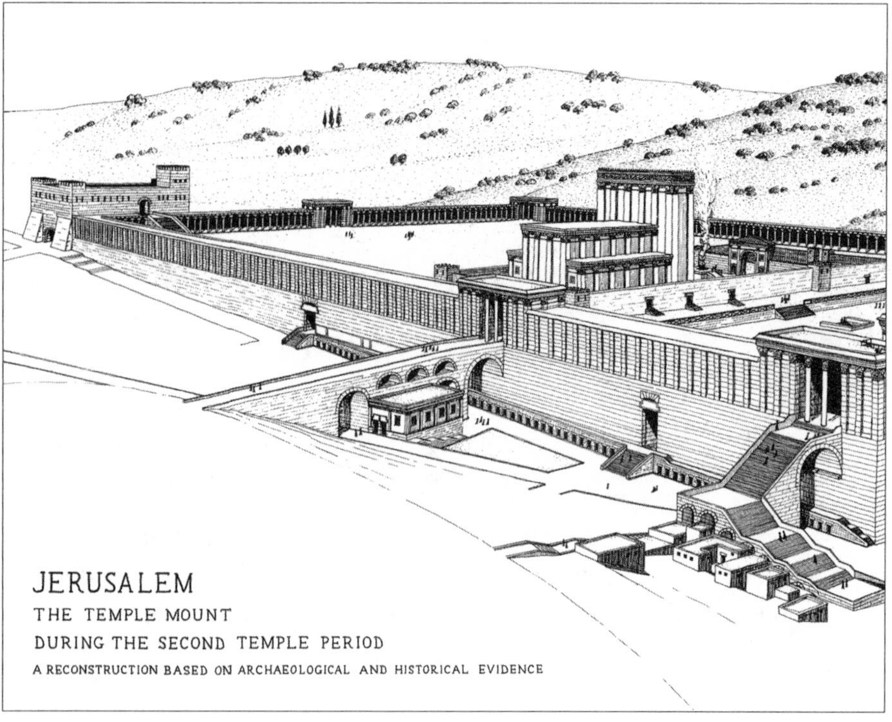

The Second Temple in the early Roman Empire: Herod's Temple Mount, based on archaeological and historical evidence, a view from the southwest.

> For the Lord has chosen Zion;
> He has desired it for his habitation.
> "This is my resting place forever.
> Here I will reside, for I have desired it. . . .
> There I will cause a horn to sprout up for David;
> I have prepared a lamp for my anointed one."
>
> (Psalm 132.13–14, 17)

The house of David (that is, the kings of David's line) and the house of God (that is, the temple in Jerusalem) came bound together in Jewish tradition. In 586 B.C.E., Babylon terminated both, destroying Solomon's building and taking the last Davidic king into captivity. Rebuilt by returning exiles and enhanced by the Hasmoneans, the Second Temple reached its height of splendor thanks to the talents and vision of Herod the Great. Herod, ingeniously combining backfill and huge retaining walls—still visible today as Jerusalem's Kotel, the Western Wall—enlarged the temple precincts to some thirty-five acres. Its most exterior courtyard, the Court of the Nations, was Jerusalem's largest public space. This was the space within which Jesus proclaimed his message of God's coming Kingdom; this was the space within which his apostles, after his death, continued his mission; this was the space from which, prophesied Paul, quoting Isaiah, "the Redeemer will come"—that is, where the returning messiah would appear (Romans 11.26; Isaiah 59.20). Both actually and imaginatively, both before its destruction in 70 C.E. and even thereafter, Herod's temple was a major staging area of the gospel movement.

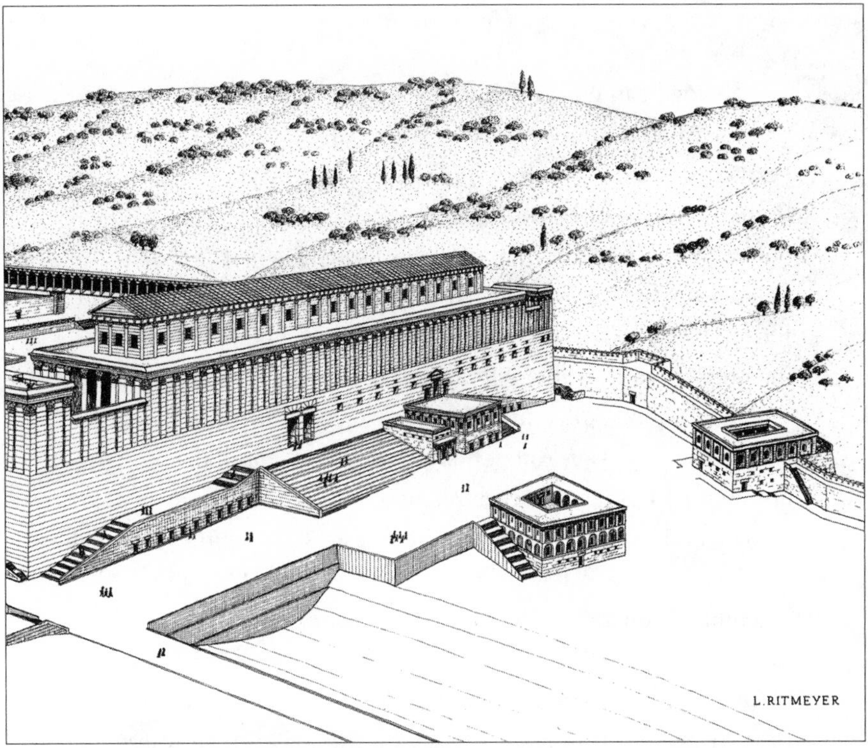

Reconstruction by Dr. Leen Ritmeyer.

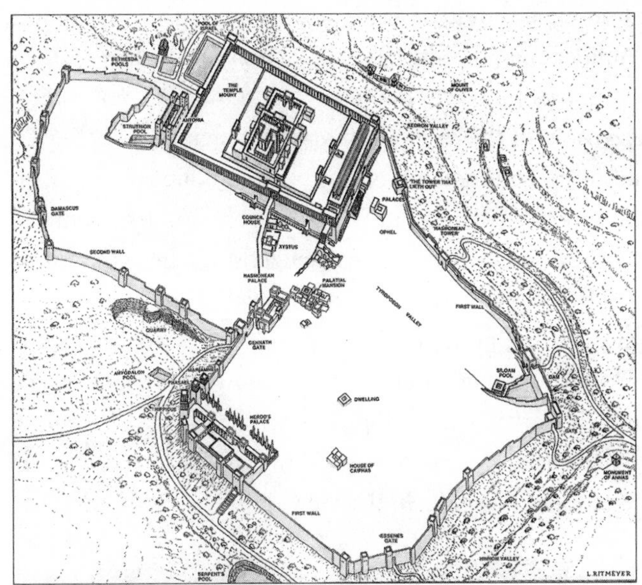

Change came from without. Trouble more often came from within. Alexander swept through the Middle East, conquering Persia in 332 B.C.E. But his empire, upon his early death, devolved to the families of his feuding generals. The military and political power of two of these families, the Ptolemies of Egypt and the Seleucids of Syria, seesawed unstably in the Eastern Mediterranean. Judea lay exactly between their two territories, perpetually tempting one side or the other with an opportunity for expansion.

In 198 B.C.E., Antiochus III of Syria seized Judea from Ptolemaic Egypt. His successor, Antiochus IV, sought to consolidate his government by extending Greek religious and political culture at regional sites. (This blending of Greek with local cultures is what scholars mean by "Hellenization"—that is, "Greek-ification.") He had little reason to think that Jerusalem would pose any sort of problem. After all, a member of the large Zadokite high priestly family there had already approached him with just such a project in mind.

One Zadokite brother, Onias, was the Jewish high priest; another brother, Jason, wanted to be. Jason proposed to Antiochus that Jerusalem should be Hellenized, bringing it more directly under Antiochene administration. Granting Antiochene citizenship to upper-class Jerusalemite males would in effect make Jerusalem an extension of the Syrian capital. This change in its legal status would bring considerable economic and political benefits to the Jewish city. And Jerusalem would now house a key educational and cultural institution of Greek citizenship: the gymnasium.

With the gymnasium came special complications. Greeks exercised in the nude. Jewish males doing so would expose their circumcision, a condition that Greco-Roman culture regarded with both derision and horror. Young Jewish men committed to Hellenization "made foreskins" through the cosmetic surgical procedure of epispasm. In the view of the writer of 1 Maccabees, they thereby "abandoned the holy covenant, joined with the pagans and sold themselves to do evil." Circumcision literally embodied the covenant between God and Abraham. To surgically undo circumcision, in the eyes of the author of 1 Maccabees, was to undo being a Jew. The Jewish priest Jason obviously saw things otherwise. Empowered by his Seleucid patron, he ousted his brother Onias (who fled to Ptolemy in Egypt) and embarked upon the project of modernizing his people and his capital.[3]

What began as an aristocratic Jewish initiative—and as a fraternal power struggle—soon deteriorated into a violent clash of cultures between Syrian Greeks and Jerusalem. Some Jews welcomed these changes; others resisted them. Angered by opposition, Antiochus IV pushed harder, mandating further Hellenization of Judea. Finally, in 167 B.C.E., the altar of Jerusalem's temple served as a site of pagan cult—the abominable "desolating sacrifice" reviled in a contemporary document, the prophecy of Daniel. These events culminated in the Maccabean Revolt of Hanukkah fame (166 B.C.E.).[4]

The success of the Maccabean Revolt had a defining effect on the politics of the region. Its repercussions were felt long after the Hasmoneans, that priestly family who led the rebellion, were in their turn pushed from power. For now, though, the main point to bear in mind is that, through the Hasmoneans, Rome became immediately involved with Judea. Entering the scene as a republican ally, within a century Rome grew into an imperial overlord.[5]

Once again, fraternal rivalry for the high priesthood—between Hasmonean brothers this time, not Zadokites—led to foreign intervention. The Roman general Pompey, in order to quash this destabilizing regional in-fighting, conquered Jerusalem in 63 B.C.E. He entered the sanctuary of the temple, in Jewish eyes thereby defiling it. He tore down the city walls. He deprived

Jerusalem of revenue-yielding territories. Diminished and humiliated, the city shriveled.

Soon, however, the proverbial shoe was on the other foot. Two waves of civil war engulfed Rome, first between Pompey and Julius Caesar and then, with Caesar's assassination in 44 B.C.E., between Mark Antony and Octavian. Octavian's victory in 31 B.C.E. finalized Rome's bloody transition from republic to empire. In Judea, meanwhile, Hasmonean priestly brothers continued to squabble between themselves. But real power had already shifted to another family, one that had backed Rome's winners, and to whom accordingly Rome awarded control of local military matters: the family of Herod the Great.

It was Herod who built Jesus' Jerusalem. Ruling from 37 to 4 B.C.E. over widespread territories—Judea, Transjordan, Samaria, the Galilee, and the Golan—Herod had consolidated his power, and buffed his social credentials, by marrying into the regal Hasmonean family. Fearing the popularity of his younger brother-in-law, who was then serving as high priest, Herod had him assassinated. He then turned the position, traditionally held for life, into a political revolving door. He, Herod, would name the high priest, frequently a *cohen* ("priest") from abroad with no threatening local connections. And at will, Herod would replace him.

Though he undermined the institution in this way, Herod enormously enhanced it in another. Individual high priests might come and go, but they executed their office within one of the most imposing and impressive settings in the ancient world: Jerusalem's temple. Centuries after its destruction, the rabbis—no fans of Herod—would still recall, "Whoever has not seen Herod's temple has never seen a beautiful building."[6]

Herod was a master builder, and grand public works were part of the repertoire of power in antiquity. More than vainglory was at stake, for the display of power went far toward maintaining order. But by so expanding and beautifying Jerusalem in general and the temple in particular, Herod also made a point against his aristocratic priestly in-laws. Kingship trumped priesthood. While, back in the day, Zadok may have anointed Solomon, it was the monarch alone who had had heaven's mandate to build the temple in which priests would serve. The Hasmoneans, after their successful revolt against Antiochus IV, had (controversially) combined the two offices, high priest and king. But biblically—and, under Herod, unambiguously—these were once again separate. And the king—again, unambiguously—was the superior figure. After all, he controlled the army.

Herod took the older Hasmonean sacred precincts and, through an ingenious combination of backfill and powerful retaining walls, increased its surface area to some thirty-five acres. This wall around the irregular rectangle of the temple complex, still visible today as Jerusalem's Western Wall, the Kotel, ran for almost nine-tenths of a mile. Within, nested courtyards subdivided sacred space. At the heart of the whole, facing east, was the two-chambered sanctuary itself, its innermost room completely empty, the earthly abode of Israel's god. Facing this structure was the courtyard of the priests, the area of active sacrificing. Adjacent to the priests' area stood the court for Jewish men; exterior to that, the women's court.

Surrounding these three inner courts was the vast and beautiful Court of the Nations. It was the largest area within the whole compound. There, pagans too could collect, admire the building, contribute to its overhead costs, and otherwise indulge in religious tourism. Jews entering the temple precincts to make their offerings had to traverse this stone mesa to reach their own courts. Pilgrims and pagan visitors wishing to donate toward the temple's operation could change their various currencies into the Tyrian shekels accepted by the temple. It was for this reason that the tables of the moneychangers were also set up in this exterior court, under the stoa that ran along its perimeter. (In antiquity, free cities often minted their own coins. There was no single currency. Besides this, Tyrian shekels had a stable silver content.) The Court of the Nations would have been the noisiest, the busiest, the most animated, and often the most crowded space in the entire temple complex.[7]

THE GOSPELS, JESUS, AND JERUSALEM

How often would Jesus have gone to Jerusalem, and so to the temple? During his childhood, says Luke's gospel at 2.14, Jesus and his family went up every year for Passover. But what about as an adult, after he started his mission? On this question, our sources diverge significantly.

Mark—which most scholars regard as the earliest gospel—frames Jesus' mission all within one year. And, save for a brief stop in Jericho, Mark's Jesus works exclusively in and around the Galilee. Only once did Jesus go to Jerusalem, claims Mark, arriving with other pilgrims in the week before Passover, which Mark describes as the triumphal entry. At that point, Jesus causes an incident in the temple, overturning the tables of the moneychangers. This scene is thus set in the Court of the Nations.

His action, in Mark's telling, earns Jesus the deadly hostility of the priests. Dramatically, it sets up the finale of Mark's story. Fearing Jesus' popularity, the priests conspire to arrest him by stealth after the Passover meal, "lest there be a tumult of the people." Condemning him for blasphemy at a night trial before the priestly council, the Sanhedrin holds a plenum meeting again in the morning. Thereafter, the priests importune Pilate to execute Jesus. Rome's prefect, bullied into cooperation, then crucifies Jesus as "King of the Jews." Matthew and Luke, the other two synoptic gospels—so called because they each follow Mark closely—repeat Mark's basic sequence of events. In these three related traditions, Jesus in the course of his mission makes one single trip to Jerusalem that, because of the priests, proves fatal.[8]

John's gospel, by contrast, tells a very different story. John depicts Jesus as frequently in Jerusalem. Already in chapter 2, Jesus teaches within the temple's exterior court. And already in chapter 2, John's Jesus stages this incident with the moneychangers. Coming as it does at the very beginning of John's gospel, Jesus' action does *not* inaugurate events in the final week of his life and has nothing to do with his eventual execution. Dramatically, the scene goes nowhere.[9]

John's Jesus then continues his mission in Judea, passing through Samaria on his way back to the Galilee. In chapter 5, he is back in Jerusalem for another feast. In chapter 7, he goes up for Sukkot (the "feast of Tabernacles," in the fall). Evidently he then stays in Jerusalem for several months, until December, and the "feast of Dedication" (celebrating the Maccabees' purification of the temple, root of the modern Hanukkah). Later, Jesus crosses into Transjordan, and then returns to Jerusalem for Passover yet again, his final trip. The mission of John's Jesus, in brief, is more Judean than Galilean. And it is emphatically Jerusalem-centered.[10]

We have no place to turn outside of the gospels for information about Jesus of Nazareth's itinerary. And indeed, given the distance in time and in place between the mission of the historical Jesus (late 20s to early 30s C.E., in the Galilee and Judea) and the later composition of these gospels (between 75 and 100, somewhere in the Greek-speaking Diaspora?)—a gap of some forty-five to seventy years—we have to wonder what information the evangelists themselves could have had to draw upon.

Jesus' itinerary in Mark's gospel differs considerably from that of John's. It is possible that neither narrative accurately relates the movements of the Jesus of history. Were we to judge between the two itineraries, however, it is John's that seems the more plausible. For one thing, the community of Jesus' followers, according to Paul, the Acts of the Apostles, and Josephus, settled in Jerusalem shortly after his death, and remained there. And a sporadic but repeated Jerusalem mission, as we will see, provides a better nexus of explanation for Jesus' death. Also, a public mission of less than a year seems too little time to develop a movement as tenacious as Jesus' was. And, as we know from one of Paul's letters, the epistle to the Galatians, small assemblies of Jesus' followers within about five years of his death already existed in Judea. This last fact also supports the idea of a prior Judean mission.[11]

Finally, Jerusalem, with its three biblically mandated pilgrimage festivals, was a magnet for Jews throughout the Roman Empire and beyond. It was there that Jesus would have been guaranteed his largest Jewish audience. Again, John's gospel points in this direction. When Annas, a chief priest, questions Jesus "about his disciples and his teaching," John's Jesus answers, "I have spoken openly to the world. I have always taught in synagogues and in the temple, where all Jews come together." Jerusalem would be an ideal place to maximize a mission to Israel—a point that Jesus' later followers, after his crucifixion, evidently realized as well: after all, they settled there. All of these reasons, taken together, seem to favor the *sort* of itinerary depicted in John as opposed to that of Mark, Matthew, and Luke.[12]

Most New Testament scholars, however, favor the synoptic gospels when reconstructing the historical Jesus. There are good reasons for this. The main one is the strong contrast between the ways that the Synoptics present their main character and the way that John does his. The Jesus of the synoptic tradition is a charismatic healer, a holy man, and an exorcist. His preaching centers on the good news of the coming Kingdom of God. And Jesus frames his call to repentance in terms of the Ten Commandments.

Asked about the greatest of the commandments, the Jesus of the synoptic tradition responds by quoting Deuteronomy 6.4 (love of God) and Leviticus 19.18 (love of neighbor). These two quotations, and the sentiments that they evoke, represent a common two-word code used by ancient Jews to refer to the Two Tables of the Law, namely "piety" toward God (the first five commandments) and "justice" toward other people (the second five).[13]

Elsewhere, the Jesus of the synoptic tradition quotes these divine directives forthrightly. "You know the commandments: 'You shall not murder. You shall not commit adultery. You shall not steal. You shall not bear false witness. You shall not defraud. Honor your father and your mother.'" Such a message coheres well with what we know of John the Baptizer, Jesus' great predecessor. John's teaching, too, according to Josephus, also featured the Ten Commandments. And such a Jesus fits in easily among other such contemporary and near-contemporary Jewish charismatic figures, less well known to us, such as Honi the Circle Drawer (who, through prayer, could cause rain to fall) or the Galilean Hanina ben Dosa (who, like Jesus, could heal people even from a distance).[14]

As a character in the gospel story, by comparison, the Jesus of the fourth gospel is an eerie loner, a stranger from heaven. Supremely and serenely in charge of his own circumstances, he moves untroubled through an atmosphere charged with hostility. Time and again, plots against Jesus fail because the predestined time for his death—which Jesus himself knows—has not yet arrived. He preaches incessantly, not about the Kingdom, but about himself. And he cannot say enough about his own divine identity.[15]

The terms of that identity—the "true vine"; the "lamb of God"; "the gateway"; "the way, the truth and the life"—are symbolically rich and complex. They seem drawn from a Christian tradition that has had the chance to evolve, to reflect upon itself, and to develop in sophisticated ways, in the four to seven decades between Jesus' crucifixion and the fourth evangelist's composition. This observation is equally true of this gospel's introduction of Jesus as God's *Logos*, the divine eternal "Word." John's heavily theological presentation of his mysterious hero, in short, means that his Jesus seems more at home in a late first-century, natively Greek, and possibly gentile context than he does in an early first-century Palestinian, Aramaic, Jewish one.

In terms of the historical plausibility of the gospels' depictions of Jesus of Nazareth, in other words, the synoptic material is simply much more usable. This reasonable scholarly reliance on the synoptic *Jesus*, however, has led to scholars' depending as well on the synoptic *itinerary*. And the problem with that itinerary—Jesus in Jerusalem only once, at the very end of his mission; otherwise mostly if not solely in the Galilee—is not only the way that it fails to speak to the evidence of early Jesus-following communities throughout Judea. Reliance on the synoptic tradition on this point about how often Jesus during his mission went up to Jerusalem also compounds the historical problem of explaining why Jesus was crucified. We will shortly see why that is so, and how John's gospel provides a solution to this problem.

But modern historians are not alone in being troubled by the very linear movement of Mark's, Matthew's, and Luke's Jesus. The evangelists' Galilean emphasis also presented a structural problem for the synoptic writers themselves. Their exclusive focus on a Galilean mission makes it difficult for them to connect the Galilean Jesus with his Roman cross.

This is because, for the whole of Jesus' lifetime, the Galilee was an independent Jewish territory ruled by Herod Antipas, one of the sons of Herod the Great. Another of Herod's sons, Archelaus, had once ruled Judea. The reign of both sons began only with their father's death, in 4 B.C.E. But Archelaus proved inept, and Augustus finally removed him in 6 C.E. Thereafter, Judea—and Judea alone—was placed under Roman provincial rule. No Roman authority presided over the Galilee.

The Roman provincial governor or "prefect," together with his three thousand troops—local pagans in the employ of Rome—exercised authority *only* in Judea. He was in Jerusalem only rarely. Most of the time, the prefect and his troops were garrisoned on the coast, in Caesarea, a magnificent harbor city—another one of Herod's splendid architectural accomplishments—with a mixed population of pagans and Jews. The prefect and his army went up to Jerusalem only three times a year, to help maintain order when the city was especially, exceptionally crowded. That is to say, the prefect too went up for the pilgrimage holidays: Sukkot (in the fall), Passover (early spring), and Shavuot (late spring). The only time that Jesus could have encountered Roman forces—the prefect and his soldiers—was when he went up to Jerusalem, to celebrate one of these holidays.

By focusing so resolutely on the Galilee, and on local resistance to Jesus' message there, the synoptic writers created a logical gap in their own stories that they needed to close. The prime problem was that none of the intra-Jewish religious arguments featured in these gospels—Jesus' testy encounters with scribes and with Pharisees—could account for Jesus' very political, Roman death.

Pilate, as indeed *any* prefect, would have understood little and cared less about intra-Jewish religious debates. Can someone heal on the Sabbath? Pluck grain on the Sabbath? Cast out demons on the Sabbath? Why should the prefect care? And he had better things to do than to intervene in such arguments, much less to execute summarily those Jews participating in them. In short, the synoptic writers' Galilean scribes and Pharisees, no matter how hostile, could never have prevailed upon Pilate to have Jesus killed.[16]

It is for this reason—the need to account for how and why Jesus, once in Jerusalem, is killed by Rome—that synoptic tradition dramatically emphasizes the story of Jesus' overturning the tables of the moneychangers. The scene in the temple provides their story's structural turning point, the pivot that moves the plot along. Jesus' Galilean opponents thereafter fade from view. They are, through this scene in the temple, replaced by Jerusalem's priests. From this point forward, priestly hostility drives the story's action.

According to the Synoptics, it was this incident over the moneychangers' tables that first brought Jesus to the attention of the priests. The priests seem to take his action as a criticism of themselves, or perhaps as a threat to their authority. On the spot, they resolve to neutralize him permanently. "And the chief priests and the scribes heard it"—that is, Jesus' condemnation of the temple's being "a den of robbers"—"and they sought a way to destroy him; for they feared him, because all the multitude was astonished at his teaching." With the priests, Jesus (finally) gains Judean opponents. The rest of the story of the Passion relates how the priests manipulate Pilate into doing their will.[17]

Scholars who rely on the synoptic itinerary also focus, like the synoptic evangelists themselves, on this incident. They assume that the historical Jesus did perform such an act, and then they interpret his gesture. Did the overturned tables signal Jesus' condemnation of the temple as an institution? That is to say, did Jesus in principle oppose sacrifices as a way to worship? Some scholars say yes; others, no. Or was Jesus objecting not to the temple itself, but to the way that the priests ran it? Other scholars prefer this second interpretation. Whether they understand Jesus' action to indicate his supposed hostility to the temple or to what it represented—financial exploitation? oppressive purity regulations? an elite, urban, Judean tradition versus a peasant, popular Galilean tradition?—these scholars use Jesus' supposed opposition to the temple to explain the priests' mortal opposition to Jesus. In these reconstructions, the priests were hostile to Jesus because, first, Jesus had been hostile to them. They may get Pilate to do the job, but the priests—so goes this argument—are really the ones who wanted Jesus dead.[18]

Did the historical Jesus, sometime around the year 30 C.E., enact this scene at the temple at the very beginning of his mission (so John), or at its very end (so Mark, Matthew, and Luke)? Three gospels, the Synoptics, say one thing; only one gospel, John, says another. That fact in itself may seem to resolve the issue right there. Three outweighs one.

But the synoptic gospels, Mark, Matthew, and Luke, all share some sort of literary relationship with each other. Scholars debate which evangelist read the other(s) first. (I think that Mark is the earliest, and that Matthew and Luke, each independently, read Mark.) But scholarly consensus holds that all three, in some way, influenced each other. Thus they do not represent three individual independent sources.[19]

John's relationship to these three gospels is also uncertain. John may also have known one or some of the Synoptics—this question, also, is debated—but he is clearly and radically independent of them too, telling a very different story in a very different way. My point is that, on the question about the sequence of events during Jesus' mission circa 30, in terms of these gospel accounts, we do *not* have a split three-to-one decision. We have a one-or-the-other decision: do we go with the synoptic chronology/itinerary or with the one offered by John?

All four gospel stories confront us with interlocking questions about the Jesus of history. (1) Did Jesus during his mission go more than once to Jerusalem? (2) How did Jesus of Nazareth regard the temple and Jerusalem? (3) Did Jesus cause an incident with the moneychangers' tables in the temple, and if he did, what did he mean by it? (4) Why did Jesus end up on a cross?

And over all of these is the question most relevant to our effort here: why would the earliest community of Jesus' followers have settled *in* Jerusalem, if Jesus himself had condemned the city together with its beating heart, the temple itself? Why would the first community have settled in Jerusalem, if the city and the chief representatives of its temple, the priests, had condemned Jesus to death and brought about his execution? And if Jesus himself were for some reason hostile toward the holy city, why would his closest followers, so soon after his death, have chosen to make Jerusalem the center of their new movement?

Fortunately for our attempts to answer all of these charged questions, we have other first-century sources that can help to fill in the gaps in our gospel evidence. We have, first of all, the seven undisputed letters of Paul, who writes before the temple's destruction in 70. We have the Dead Sea Scrolls (roughly mid-second century B.C.E. to 68 C.E., when Roman legions destroyed the site at Qumran). These preserve the library of the Essene community, which also gives us a valuable perspective on Jewish attitudes toward Jerusalem's temple.

And finally, we have the works of Josephus, the *Jewish War* and the *Antiquities of the Jews*. True, Josephus wrote these with postwar retrospect; but he still provides valuable information about the temple, about popular attitudes toward the temple, and about the many and various messianic and prophetic Jewish movements that flourished and failed throughout the first century. Triangulating by means of these sources, we can navigate our way through the gospels' conflicting traditions about Jesus and Jerusalem.

PAUL AND THE TEMPLE

Paul's letters date to the mid-first century, some two to three decades after Jesus' death. Paul's native language was Greek, which means that he used a biblical tradition different from the one that the original disciples, and Jesus himself, would have been familiar with. Jesus and his original community heard scriptures in Hebrew, or perhaps in Aramaic. Paul knew the Septuagint traditions, third- and second-century B.C.E. translations of Jewish scriptures from Hebrew and Aramaic into Greek, considered authoritative by Greek-speaking Jews.

Did Paul also know Aramaic and/or Hebrew? On this as on so many other points, scholars are divided: some say yes, others no. What really complicates this question are the stories about Paul that appear in the later Acts of the Apostles.

Acts seems to have been written toward the end of the first or the beginning of the second century. It narrates traditions about the original postcrucifixion community of Jesus' followers in Jerusalem. I will refer to these traditions frequently in the course of our study here. But Acts also and particularly relates many stories about Paul. This material greatly amplifies what we can glean about Paul from his own letters.

Unfortunately, however, the relationship between the letters and this later story about the apostles is complicated. Paul sometimes offers no support for Acts' claims, and other times his letters actually contradict them.

For example, Acts states that Paul studied under the sage Gamaliel in Jerusalem. In Philippians, however, where Paul boasts about his Jewish credentials, he says: "Circumcised on the eighth day, of the people of Israel, of the tribe of Benjamin, a Hebrew born to Hebrews; as to the Law a Pharisee; as to zeal a persecutor of the assembly; as to righteousness under the Law, blameless." If Paul had studied under so eminent a figure as Gamaliel, shouldn't we expect to see him say so here?[20]

Acts further claims that, while in Jerusalem, Paul witnessed and consented to the death of the Christ-follower Stephen. In his own letters, Paul himself, three different times, emphasizes his past as a violent persecutor. He thereby highlights his divine epiphany, that moment of dramatic reversal when he transformed from opponent of the Christ-movement to apostle. But he nowhere in this connection mentions anyone named Stephen.[21]

Further, the itinerary implicit in Paul's letters cannot be made to square with that of Acts. Acts introduces us to Paul in Jerusalem, where, "breathing threats and murder," Paul seeks to extend persecution to Damascus in Syria. And it is while on the road *to* Damascus that the Paul of Acts has his encounter with the risen Christ. In Galatians 1.17, however, after receiving his call to be an apostle, Paul speaks of "*returning* to Damascus," not, as in Acts, going there for the first time. And whereas Acts depicts Paul going back to Jerusalem and meeting with the apostolic community there very shortly after receiving his call, Paul himself asserts heatedly that he went up to the city only several *years* thereafter, at that point meeting only with Peter ("Cephas") and with James, the brother of Jesus. "When he [that is, God] who had set me apart before I was born, and had called me through his grace, was pleased to reveal his son to me, in order that I might preach him to the gentiles, I did not confer with flesh and blood, *nor did I go up to Jerusalem to those who were apostles before me*, but I went away into Arabia, and again I returned to Damascus. Then after three years I went up to Jerusalem. . . . In what I am writing to you, before God, I do not lie!"[22]

Finally, this pivotal moment in Paul's life, when he turns from persecutor to apostle, is presented quite differently in our two different sources. Acts foregrounds an auditory experience to a *blinded* Saul. Paul emphasizes, quite precisely, *seeing*. And whereas Acts repeatedly depicts Paul as preaching first to Jews and then, only after setbacks, to pagans, Paul states that, from the time of his vision of the risen Christ, he went to pagans first: it was for this reason, he states firmly, that God had formed him "in the womb."[23]

Was Paul really a citizen both of Tarsus and of Rome? Was his Hebrew name truly "Saul"? Did he in fact complete his journey to Rome, as he had intended? Did he indeed ever reach Rome at all? Paul's letters cannot help us to answer any of these questions: he says nothing on these issues. And the pattern of direct conflicts and curious silences that marks Acts' relationship to Paul's letters more generally cannot but undermine a robust confidence in Luke's material. If Luke had had access to Galatians and to 1 Corinthians, for instance, he clearly did not use them.[24]

One episode related by Luke, however—whether it actually happened or not—coheres nicely with an aspect of Paul's own message. Acts 21.26 depicts a law-observant Paul as worshiping in the temple. Paul's own letters display his high regard for the temple as well.

Paul refers positively to the temple in four distinct connections. The first has to do with the way that the temple sacrifices represent a meal shared between God and his priests. Urging the assembly in Corinth to regard the eucharistic bread (Christ's "body") and the wine (Christ's "blood") as creating "communion"—that is, an intimate and unifying relationship—between believers with each other, and with Christ, Paul continues: "Consider the practice of Israel: Are not those who eat the sacrifices sharers of the altar?"[25]

This rhetorical question expects the answer, "Yes." Paul points to Jerusalem's cult offerings as exemplifying the bond created by "eating together," whether with Christ and this gentile community (with the eucharist as a kind of imitation of sacrifice), or with God and his priests (who "share" a meal through the flesh of sacrifice offered at the temple). Sacrifice to pagan gods likewise effects such a union, he warns. Distinguishing between "idols" (cult statues that represent these gods) and the gods themselves (whom Paul dismisses as *daimonia*, "lower gods" or "demons"), Paul warns his people: if you eat the meat sacrificed to these gods, you partner with them, too. The point for our purposes here is to note that, as far as Paul is concerned, the altar in Jerusalem creates this divine-human sharing around sacrificial food. For Paul—and, thus, for his mid-first-century gentile audience in Corinth—the temple's sacrifices both illumine and exemplify how the eucharistic offering works.[26]

A second way in which Paul positively uses ideas drawn from the Jerusalem temple concerns his congregations. The temple provides the ideas and images through which Paul describes the effects of God's spirit or of Christ's spirit on his baptized gentiles. By receiving this spirit, he says, these gentiles have been made both "pure" and "holy." These two words may sound like moral abstractions to us. In fact, they refer directly to the rules in Leviticus, where God details how a sacrifice was to be brought to his altar.

To approach the altar of God, instructs the Torah, the worshiper needed to be in a state of purity. Jewish purity rules, not unlike pagan ones, emphasized abstention from sex, and certain rituals involving water (a common medium of purification in many cultures). Through observing such rituals and behaviors, the person prepared for his encounter with the divine around the altar. Further, Leviticus instructs, the animal offered should be "pure" (whole, unblemished), and also "holy." The word that we translate as "holy" can also be translated as "dedicated" or as "separated out." Separated from what? From what is "common," which is to say, "not dedicated" (understood: to God). Something set apart for God is dedicated to him.[27]

Echoing Leviticus, Paul says that his ex-pagan gentiles, by turning *from* the worship of idols and demons (thus from the sorts of sexual behaviors that Jews associated with such religious activities), and by turning *to* the god of Israel, have achieved "holiness." That is, they are "separated out" from other, pagan gentiles, the ones who do not know God. Their new sexual and ritual behavior indexes their new state of the "purity" that God, through Christ, has called them to. They themselves, metaphorically, become a pleasing "offering to God," their support for Paul's mission the "sweet savor" of a God-pleasing sacrifice.[28]

Third: as vessels of God's spirit, these special ex-pagan gentiles, Paul claims, resemble God's temple itself. "Don't you know that you are God's temple, for God's spirit dwells in you? . . . God's temple is holy/separated/dedicated, as you are." "Your body is the temple of holy spirit." "We are the temple of the living God."[29]

Theologians will sometimes point to these verses to argue that, for Paul, the physical, Jewish temple back in Jerusalem has been replaced or surpassed by this new, "spiritual" and metaphorical "temple," the diaspora Christian communities. Given that, since 70 C.E., no temple in Jerusalem has stood, this claim can seem to be simple common sense.

But that is not what Paul says. Paul writes before 70. He never imagined a world without the temple. On the contrary: Paul praises his new communities by comparing them to this institution, which he valued supremely. Had he valued the temple less, he would not have used it as the defining image for his assemblies. Mid-first century, then, on the topic of the temple, Paul's thinking is not "either/or" but "both/and." God's spirit dwells *both* in Jerusalem's temple *and* in the "temple" of the believer and of the community. As the Jesus of Matthew's gospel will declare, two generations or so after Paul, "He who swears by the temple, swears by it *and by him who dwells in it*"—that is, by the god of Israel.[30]

Fourth and finally, Paul mobilizes traditionally pious ideas about Jerusalem's temple when referring to it directly. In the opening verses of Romans 9, listing the privileges that God has given his "kinsmen, the Israelites," Paul mentions specifically Israel's status as God's sons, the "glory," the covenants, the giving of the Torah, the "worship," the promises, the patriarchs, and the messiah.

I put "glory" and "worship" in quotation marks, because these English translations so obscure Paul's positive reference to Jerusalem and to the temple. The Greek word behind the English "glory," *doxa*, refers to the glory of God's presence. The word thus points to Jerusalem, and specifically to the temple, as that place on earth where God "dwells." (Matthew's Jesus, cited just above, voices the same conviction.) And the Greek word *latreia*, behind the English word "worship"—which to us cannot help but sound like some sort of prayer service—actually means "cult," that is, sacrifices. Paul thereby refers to both practice and place: the cult of offerings commanded by God in Exodus, Leviticus, Numbers, and Deuteronomy, and enacted in Paul's lifetime before God's sanctuary, at his altar in the holy city—holy because of God's special presence there.

In sum: Paul *does* object to sacrifice—but only to pagan sacrifice, which is offered to "demons," that is, to pagan gods. Jewish sacrifices to the god of Israel he praises. And he likens his communities, in positive ways, both to those sacrifices themselves and to the holy place where those sacrifices are offered: the temple in Jerusalem. The temple, its cult, Jerusalem itself as the place of God's presence: all these he holds to be defining privileges of his "kinsmen," Israel. If Paul, some twenty years into this movement around the mission and memory of Jesus, is so positive about the temple and its sacrifices, then the likelihood of Jesus himself having held and broadcast a negative view diminishes accordingly.

THE ESSENES AND THE TEMPLE

We do find a stridently negative attitude toward Jerusalem's temple—not in proto-Christian sources, interestingly, but in unimpeachably Jewish ones: the Essene library of the Dead Sea Scrolls. To understand why this is so, we need to understand as well the complicated history behind this community. And for that, we need to turn our gaze back a century and a half, away from Jesus' and Paul's lifetimes and toward the turbulent fight for freedom led by the Hasmonean family against Greek Syrian rule. The roots of Essene alienation from the temple extend back in time to the mid-second century B.C.E., and the days of the Maccabean Revolt.

The success of that revolt simplified some things, but it complicated others. The war had loosened the grip of the Seleucid ruler Antiochus IV on Judea. It arrested efforts, both external and internal, to Hellenize Jewish traditions through the surgical removal of circumcision (epispasm). It repudiated the relaxation of food laws and the worship of other gods alongside of the god of Israel. And it introduced Rome, the Hasmoneans' new ally, into the region's shifting political mix. The temple, purified and rededicated after the defiling pagan sacrifices of 167 B.C.E., was back in operation. After 160, relative quiet prevailed.

The question of who would be high priest, however, remained unsettled; and for seven years, the position remained empty. Radical Hellenizers (like the erstwhile Zadokite high priest Jason) were out. Yet, given the broad administrative duties of the office, and Judea's continuing status as a Seleucid province, the priest had to be someone who could work with the Greek Syrian government.

Just at this juncture, however, Antiochus died, and Seleucid power began to fissure. The ensuing civil war between Syrian strongmen presented the Hasmoneans with a surprising and, for them, a happy opportunity. One of the Syrian contestants for power, in order to gain an ally, elevated Jonathan, Judah Maccabee's brother, to the high priesthood (152 B.C.E.; Judah had fallen in battle eight years earlier). Jonathan's brother and successor, Simon (fl. 142–134), went further yet: achieving autonomy from Syria for Judea, he combined in himself the functions of both high priest *and* king.

These arrangements did not please everybody. One man, a Zadokite priest, left Jerusalem in 152 B.C.E. when Jonathan assumed office. (Had Jonathan driven him out?) This man joined with, and assumed the leadership of, a sectarian priestly group. His followers called him the Teacher of Righteousness. They referred to themselves as the Sons of Zadok, and as the Sons of Light. In the first century C.E., the Roman naturalist Pliny the Elder, and Jewish writers Philo of Alexandria and Josephus, identified this group as the Essenes. This is the community that collected and preserved the library recovered, almost two millennia later, in the caves of Qumran, the Dead Sea Scrolls.[31]

We can discern many areas of overlap, both in terms of religious mentality and in terms of social behaviors, between these Dead Sea sectarians and their later contemporaries, the assembly of Jesus' followers in Jerusalem. Both communities expressed intense messianic speculations. Both voiced vivid apocalyptic hopes. Both communalized property. Both advocated sexual renunciation, on the part of some members, in preparation for the impending Endtime. Socially and spiritually, in other words, a vivid expectation of the Endtime seems to have evoked similar beliefs and behaviors on the part of the two communities.[32]

We will explore these similarities further on. Here, however, we must note instead a strong point of contrast. Whereas the Christ-follower, Paul, evidently revered the temple in Jerusalem, the priestly Essenes reviled it.

Their loathing was born of intense resentment and feelings of injury. These members and allies of the Zadokite high priestly dynasty had lost the power struggles of the Hellenistic period. Theirs had been the family sanctioned by biblical tradition. The Hasmoneans—priests, but not Zadokites—in their view had usurped their rightful position. They named the empowered Jonathan "the Wicked Priest," the evil persecutor of "*the* priest," that is, of their anonymous Zadokite leader. So intensely did they hate their Hasmonean rivals that they actually rejoiced when, in 63 B.C.E., the Roman general Pompey conquered Jerusalem and defiled the temple: after all, the temple had already been defiled, as they saw it, by their upstart priestly opponents. "The Wicked Priest . . . forsook God . . . he robbed and amassed riches . . . heaping sinful iniquity upon himself. And he lived in the ways of abominations, amidst every unclean defilement." The New Testament's gospels are considerably kinder to Caiaphas.[33]

That part of the Essene community that lived by the Dead Sea—in strong contrast to the community of Jesus' followers, who settled in Jerusalem—seems to have refused any contact with Jerusalem's temple. In addition, they measured time by a solar calendar, not by Jerusalem's lunar one, so that their biblical holidays remained out of synch with those of the rest of the nation. So they waited, their apocalyptic convictions compensating for their current displacement. Once the final battle between Light and Darkness was won, they believed, there would come a new temple, built to their specifications and, finally, run by themselves. This scenario is detailed in the *Temple Scroll*.

In the meanwhile—hostile, patient, learned; utterly faithful to their group's revelations—they awaited the End of Days, which they knew was surely coming. The Essenes thus present the strongest contrast imaginable to Jesus' community in Jerusalem. There in the capital, Jesus' followers frequented the temple and evidently esteemed its sanctity. They too awaited the End of Days, but without the hostility to and alienation from Jerusalem's priesthood that defined the community of the Scrolls.

POPULAR PROPHETS AND THE TEMPLE

At what point did prophecy function as politics by other means? To what degree was insurrection undergirded or inspired by strong religious convictions? These questions recur continuously when one reads about the popular actions—and the muscular Roman responses that they called forth—in Josephus' review of the years preceding the outbreak of the War.

For example, Josephus traces the War's origins in 66 C.E. back six decades, to the rebellion begun by Judah the Galilean and Zadok the Pharisee in 6 C.E. "These men sowed the seed of every kind of misery, which so afflicted the nation that words are inadequate . . . until at last the very temple of God was ravaged by the enemy's fire."[34]

The changes in Judea's government following Herod's death had triggered this Judah's rebellion. Herod had divided his kingdom between his three remaining sons, with Archelaus assuming control over Judea, thus Jerusalem. Heavy-handed and insecure—a bad combination—Archelaus caused the slaughter of several thousand Jews in the temple at the beginning of the Passover festival in 4 B.C.E. He subsequently suspended the rest of the weeklong holiday of Unleavened Bread, and then sailed off to Rome, to have his father's will ratified by Augustus. In his absence (or, more likely, in the power vacuum created now that Herod was gone), the country careened into anarchy and anti-Roman violence, some of it launched from the temple complex itself. It took the troops of the Roman legate, Varus, coming down from Antioch, to restore order. Josephus recounts these events in book 17 of his *Antiquities.*

Varus pacified the country, crucifying some two thousand rebels outside the walls of Jerusalem. But he also allowed a delegation of fifty Jews to go to Rome to contest Herod's will before Augustus. These men sought their region's *autonomia,* "self rule."

This word, in its ancient Judean context, does not mean what it sounds like it means to us. To ask for "autonomy" was not to ask for "independence." Rather, these men petitioned Augustus to let Rome assume authority over Judea by administering it as part of the province of Syria. For them, "autonomy" meant no more Herodian kings. They sought instead a reversion to the good old days, as under Persia, or even as under the Seleucids or Ptolemies after Alexander the Great. They wanted the rule of a high priest, coordinated with a local provincial governor who in turn represented a distant emperor.[35]

Within ten years—which is to say, in 6 C.E.—these men got what they had asked for. Augustus finally deposed the hapless Archelaus. Rome would administer Archelaus's former kingdom through a local governor or "prefect," stationed in Caesarea; the prefect would coordinate with the high priest, also a Roman appointee, who would remain in Jerusalem. Both were subordinate to the regional Roman legate in Antioch; and everyone was subordinate to the emperor in Rome.

Further, because of its new provincial status, property in Judea would need to be assessed with an eye toward collecting the taxes necessary to fund its new Roman administration. This was the issue that had galvanized Judah and Zadok's rebellion—the rebellion, claimed Josephus, that, sixty years later, led to the War. One man's *autonomia* was another man's outrage. The men sent by Varus to Rome back in 4 B.C.E., in other words, finally—one long decade later—were granted their appeal. Judea would be administered without the imposition of Herodian kings.

Rome must have been startled, then, when once again rebellion broke out.

With cries of "No king but God!" Judah rallied Judean support. He thereby framed paying the tax—or, rather, *not* paying the tax—as a religious issue. These men were certain, reports Josephus, that "Heaven would be their zealous helper, . . . furthering their enterprise until it succeeded." Judah's military assertion was thus also a prophetic one. Judah and Zadok might start the tax revolt; but God, they were convinced, would finish it. Their call to military action, in other words, was framed, and buoyed, by prophecy.[36]

Much of this unrest, whether under Archelaus or immediately after his dismissal, occurred in and around the temple. Archelaus's unhappy debut at Pesach in 4 B.C.E. was followed, fifty days later, by more violence during the next pilgrimage holiday, Shavuot (or, in Josephus' Greek, "Pentecost"). Holiday crowds always had the potential to destabilize Jerusalem. And as the largest public space in the city, as well as the object of strong religious feeling, the temple itself invariably served as a flashpoint for unrest. Judah and Zadok, in 6 C.E., had fought to liberate not just Judea in general, but the city and the temple in particular.[37]

In the event, Rome prevailed. The rebels were defeated, the tax collected, and the prefect together with the high priest began their joint enterprise of governing Judea.

Josephus speaks of many other prophetic figures—some militantly insurgent, like Judah the Galilean, others not—who preached and gathered followings in the decades before the War. Because we are focusing particularly on Jesus of Nazareth, I want to restrict our attention at this point to two such prophetic figures who were active in the early part of the century, namely John the Baptizer and Jesus himself. Both seem to have proclaimed the coming of God's Kingdom; both seem to have coupled this teaching with a call to repentance. John evidently enhanced his prophetic authority by his extreme personal asceticism; Jesus, by his ability to exorcise demons and to heal.

John, said Josephus, also preached purification of the body—that is, water-immersion, a procedure frequently described in Leviticus and Numbers—"after the soul had been purified by right conduct." New Testament scholars frequently assert that John pitched this procedure as an alternative to the temple. John taught that forgiveness was attained through repentance plus immersion, they say, as opposed to repentance, immersion, and then, the next time the penitent was in Jerusalem, making an offering in the temple.[38]

This seems unlikely, however. One of the main goals of purification pre-70 C.E. was to enable the worshiper to enter the temple area: this is why so many immersion-pools pock the terraces still visible today on the southern side excavations below the Temple Mount. The south side gates were the main entry to the precinct. Immersion preceded entering the temple complex. In other words, before Rome erased Jerusalem and its cult in 70, "purification" cohered with "temple." It was not an alternative to it. And no anti-temple traditions attach to John, whether in the gospels' accounts or that of Josephus.

Also, as we have already seen, Josephus emphasized John's teaching "piety and justice," the common two-word code for the Ten Commandments. (Again, "piety" indicated the First Table of the Law, the rules governing a person's relationship with God; "justice" indicated the Second Table of the Law, the rules governing a person's relationship with others.) "Piety" in John's period and within his culture again points to the temple: that was the biblically mandated place for enacting proper deference to God. (Think again, also, of Paul's list of Israel's privileges in Romans 9, where he links the giving of the Law with the temple and with its cult.) The temple provided a key context for understanding and the place for enacting those traditions that had grown up around these first four commandments.

What about Jesus? The gospels present many incidents that presuppose Jesus' positive orientation. For example, after purging a man of leprosy, the synoptic Jesus says, "Go, show yourself to the priest, and offer for your cleansing what Moses commanded, as a proof to the people." "What Moses commanded," detailed in Leviticus 14, involved an elaborate protocol of physical examinations, immersions, and offerings, spread out over a week (two pigeons, two lambs, one ewe, a mixture of flour and oil, and a unit of oil itself). This sacrificial ceremony in Jesus' lifetime would have been enacted in Jerusalem, terminating at the temple.[39]

Matthew provides us with another bit of material on this question of Jesus and the temple. In the course of his Sermon on the Mount, Matthew's Jesus counsels his hearers on how to behave when making a "gift before the altar." If the worshiper has a problem with another member of the community ("your brother"), he should reconcile with that person first. Only then complete the offering, teaches Jesus. The point to note is that this story presumes that Jesus' followers would make temple offerings.[40]

The fourth gospel's Jerusalem-centered story implies that Jesus would have been involved with purity rituals when he was in the capital, given how much of his time he spent within the temple complex. Even later, ex-pagan gentile hearers of this gospel would presuppose the same: nobody in antiquity, Jewish or pagan, would ever have entered a sacred precinct without first undergoing some sort of purification. The details of that ritual would differ according to the god involved; the principle of human purification to approach divinity would not.[41]

Finally, all four gospels depict Jesus going up to Jerusalem for his last Passover in advance of the feast, entering the city with crowds of other pilgrims. What is he, and what are they, doing there all together at the same time? Once again, ancient Jewish practices of purification underlie the surface of the story.[42]

We think of "Passover" as a point in time, beginning on one specific date. In antiquity, however, the holiday, linked with the seven days of the feast of Unleavened Bread, spread out over a zone of time, a period that could stretch into three to four weeks. Travel to the city would bring the pilgrim there no later than seven days *before* the actual beginning of the holiday. Jews would go up to Jerusalem early because the Bible required that they undergo a weeklong process of purification preparatory to the feast, a purification requiring water and the ashes of a red heifer.

This was because most people were in a state of impurity most of the time. Menses, semen, childbirth, burial of the dead: all of these (more-or-less inevitable) occurrences rendered a person "impure." Impurity, in other words, was a (natural) state that a person moved into and out of. It implied no "sinful" condition or permanent status; rather, it simply limited a person's access to the temple. The remedy for impurity was purification—usually some combination of washing and waiting.

God had commanded Israel to eat the commemorative Passover meal in a state of purity. The most virulent form of impurity came from contact with a human corpse. Scripture specified a seven-day rite that removed corpse impurity, which required worshipers to be sprinkled with a special "water of cleansing" on the third and the seventh day of the rite. (The Bible details this ritual in Numbers 19.) After this, together with immersion, the celebrant was properly prepared to observe the holy day.

Only once the seven-day purification process was complete, by the afternoon of 14 Nisan, would the active sacrificing in the temple begin. The Synoptics, in presenting the Last Supper itself as the Passover meal, thus further imply that at least one of Jesus' circle of disciples had been up to the temple to offer the lamb during the afternoon of the day of 14 Nisan. That would have been the only way to secure "*the* Passover," that is, the sacrificial meat at the ceremonial center of the meal. Finally (since Jewish days begin at nightfall) a few hours later, the evening of 15 Nisan, the holiday meal would begin. Unleavened Bread (*matzah*) would be observed for the rest of the week. More ceremonies in the temple marked the close of the holiday. And then, slowly, Jerusalem would empty out as pilgrims began to make their way home. When John's gospel presents Jesus going up to Jerusalem for a feast, this week-long ritual would have preceded the process of celebration. Each trip would require a stay of several weeks.

Both John the Baptizer and Jesus of Nazareth thus seem to have incorporated Jerusalem and the temple in positive ways as part of their missions, and especially as part of their prophecy of the coming Kingdom. They had good biblical reasons for doing so. Those passages in scripture that speak of God's Kingdom also foreground Jerusalem, and specifically *har bayit Adonai*, the "mountain of the Lord's house," that is, of God's "house," the temple. Isaiah, for example, foresees the day when all humanity, both Israel and the nations, will gather there to worship God. "I am coming to gather all nations and tongues, and they will come and see my glory," God says, speaking through the prophet. Assembling on "this mountain," the mountain of the Lord's house in Jerusalem, all of these peoples will feast together on a meal made by God himself. "Their burnt offerings and their sacrifices will be accepted on my altar," God says of the last days, concerning the foreign-born who have joined themselves to Israel, "for my house"—that is, the temple—"will be called a house of prayer for all the nations." When the Kingdom comes, sing these biblical traditions, it comes in Jerusalem.[43]

Neither figure, John or Jesus, seems to have linked his prophecy to a call to violent resistance against any political leader, whether Jewish or Roman. God, not human armies, would establish his Kingdom (in some versions of the prophecy, through the agency of his messiah). And the Jesus of the synoptic tradition, in striking contrast to his fellow Galilean, Judas, specifically teaches that Judeans should pay the Roman tax.[44]

Nonetheless, both men died violent deaths. Antipas, another of Herod's sons and the ruler of the Galilee, had John arrested, imprisoned, and then beheaded. According to Josephus, the problem was John's popularity. He had gathered such a large and committed group of followers that Antipas, within whose territory John ranged, feared "sedition." Why specifically, apart from the number and the enthusiasm of John's followers, Josephus does not say. What the prophetic John said, in other words, and what he taught, seems to have mattered much less than did the size and the enthusiasm of the crowds attending to his message. It was the numbers and the commitment of John's followers that made Antipas nervous, not what John was telling them.

But against Jesus, in the Galilee, Antipas never made a move. This implies that Jesus' popular following there was noticeably smaller than John's near the Jordan had been. Had things been otherwise, Antipas would have struck Jesus, too.

If so—that is, if the number of Jesus' Galilean followers occasioned no alarm on the part of (Jewish) Galilee's ruling authority, Antipas—then things must have changed significantly during Jesus' final Passover in (Roman) Judea, in Jerusalem. There, Rome moved decisively against Jesus. And he died by crucifixion, a manner of death reserved particularly for insurrectionists. The titulus over his cross read "King of the Jews." These data all point in the same direction: because of the size and enthusiasm of the crowds around Jesus in the city during that holiday, the Romans, too, like Antipas vis-à-vis John, were concerned about sedition.

The titulus over the cross, "King of the Jews," gives us just a bit more information: those crowds were proclaiming Jesus the messiah. Crucifixion—an ugly, slow, highly visible form of public execution—was Pilate's way of disabusing the crowds of that idea. Had Pilate had a problem with only Jesus himself, he could have neutralized Jesus easily, by any of the many means that the prefect had at his disposal. The crucifixion points—and points us—in another direction: away from Jesus himself, toward those watching him die. Pilate did not have a problem with Jesus. Pilate had a problem with the crowds who followed him.[45]

◆◆◆

From this brief review of material about attitudes toward the temple evinced in Paul's letters, in the Dead Sea Scrolls, in the gospels, and in Josephus, a few points clearly emerge.

Hostility toward Jerusalem's temple, toward its priests—especially the high priest—and toward the way that it was run characterized only one body of materials: the Dead Sea Scrolls. That hostility and those criticisms were generated by very specific political circumstances, namely the Hasmoneans' disruption of Zadokite high priestly privilege. The internal Seleucid power struggle that followed from the early death of the Syrian Greek ruler Antiochus had led to Jonathan's surprising—and totally unanticipated, and biblically irregular—appointment as high priest. That was a black day, as far as the Zadokite Teacher of Righteousness was concerned.

Jonathan's younger brother Simon later consolidated political power further, and his descendants, the heads of a now independent Jewish state, were recognized as "kings." This only increased Essene disapproval. High priests but not Zadokites, the Hasmoneans were now kings, but obviously not of David's line. (Priests, *cohanim*, were a clan within the tribe of Levi; David had been a lay Israelite from the tribe of Benjamin.)[46]

These scriptural irregularities might be what stands behind the Essenes' expecting not one but (at least) two messiahs at the End of Days. The first and more important would be the messiah son of Aaron, the priestly messiah. (Priests, like kings, were anointed when they took office; and Aaron, Moses's brother, had been the first high priest of Israel.) The second "anointed one," the messiah son of David, a warrior like his namesake, would take part in the apocalyptic battle. And finally, in those days, the defiled temple of their enemies would be destroyed, and the true temple—the pure and perfect temple, the one run the way that the Essenes thought it should be run—would be secured. When he established his Kingdom, God would put things right.[47]

Even the Essenes, then, were not antitemple per se. They were against the Hasmoneans' temple. If anything, their elaboration of purity rituals, and their enormous (and compensatory) attention to what the final temple would look like and how it would run underscores the intense temple commitment of this priestly group. And all of the other sources that we examined present early first-century figures—Judah and Zadok in 6 C.E., John the Baptizer and Jesus of Nazareth in the late 20s–early 30s C.E., Paul in the late 40s–late 50s C.E.—who view the temple and its operations positively.

What sense, then, are we to make of that story, presented both in the synoptic gospels and in John, wherein Jesus seems to repudiate the temple, and enacts its so-called "cleansing" by overturning the tables of the moneychangers?

TWO

GOD'S HOLY MOUNTAIN

A positive orientation toward the temple and its cult seems to have been a virtually universal index of Jewish piety in the period before the first revolt against Rome. Particular priests might come in for criticism; the temple itself did not. We have inferred from the gospel stories that Jesus himself shared in this orientation. And that inference is supported by two later facts: first, his earliest followers, after his death, chose to settle in Jerusalem and to participate in normal temple worship; and, second, Paul's letters—our earliest source for the movement around Jesus—express such piety as well. If Jesus himself ever issued a condemnation of the temple and its operations, in other words, his first followers, Paul included, knew nothing about it.[1]

THE TABLES OF THE MONEYCHANGERS

Such a reconstruction, however, seems contradicted by a famous gospel episode, related both in John and in the synoptic tradition. I speak of "The Cleansing of the Temple."

This is John's version, set at the very beginning of Jesus' mission, John 2.13–16:

> 13 The Passover of the Jews was at hand, and Jesus went up to
> Jerusalem. 14 In the temple he found those who were selling
> oxen and sheep and pigeons, and the moneychangers at their
> business. 15 And making a whip of cords, he drove them all, with
> the sheep and the oxen, out of the temple; and he poured out the
> coins of the moneychangers and overturned their tables. 16 And
> he told those who sold the pigeons, "Take these things away; you
> shall not make my father's house a house of trade."

And this is Mark's version, set at the close of Jesus' mission, Mark 11.15–17:

> 15 And they came to Jerusalem. And he entered the temple and
> began to drive out those who sold and those who bought in the
> temple, and he overturned the tables of the moneychangers and
> the seats of those who sold pigeons; 16 and he would not allow
> any one to carry anything through the temple. 17 And he taught,
> and said to them, "Is it not written, 'My house shall be called a
> house of prayer for all the nations'? But you have made it into
> a den of robbers."

The scene functions differently in its two different literary settings. John segues immediately to a seeming prediction of the temple's destruction: "Destroy this temple, and in three days I will raise it up." This turns out to be a heavily symbolic reference to Jesus himself. "But he spoke of the temple of his body. When therefore he was raised from the dead, his disciples remembered that he had said this."[2]

Mark, by contrast, needs this scene for purposes of plot. Mark has to introduce hostile priests into his story, to account for resistance to Jesus in Jerusalem where, according to the evangelist, Jesus has only just arrived. Putting the episode's Markan function aside for the time being, however, both passages, John's and Mark's, clearly sound a negative tone. Jesus in both stories appears to enact some sort of moral condemnation of the temple and of its activities.

In the traditional interpretation of these passages, Jesus "cleanses" the temple of trade, which is consequently held as compromising the temple's rightful function as a place of prayer. Getting and spending in the temple by implication defiles it, whether morally, spiritually, or both. John's Jesus states so plainly ("You shall not make my father's house a house of trade"). Mark's Jesus, quoting Isaiah 56.7, seems to favor prayer over sacrifice ("My house shall be a house of prayer for all the nations"). Clear from both passages is a ringing disapproval of changing money and of selling sacrificial pigeons (and, according to John, of selling sheep and oxen as well). Mark's Jesus, besides emphasizing prayer, seems further to accuse the tradesmen of dishonesty: they are "robbers."[3]

John's version, albeit very dramatic, is also historically impossible. Sheep and oxen were never penned within the temple precincts: they would have turned the outer court into a barnyard. (Pigeons, kept in baskets, posed no such problem.) Mark's version is odd in other ways. For instance, the quotation from Isaiah 56.7 does not really suit its evangelical context. In Jesus' day, for those pagans gathered in the Court of the Nations, the temple would have been functioning already as a "house of prayer." Pagans could not bring sacrifices in the Second Temple: offerings were brought through the interior courts, to which they had no access. But they surely could pray. Also, the Isaiah text itself does not support prayer over-against sacrifice. The preceding clause in the prophetic scripture foretells that, at the end of days, gentiles would be able to offer sacrifices at the temple: "*their burnt offerings and their sacrifices will be accepted on my altar*; for my house will be called a house of prayer for all peoples."

A second historical issue also looms: the problem of empirical description. Mark follows his depiction of Jesus' action against the moneychangers by saying, in verse 16, that Jesus "would not allow anyone to carry anything through the temple." But the temple plaza was enormous, and it had several points of entry and egress. How does Mark imagine Jesus' preventing anyone from carrying anything into or out of such a huge area? Jesus would have needed an army. And the army that we know actually *was* present—Roman soldiers up from Caesarea with Pilate, stationed at intervals on the roof of the surrounding stoa precisely to insure that things ran smoothly—would have to have been singularly derelict or incompetent to permit such a disruption. Mark's scene, in other words, is untroubled by a strong sense of realism.

Finally, again with Mark, we have a problem with the standard English translation of this passage. Mark's condemnation of the temple as "a house of robbers" has caused no end of confusion. The word for "robbers"—*lēstai* in Greek—reappears at Mark 14.46, when Jesus protests that the arresting party has come for him as if he were a "robber" (singular, *lēstēs*). And the word appears again at Mark's crucifixion scene, where Jesus is hanged between two otherwise unidentified "robbers" (so the Revised Standard Version [RSV], at Mark 15.27). The uninformed reader can walk away with the impression that Rome crucified people for larceny.

A *lēstēs*, however, was not a "thief." *Lēstai* were political brigands—militants, rebels, insurrectionists. That is how Josephus uses the term. The Greek of Mark's sentence actually means something like, "You have turned the temple into a hiding place for revolutionaries." The appearance of such a politically laden word in traditions clustering around the Passion narratives is intriguing: someone accused of being a *lēstēs* could quite easily wind up on a cross. Paired with the rest of Mark's episode, in its context here in the temple's outer court, however—Jesus' action against moneychangers and pigeon sellers—this statement makes little sense.

But looking at this episode, whether in Mark's version or in John's, as a protest against changing money, or perhaps (given the pigeons, and John's stampeding quadrupeds) against making sacrifices, also makes little historical sense. The purpose of Jerusalem's temple, as of any ancient temple, was to serve as the site for sacrifices. Jewish protocols of sacrifice had been detailed in four of the five books of the Torah. They were preserved in tradition as the commands of God to Moses for Israel at Sinai. "To think of leaving off those sacrifices is to every Jew plainly impossible," wrote Josephus, who goes on to say that his people "would rather give up their lives than the worship which they are accustomed to offer God." Money changing and access to unblemished offerings were support services. They were set up to assist and to accommodate worshipers, such as Mary and Joseph, Jesus' parents, when they came to the temple after Jesus' birth and offered pigeons. Taken as a protest against sacrifice as such, in short, this scene hovers between incoherent and impossible.[4]

Aware of this historical problem, some scholars have argued that Jesus' imputed words in the temple court reflect a negative attitude toward the temple only on the part of the later evangelists, not of Jesus himself. Writing in the period after 70, in the wake of the war with Rome, the evangelists themselves condemned the workings of an institution that no longer existed, these scholars maintain. But the gospels' words, they insist, do not correspond to the meaning of the historical Jesus' actions.

Many modern scholars therefore scissor out as later evangelical editorial additions Jesus' negative *statements:* "Take these things away; you shall not make my father's house a house of trade" (John 2.16). "Is it not written, 'My house shall be called a house of prayer for all the nations'? But you have made it into a den of robbers" (Mark 11.17). Instead, they focus on a different aspect of Jesus' performance: his deed. The historical question accordingly shifts from, "What did Jesus mean when he spoke these words?" to, "What did Jesus mean when he performed this act?" The condemnatory words, say these scholars, come from the later evangelists. But the action of overturning the tables itself, so goes this argument, was a remembered event of the historical Jesus of Nazareth himself. What would Jesus have meant by making such a gesture?

Here, we can draw connections between Jesus' action and the apocalyptic content of his good news, namely that the Kingdom of God was at hand. Belief in the establishment of a renewed, enlarged, and improved temple coheres with this message. We have already noted this belief attested in the *Temple Scroll* of Qumran. Other Jewish apocalyptic texts and traditions mention an improved Endtime temple as well. And the Bible presupposes it: after all, at the End, according to Isaiah, the temple has to accommodate all humanity. So also the Book of Tobit, a text set in the period of the Assyrian invasion of the northern kingdom of Israel—that is, in 722 B.C.E.—but actually written in the period just before the Maccabees (c. 200 B.C.E.): "They will rebuild the House of God. . . . the House of God will be rebuilt there [in Jerusalem] with a glorious building for all generations forever."[5]

Overturned tables, in this reading, simply and visually reinforced Jesus' prophetic message. He symbolically enacted the *current* temple's coming *apocalyptic* destruction. At or as the End of the Age, God would demolish the standing temple, Herod's temple, in order to replace it with the final, glorious, eschatological temple of the Kingdom, one "not made by the hand of man." Such a prediction of destruction would imply no censure of the current temple. Jesus made no such negative judgment. His action functioned, rather, to prophesy visually the approach of the End.[6]

This interpretation is possible, even credible. It coheres with other apocalyptic Jewish themes about a new temple at the end of the age. And it has the great virtue of making sense of all the other positive traditions about the temple that we have seen in Paul and in the gospels, and that we will see later in Acts, which depicts the original apostolic community's frequenting the temple. Jesus' later followers, on this construction, valued the temple because Jesus himself had valued it, too. His visual prophecy of its impending destruction, enacted in the Court of the Nations, neither pronounced nor implied any condemnation of the temple or of the temple's function. It was simply another way of announcing the nearness of the Kingdom.[7]

The theme of the temple's and of the city's destruction hangs heavily over all the gospels' accounts. Elsewhere in their stories, the evangelists portray Jesus as forthrightly predicting the temple's impending demise. "Do you see these great buildings?" asks Mark's Jesus. "There will not be left here one stone upon another that will not be thrown down." "Destroy this temple," John's Jesus predicts, "and in three days I will raise it up." Matthew and Luke both present Jesus' saying, "Behold, your house [meaning: the temple] is forsaken [and desolate]." Further, Luke portrays Jesus as mourning over the city, foreseeing its demolition. Finally, before the Sanhedrin, Mark's Jesus is accused of saying that he will destroy the temple himself. And at the trial of Stephen in Acts, his accusers likewise claim that "we have heard [Stephen] say that this Jesus of Nazareth will destroy this place"—that is, the temple.[8]

Did Jesus, circa 30 C.E., indeed predict the coming destruction of the temple? Since all of the gospels were written after the fall of Jerusalem in 70, it is difficult to say. Perhaps, though, this theme, presented in so many different versions in all of these various New Testament texts, indeed represents the garbled recollection of a genuine prophecy by Jesus of Nazareth: namely, that God would replace the current temple with the final one at the End of the Age.

Perhaps. But on this point we encounter another awkward silence, this one emanating from Paul.

Paul's letters antedate the gospels by one or two generations. He is the *only* New Testament author who unquestionably lived before the Roman destruction of Jerusalem. Paul personally knew Peter, John, and probably others among the original disciples. His instructions to his gentile congregations on the looming approach of God's Kingdom—associated, in this postresurrection phase of the movement, with Jesus' imminent glorious second coming—are a vivid and vital part of his gospel, which he claims to have by prior tradition, through the original apostles themselves. For example, in his earliest letter, 1 Thessalonians, Paul says, "This we declare to you by the word of the Lord," and he then goes on to describe events at the End. "I delivered to you as of first importance," he repeats to his Corinthian assembly, "what I also received," that is, traditions about Jesus' death and his resurrection appearances, which Paul goes on to link to Jesus' impending return.[9]

Here, then, is the problem. If Jesus had actually made such a spectacular prophecy of the temple's destruction (as Mark's thirteenth chapter depicts him doing); or if he had *enacted* such a prophecy so dramatically at such a key moment in his mission (the scene in the temple's court with the moneychangers, as decoded by modern scholars); if Paul were colleagues with those men who must themselves have known that prophecy (they had been with Jesus in Jerusalem that Passover); and if Paul himself throughout his letters proclaims the signs of the coming Kingdom to his own communities, then *why does Paul evince no knowledge of Jesus' prediction?*

We have only seven letters from Paul. He was an active apostle for close to thirty years. Clearly he dictated more than seven letters in all that time. The greater part of his correspondence is lost—which may have included, for all we know, his definitive description of Jesus' action in the temple's court and his prediction of the temple's destruction. Yet in the letters that we do have, Paul's eschatological teaching about the approaching Endtime represents traditions that, he himself claims, go back to Jesus and to his earliest followers. And there are so many places in his letters where he does describe events at the End: in 1 Thessalonians 4, on Jesus' second coming and the Endtime resurrection of the dead; in 1 Corinthians 15, on the same themes; in Romans chapter 8 (cosmic redemption), or chapter 11 (the salvation of all humanity, both Israel and the nations), or chapter 15 (on all these themes). Yet he nowhere tells any of his communities that, according to "the word of the Lord," the destruction of the temple would signal the Kingdom's approach.[10]

The temple fell in 70 C.E. All of the evangelists wrote after 70 C.E. The source of the gospels' predictions of the temple's destruction may very well have been the historical event itself—an event that Jesus and his contemporaries, such as Paul, never saw coming. But if that is the case, then we still need to ask two questions, one literary, the other historical: How, at a literary level, do these retrojected predictions of the temple's demise function to move the plot along within the two quite different stories that Mark and John tell? And how, historically, do issues involving the temple relate to the reasons why Jesus of Nazareth was crucified?

THE FEASTS OF THE JEWS

Let's approach these two different sets of questions, the literary and the historical, by reviewing, thus comparing, the two different itineraries of Jesus' mission that our New Testament sources offer us.

In Mark, Matthew, and Luke, Jesus goes to Jerusalem for Passover only once, at the end of his mission. Other pilgrims celebrate his entry, hailing him as the messenger of the coming Kingdom. And the crowd's cries conjure kingship, specifically that of David. Thus Mark: "Blessed is the coming Kingdom of our father David!" So also Matthew: "Hosanna to the Son of David!" "Blessed is the king who comes in the name of the Lord!" Luke's crowd shouts. This messianic or kingly entrance then leads immediately to the scene at the temple, where Jesus overturns the tables of the moneychangers. In consequence of that action, Jesus earns the enmity of the priests: They resolve to destroy him. But, states the synoptic tradition, Jesus was hugely popular. For this reason, the priests realize that they must arrest him by stealth, "lest there be a tumult among the people." In the synoptic scenario, in other words, the size and the enthusiasm of Jesus' following among the holiday crowds in the city means that Jesus must be arrested covertly.[11]

That Thursday night after the Passover meal, in the evening of 15 Nisan, the synoptic gospels' hostile priests get their chance. A crowd of Jews sent out by the chief priests captures Jesus in the garden of Gethsemane. They then lead him to a fully assembled Sanhedrin, the ruling priestly council. There the high priest confronts Jesus with the question, "Are you the messiah, the son of [God]?" In Mark, Jesus dramatically affirms the identification: "I am. And you will see the son of man"—Jesus' self-designation of choice in this gospel—"seated at the right hand of the power [that is, God] and coming with the clouds of heaven." The high priest deems this statement blasphemous, and the council condemns Jesus to death. After the full Sanhedrin convenes a second time early the following morning, it hands Jesus over to Pilate, who (unprompted) asks, "Are you king of the Jews?" to which Jesus answers, "So you say."[12]

At this point—somewhat inexplicably, given that Jesus' popularity had required the priests to work by stealth only a few hours before—a hostile crowd suddenly appears. They insist that Pilate release Barabbas, a known insurrectionist and murderer, rather than Jesus. The reluctant Pilate, wishing to please the people, does so; and he then hands Jesus over to be crucified between two other insurrectionists, "robbers" in the RSV translation. The charge over Jesus' cross reads "King of the Jews." Jesus dies a few hours later, before the beginning of the Sabbath. His Sabbath-keeping female followers therefore wait until Sunday morning to visit his tomb, which, they discover, is empty. The other two synoptic gospels, Matthew and Luke, vary in detail but generally adhere to the same story line as Mark.

John's story line is dramatically different. His Jesus goes to Jerusalem repeatedly. Shortly after his (offstage) immersion by John the Baptizer, Jesus enters the city for Passover, when he enacts the scene in the temple. At that point, Jesus names "the Jews" as the destroyers of the temple, in a prophecy that actually concerns not the temple's destruction so much as his own resurrection ("'Destroy this temple, and in three days I will raise it up.' . . . But he spoke of the temple of his body"). This disruption causes no complications for Jesus, neither when he performs it nor when he returns to the city for another feast, three chapters later. Indeed, whenever he enters Jerusalem, John's Jesus teaches in and around the temple complex. In terms of Jesus' reception in Jerusalem, and in terms specifically of his later arrest and arraignment, John's temple scene is utterly irrelevant.[13]

Only during his final trip for Passover is Jesus hailed by the crowds in messianic terms. "Blessed is the one who comes in the name of the Lord: The King of Israel!" Unbeknownst to Jesus' followers, however, the chief priests and Pharisees, well before the holiday, had already convened a full meeting of the Sanhedrin to discuss Jesus' fate and to settle on a course of action. What in John's story caused their alarm, if not the scene in the temple? The priests, says John, were worried about the potential political and military consequences of Jesus' raising Lazarus from the dead. (Why or how this should concern the Romans is nowhere explained.) Afraid that, on account of Jesus' performing such signs, the Romans might "come and destroy both our holy place"—that is, the temple—"and our nation," the council at this earlier point resolved to seek his death. As the high priest Caiaphas observes, "It is better for you that one man die for the people than to have the whole nation destroyed."[14]

That Thursday night, 14 Nisan, Jesus shares with his disciples a final meal. (This "last supper" is *not* a Passover meal which, according to John's chronology, would occur only on the following night, a Friday.) Walking in a garden thereafter, Jesus is captured. The arresting party is comprised of the temple police (Jerusalemite locals) and a detachment of Roman soldiers (men who had come with Pilate from Caesarea). They lead Jesus to Annas, Caiaphas's father-in-law, who questions Jesus "about his disciples and about his teaching." Jesus responds by saying that he has always taught openly, both in synagogues and in the temple "where all Jews come together. I have said nothing in secret." Jesus is then brought to Caiaphas the high priest, though no dialogue passes between them.[15]

In the morning, the priests walk Jesus over to the praetorium and Pilate. Pilate immediately asks, unprompted, "Are you the King of the Jews?" After some back-and-forth, and the release of Barabbas, a "robber" (so the RSV: the word again is *lēstēs*, "revolutionary"), the reluctant Pilate bows to the will of the priests, their police force, and a suddenly assembled, hostile crowd of Jews. (Again, and like the synoptic evangelists, John does not trouble to explain how Jesus' extreme popularity, which necessitated the ambush in the garden, fits with his extreme *un*popularity within hours of his arrest, literally from dark to dawn.) Jesus is nailed to the cross early Friday afternoon, at about the same time that the Passover lambs are being slaughtered in the temple. He hangs beneath the charge "Jesus of Nazareth, King of the Jews." Jesus is buried before Friday nightfall, just before the Passover feast begins. Early the following Sunday morning, Mary Magdalene discovers that the tomb is empty. Shortly thereafter she meets the risen Christ, who later that day appears to the assembled disciples as well.[16]

The Synoptics and John relate two versions of what is clearly the same basic story. It is their variations, however, that may give us some historical purchase on their respective accounts. We see these most clearly if we compare their narrative chronologies, that is, the sequence of events shaping their stories. Since Matthew and Luke closely follow Mark, I will let Mark represent the synoptic tradition. And since I think that Mark wrote prior to John, I will number the individual episodes shaping each gospel according to the sequence of events in Mark.

JESUS' ITINERARIES IN MARK AND JOHN

Mark	*John*
1. Mission (Galilee)	1. Mission (Galilee/Judea/Jerusalem)
	4. *"Cleansing of the Temple"*
	5. Teaching on the Temple Mount
	8. Sanhedrin "trial" (ch. 11)
2. Jerusalem for final Passover	2. Jerusalem for final Passover
3. Triumphal entry	3. Triumphal entry
4. *"Cleansing of the Temple"*	
5. Teaching on the Temple Mount	5. Teaching on the Temple Mount
6. Final meal (Passover)	6. Final meal (pre-Passover)
7. Ambush and arrest (Jewish mob)	7. Ambush and arrest (temple police plus Roman soldiers)
8. Sanhedrin trials	8. Hearing before Annas
9. Interrogation before Pilate	9. Interrogation before Pilate
10. Crucifixion as "King of the Jews"	10. Crucifixion as "King of the Jews"

Item 4, the "Cleansing of the Temple," as we have noted, skips around in the sequence of events between these two different gospel traditions. Two other major differences between them should also be noted. One is the social makeup of the group arresting Jesus. The synoptic gospels, item 7, feature a Jewish "crowd" or "mob." John, instead, names temple police, thus, agents of the high priest, who work in concert with a detachment of Roman soldiers, thus, agents of Pilate. Finally, item 8, relating Jesus' experience with the priests just before his execution, is also very different. Was Jesus "tried" before the full Sanhedrin and charged with blasphemy (so Mark), or was he merely interrogated separately by Annas, and then (presumably) by Caiaphas (so John)? John's gospel, in other words, depicts no full priestly council the night of

Jesus' arrest and, even more strikingly, no charge of blasphemy. For John, what motivates the Sanhedrin's decision about Jesus—taken even before Jesus comes up to the city for the last time—is politics, not piety. The Sanhedrin fears Rome.

We will examine these differences momentarily, to try to discern what the history behind these divergent stories might be. Toward that same end, however, we should also note where the two traditions *agree* with each other. If we bracket out item 4, the floating story about the "Cleansing of the Temple," the two gospels present the same sequence of events for Jesus' final sojourn in Jerusalem. In both traditions, Jesus journeys to Jerusalem for his last Passover (2). Rapturous crowds greet him, proclaiming messianic titles and themes (3, the "triumphal entry"). Jesus then teaches on Temple Mount (5). Later, he and his disciples share a final meal (6), after which Jesus is ambushed, arrested (7), and variously interrogated by Jewish and Roman authorities (8 and 9). Before nightfall on Friday, Jesus dies crucified as "King of the Jews" (10). Both the Synoptics and John, in other words, follow in the same order for these final events. Their details diverge; their respective outlines, however, converge.

I suggest, then, that we start with what we know to be firm historical facts, and then reflect on these gospel traditions with these facts in mind. The firmest fact that we have about Jesus' life is his death. *Jesus was crucified, which means that he was executed by Pilate.* The messianic praises that shape gospel traditions about his triumphal entry; the claim that he was executed as "King of the Jews"; his being hanged between two insurrectionists (*lēstai*, again, the RSV's "robbers"); the fact of his crucifixion itself, a death that Rome reserved particularly for insurrectionists: the convergence of these gospel traditions with this premier historical fact points in the direction of political offense as the reason why Jesus was killed.

Pilate executed Jesus as an insurrectionist because Pilate thought that Jesus was politically and possibly militarily dangerous. "Insurrection" means armed uprising; Rome tolerated no such activities on the part of its subject peoples.

Against this reconstruction, however, stands another indisputable historical fact: None of Jesus' close followers, whether on this Passover or thereafter, once they settled back in Jerusalem, was also arrested and executed. The gospels report no mass crucifixions of Jesus' disciples, and neither does Josephus (who, had they occurred, especially at Passover, would surely have mentioned the event).

This fact immediately undermines our preceding conclusion. Had Pilate truly thought that Jesus was politically or militarily dangerous, he would have rounded up and executed his immediate followers as well. When Rome dispatched charismatic leaders, they dispatched the crowds around them, too, as Josephus narrates time and again. The fact that, of all those associated with his movement, it was Jesus alone who died implies that Pilate knew perfectly well that Jesus was *not* dangerous. (The two *lēstai* with whom he dies are nowhere presented as party to Jesus' movement.) Why, then, did Pilate execute Jesus, and specifically *by* crucifixion?[17]

And finally, reinforcing the implication that Pilate knew that Jesus was harmless, we have another fact: *after Jesus' death, the community of his earliest followers settled in Jerusalem.* Pilate remained prefect, and Caiaphas high priest, for years after Jesus' death, until 36 C.E. Evidently, from the time of Jesus' crucifixion through the rest of the length of Pilate's term of office, Jesus' followers were unafraid of being branded as insurrectionists, or of being mistaken for such. After all, they established their community in the city very shortly after their leader's execution. Nor, evidently, was Pilate concerned about Jesus' followers on this account, that is, fear of insurrection. Pilate left them alone. So again: why did Pilate execute Jesus *as though* he thought that Jesus was dangerous? Or, turning the same question a different way: *how* did Pilate know that Jesus was not truly dangerous?

Let's consider the sequence of events during the last week of Jesus' life, as supported by both evangelical traditions, which means bracketing out the scene in the temple.

A straight line connects the messianic acclaim of the triumphal entry with Jesus' death as King of the Jews. Framing both events is Jesus' boisterous popularity on that particular Passover. Of all the trips he makes to teach in Jerusalem, the triumphal entry marks only his last.

Taking seriously the pilgrim crowd's enthusiasm, further, in turn underscores two other aspects of the Passion story. The first concerns something that the evangelists do not mention; the second, something that they emphasize.

Missing in all iterations of this story is any allusion to a strong Roman response to counter the popular messianic acclamation of Jesus' triumphal entry. As one historian notes, "A public demonstration, accompanied by shouts of 'king' or even of 'kingdom,' would have been highly inflammatory. Passover was a prime time for trouble-makers to incite a crowd, and both the high priest and the Roman prefect were alert to the danger." Yet in all four gospels, this noisy, public demonstration does not lead to any effort by either authority, Jewish or Roman, to contain or cut short the crowd's enthusiasm. Jesus simply spends the rest of his time teaching in the temple courts in the week before the feast.[18]

The second aspect of the Passion story, this one emphasized in all the gospels, is the need to arrest Jesus in secret. Traditions about his public acclaim cohere with this part of the story: Jesus' popularity compels the authorities' stealth. Arresting Jesus in public, especially while he was teaching in the temple courts, might have risked riot—something that both the priests and Pilate would want to avoid at all costs. The prefect and the high priest were always on the same side of this issue. The city during the feasts was a pressure cooker; and any tumult—which could so easily careen out of control into violence—could and would cost them their jobs.[19]

On this last point—Jesus' arrest by stealth at night—we have a choice to make between the two gospel traditions about the composition of the arresting party. Was it a Jewish mob sent out by the chief priests (so the Synoptics)? Or was it a mixed contingent of temple police and Roman soldiers (so John)? If the former, we have to wonder how secret a mob action could be kept. If the latter, then Pilate was already involved in the dragnet: Roman soldiers took orders only from him, not from the priests. And if Pilate were already involved at the stage of Jesus' arrest, there would be no reason for him later to have a public hearing about and with Jesus, as all the gospel stories present. Pilate's mind would have already been made up.[20]

What, finally, about the respective "trials," one or two before the full Sanhedrin (Synoptics), one before Pilate that turns into a hearing before crowds of hostile Jews (Synoptics plus John)?[21]

If we want to hold on to a date for Jesus' arrest on or just before Passover, the likelihood of a Sanhedrin trial all but vanishes. The priests had pressing, indeed overwhelming responsibilities at the temple on account of the holiday. Besides ensuring that people had access to the required purifications for Passover, there was preparing the temple courts for the onslaught of tens of thousands of men, with sheep or goats, to be sacrificed and butchered within the temple precincts, all within a brief span of the afternoon, in the closing hours of 14 Nisan.

Josephus gives us a sense of the scope of this scene. He reports a rough census made by the priests on one Passover. They estimated that one sheep served for a dining group of ten men. (This number therefore excludes from view how many people total, adding in women and children, would have been in the city for the feast.) They counted, he says, a total of 255,600 sheep slain, thus of Jewish men sacrificing. How all this could have occurred in so few hours in one afternoon continues to mystify and confound historians; but somehow it did. The point is not Josephus' numbers per se, but the impression that they give. The priests were the ones responsible for making sure that everything ran to time, was properly done, and that the temple was cleaned and made fit for the services which would have occurred on the following day. Passover, quite simply, was one of the most hectic and most demanding days in their entire calendar.[22]

For this reason alone, Mark's depiction of not one but two full meetings of the priestly Sanhedrin, in the hours between late night and early morning—after a day of managing the sacrifices, overseeing the temple's operation, and after the priests had held their own commemorative meals—quite simply beggars belief. Matthew follows Mark, with two meetings. Luke, more reasonably, reduces the number to only one council meeting. Realistically, though, if we want to hold on to the night of 15 Nisan as the time of Jesus' arrest, the far most likely number of Sanhedrin hearings is zero.

Also, if Jesus had already been arrested, there would be no need for such (implausible and unlikely) urgency: he could easily have been imprisoned until the holiday wound to a close and the overexcited pilgrims would have left, wending their way homeward. The Jewish trial scenes, and especially Mark's and Matthew's head-to-head confrontation of the high priest ("Are you the messiah, the son of God?") and Jesus ("I am"), are powerful both dramatically and—even more so—theologically. Historically, however, in light of what we know the priests were coping with—the most harried day of their year—the likelihood of any such trial virtually vanishes.[23]

The "trial" before Pilate presents other problems of historical plausibility. The likelihood of his holding any such hearing in public was absolutely nil, in light of Jesus' popularity. Historically, Jesus' popularity is *the* condition, both necessary and sufficient, for his arrest and crucifixion. Yet in all four gospels, Jewish mobs are there, baying for Jesus' death, demanding the release of the known insurrectionist and murderer, Barabbas. Only the night before, the city's population was so sympathetic to Jesus that he had to be arrested in secret.[24]

The crowds' wholesale defection between nightfall and morning is completely unexplained in the gospels. Had the people in Jerusalem in reality been so against Jesus, there would have been no reason for Pilate to crucify him. Jesus would have posed no destabilizing threat. In addition, Pilate would have been extremely incompetent had he released a known insurrectionist, Barabbas, just because a subject crowd told him to. The hostile Jewish mob seems to be the construct of the evangelists, the better to exculpate Pilate.[25]

Once again, the scene before Pilate serves an apologetic and theological function. Rome is benign; Jews are bad. (Referring back to this scene, "Peter" in Acts 3.13 virtually says as much when he teaches about "Jesus, whom you"—Jerusalem's Jews—"delivered up and denied . . . in the presence of Pilate, when he had decided to release him.") As drama, the trial before Pilate is extremely effective. As history, the scene cannot be fit into what else we know had to have been the case—namely, that Jesus' popularity is what led him to his cross.

So why were Jesus' immediate followers not arrested and executed as well? If Pilate had truly thought for an instant that Jesus were a radical revolutionary, preaching rebellion against Rome, such a roundup would have been part and parcel of the operation. Making an example of insurrectionists, and quelling revolts, was the way that Rome ran its empire. Crucifixion broadcast Rome's zero-tolerance policy toward rebels.

Instead, what we have from the gospels is a tale of Jesus' followers, in Gethsemane—armed with "swords," no less—fleeing successfully once their leader is arrested. Were the temple police and the Roman soldiers really so incompetent?

Some scholars, who favor seeing Jesus as leading a movement of armed resistance, favor as well imagining his apostles in Gethsemane as actually armed. The gospels in English—and even in Latin—oblige this interpretation. Mark has one of Jesus' disciples draw his "sword," and then cut off the ear of the high priest's slave. Matthew's Jesus, after this event, says to this follower, "Put your sword back in its place; for all who take the sword will perish by the sword." Luke briefly embroiders this scene and has Jesus miraculously reattach the slave's ear. In John, the cutter becomes Peter, present with his "sword." Jesus scolds his disciple, but performs no healing miracle.[26]

This is a passage in the gospels where knowing not only the original Greek, but also the Hebrew that would stand behind it, matters vitally both to English translation and to historical understanding. In the original Greek text, the word translated here as "sword" is *machaira*. And one of the meanings of this word—as the ancient Latin translations tell us—is indeed "sword" (Latin: *gladius*). But this is not the first definition of this word, which is, rather, "knife," most specifically, the large knife used for the ritual sacrificing of animals. (This is the first definition of the term given in the standard academic Greek-English lexicon.) Despite the Latin and the English translations of *machaira* as "sword" in this scene, I want to urge, the word "knife" makes the most sense in historical context.[27]

Let's start thinking about these Gethsemane passages by thinking about swords. First of all, swords are large, awkward, and heavy. For that reason, therefore, and second, to know how to use them required training: in other words, swords were the weapon of "professionals," such as soldiers. Third, given their size, they would be difficult to conceal. (How do you walk around looking as if you do not have a sword on you, when you do?) Fourth: how do you cut off someone's ear with a *sword?* (Answer: very carefully.)

Finally, we have the biblical usage of the word at a key point in the Greek text of Genesis, namely the binding of Isaac. The word in the Hebrew text, *machelet*, means "sacrificial knife." The ancient Jewish translators of this Genesis text chose the Greek word *machaira* to indicate the implement in Abraham's hand. The word there, too, can only mean "knife." Isaac was to be sacrificed, that is, the arteries of his throat cut. Swords decapitate. Small precision cutting, such as a blood sacrifice would require, can only be done with a knife.[28]

In Gethsemane, then, some of Jesus of Nazareth's disciples may very well have carried *machairai*. And that makes good sense, given that they were in Jerusalem for the Passover holiday. At least some of them had come prepared to go up to the temple, to offer the Passover sacrifice. Men doing so would of necessity carry their own sacrificial knives. The city would have been replete with them. Remember Josephus' census: 255,600 paschal lambs meant at least 255,600 *machairai*. Carrying a sacrificial knife at such a holiday implies nothing in terms of armed revolt against Rome. In short: the gospels do not present Jesus' disciples as armed.

A further historical question: if Jesus had to be arrested by stealth, which group would accomplish that most quietly and efficiently, an armed mob of civilians (so the Synoptics), or a detachment of professionals (soldiers and temple police, so John)? I incline, again, toward John's description of the arresting party's personnel. The numbers that he implies, however, are impossible: John names a Roman cohort, a *speira* in John's Greek, which would comprise hundreds of soldiers, some 480 men, hardly the size for a covert operation. But John's scene does not suffer from an excess of realism, either: he also describes the entire posse as falling to the ground when they initially attempt Jesus' arrest. The historical point is this: once Jesus was arrested by this assigned contingent of police and soldiers, no subsequent conversation between Jesus and the high priest, or Jesus and the prefect, need have occurred at all. These men had their orders. At daybreak, Jesus could have gone straight to the cross.[29]

Why arrest Jesus, and Jesus alone? Because both the priests and Pilate knew that Jesus himself, thus the movement that he was leading, was in no practical way dangerous. Jesus was not fomenting insurrection. He was not rallying followers to overthrow colonial rule. He was not calling for a tax revolt. He did not agitate against Rome. He did not champion armed resistance. His followers were not armed. They were not verging on rebellion.[30]

But then the question remains: *How* did the high priest and the prefect know that Jesus was not really dangerous? For the reason that John's gospel—and only John's gospel—provides. Jesus had been up to Jerusalem for his mission on numerous occasions, and especially during the pilgrimage holidays. On those occasions, he proclaimed his message in the temple's Court of the Nations, when and where he was assured of finding the biggest crowds. He taught openly about the coming Kingdom of God, and about the need for repentance to prepare for it. He spoke of the fast-approaching redemption of the world, the resurrection of the dead, the triumph of good, the ultimate victory of peace. God, not human arms, would bring about this Kingdom. In no practical way did this message threaten Roman power, and most likely neither Caiaphas nor Pilate would ever have lost a night's sleep on its account.

So how did Jesus—and Jesus alone—end up on a cross? Again, we need to sift through motivated gospel traditions, written decades after the events that they purport to describe. What stands out in these traditions are their accounts of the triumphal entry, when Jesus himself is praised as the scion of David's house. And, as we observed above, that popular messianic acclaim connects immediately to the titulus over Jesus' cross, "King of the Jews."

Instead, extraordinarily, the gospels imply that after this outburst of popular messianic enthusiasm, nothing happened. Apparently, following this excited demonstration, Jesus simply goes on to teach on the Temple Mount—in John, as he had been doing for years—in the days before the feast.

If the traditions about the public acclaim of the triumphal entry are at all historically reliable, and if the report that Jesus moved freely around the city for the week thereafter is at all historically reliable, then we must account *both* for Pilate's and Caiaphas's initial inaction, *and* for their eventual response: the arrest and execution of Jesus, and of Jesus alone. How could the two men immediately responsible for ensuring quiet during the holiday have allowed Jesus to proceed as before, especially after such a public display of messianic enthusiasm? Again: precisely because they were already familiar with his nonviolent message, for the same reason that John's gospel—and John's alone—provides. Jesus had taught in Jerusalem many times before, during the feasts of the

Jews—precisely when Pilate would have been there, too. Jesus was a known quantity. In any practical way, his message of the impending Kingdom posed no political or military danger.

What, then, made this particular Passover different? Both evangelical traditions associate the triumphal entry with Jesus' final trip to Jerusalem. Both Mark and John, in other words, maintain that on *this* Passover, Jesus' last, the pilgrim crowds proclaimed him "messiah." The historical question then becomes, Why—especially if Jesus had been preaching the coming Kingdom for several years before this point—would the crowd suddenly do this? And why, no less surprisingly, would that proclamation finally prompt the authorities, this time, to react?

THE POLITICS OF PROPHECY

Jesus in the course of his mission had presented himself as singularly authorized (understood: by God) to announce the coming Kingdom. His ability to perform exorcisms and healings broadcast that authority. Those villages that rejected him and his message in the present, he averred, would be in worse shape on "the day of judgment" than Sodom had been. Josephus, in a problematically reworked passage of the *Antiquities*, also seems to speak of Jesus' abilities: Jesus, a *sophos* ("wise man") and a *didaskolos* ("teacher"), also worked *paradoxa*, that is, "startling deeds" or "wonders." This charismatic outreach ensured the attention, and the religious and emotional investment, of Jesus' audience, besides underscoring his personal authority. Such powers seemed a divine validation of his message.[31]

Gospel traditions also name Jesus as a "prophet"—an identity implicitly embraced by their commanding protagonist. "This is indeed the prophet!" the crowds in John's gospel proclaim. "Some of the people said, 'This is really the prophet!' Others said, 'This is the messiah.'" "He is a prophet." Matthew's crowds cry out, "This is the prophet, Jesus of Nazareth from Galilee," just after the messianic acclamation of the triumphal entry. After the crucifixion, two of Jesus' followers, according to Luke, speak of him as "Jesus of Nazareth, who was a prophet mighty in word and deed before God and all the people. . . . [W]e had hoped that he was the one to redeem Israel"—that is, the messiah.[32]

None of the gospels depicts Jesus as forthrightly teaching that he is the messiah. ("If you are the christ, tell us plainly!" a crowd—perhaps with some exasperation?—finally demands in John 10.24.) And each of the four evangelists, despite working from shared traditions, builds his own case for Jesus' messianic identity, an important if oblique datum. Had Jesus of Nazareth actually and forthrightly claimed the role for himself—a teaching that the later gospel writers would have happily used, had it existed—the evangelical depictions would be more uniform. Instead, and variously, they put the claim of Jesus' messianic status in the mouths of others. And, again variously, they each present their own reasons why and how Jesus met the criteria for such an identification.[33]

Did messianic attributions hover around Jesus' prophetic, charismatic mission? The jumble of implications that the gospels present us with make it impossible to say for certain. But after several years of announcing the coming of the Kingdom—however many years, again, we cannot say for certain—Jesus may have shifted the time frame of his prophecy, from *soon* to *now*.

That intensification of the message could well have galvanized the Passover crowd streaming into Jerusalem and celebrating his entry. Scholars of modern millenarian movements have observed that a specifically named date for the Endtime often works to raise popular attention, to spike apocalyptic enthusiasm, and to prompt fence-sitters to commit. Had Jesus named a date for the Kingdom's arrival? Was that Passover in Jerusalem to be the last before the Kingdom came?[34]

Again, scattered bits and pieces in the gospels can support such a speculation. On the Temple Mount, following his dramatic entrance into the city, the synoptic Jesus continues his apocalyptic proclamations, speaking about the signs presaging the End (Mark 13 and parallels, the so-called synoptic Apocalypse). In Luke's gospel, which consistently de-eschatologizes Jesus' message, Jesus gives a parable "because he was near Jerusalem, and because they [his crowd of followers] supposed that the kingdom of God was to appear immediately." Acts, which continues Luke's story, presents the risen Jesus as continuing to appear to the apostles "for forty days, speaking of the kingdom of God. . . . [T]hey asked him, 'Lord, will you at this time restore the Kingdom to Israel?' "[35]

It was the mounting enthusiasm of the holiday crowds—spurred this particular Passover, I suggest, by Jesus' updating, perhaps specifically naming, the Endtime—that would in turn have prompted the authorities to act. The authorities' initial *in*action gave Jesus the time to teach in the temple's court as he had always done. It is explained by the authorities' familiarity with the pacific tenor of Jesus' message, a familiarity accounted for by and only by the Johannine chronology. Jesus had taught multiple times in Jerusalem during the pilgrimage festivals; the priests and Pilate knew that, in all practical ways, he was harmless. And the authorities' eventual *re*action—Jesus' secret arrest, and his speedy execution as "King of the Jews"—is also explained by (and explained *only* by) the crowd's increasing excitement and excitability. It was to disabuse *them* that Jesus died on a cross. The crucifixion was addressed neither to Jesus nor to his immediate circle of disciples.

It was addressed to the agitated holiday crowd massed in the city that year for Pesach.

The first-century C.E. Roman orator Quintilian nicely described the social function of this Roman mode of execution: "Whenever we crucify criminals . . . [we place them] where the greatest number of people can watch and be influenced by this threat; for every penalty is aimed not so much at the offense, as at its exemplary value."[36]

The question of whether Jesus thought of himself as "the messiah" is thus irrelevant to the prior and more immediate question: why was Jesus crucified? Energized and agitated crowds who proclaimed him their messiah—and in Jerusalem, during the period around the Passover holiday, literally under Pilate's nose—would dictate Roman policy clearly enough.

But then, how do the Jewish authorities, Caiaphas and the other "chief priests," fit into this scenario?

The priests' involvement should not be erased. But neither should the gospels' foregrounding of priestly agency be taken as "gospel." Josephus, too, independently of his evangelical contemporaries, names the *protoi*, "the men of highest standing among us," as instrumental in Jesus' arrest. It was on account of their reported accusation that "Pilate . . . condemned him to the cross." Josephus is an independent witness to aristocratic priestly involvement in Jesus' arrest and execution. Jerusalem's aristocrats were the chief priests. In Jesus' generation, these were particularly men in the family of Annas—before whom, in John's gospel, Jesus makes his first stop on the night of his arrest.[37]

Annas and his family had an extraordinarily long run of prestige and power as chief priests in the period following Herod's death. Annas himself served as high priest from 6 to 15 C.E. Thereafter, five of his sons held the position. John's gospel identifies Caiaphas as Annas's son-in-law: Caiaphas held the office of high priest from 18 until 26 C.E. This family clearly knew how to exercise power in concert with whatever Roman prefect was in charge.[38]

When things went wrong in or near Jerusalem—when bursts of violence or spasms of social disorder broke out—the emperor and his legate in Antioch called to account Judea's prefect (or, after 44 C.E., its "procurator") and Jerusalem's priests. Rome subcontracted imperial rule to local aristocrats. Rome expected order in return.

This pattern preceded Roman rule. When pious protestors hacked Herod the Great's golden eagle off of one of the temple's gates, Herod not only executed the protestors. He also deposed the high priest, whom he considered in some sense responsible for letting things get so far out of hand. After Pilate lost control of a popular event in Samaria—he slaughtered an unarmed crowd following a prophet to the Samaritan holy site, Mount Gerizim—Vitellius the Roman legate not only sent Pilate back to Rome. He also relieved Caiaphas of his office. When Galilean pilgrims to Jerusalem were murdered when traversing Samaria (50 C.E.), the Syrian legate sent the high priest and other Jerusalemite aristocrats to Rome, to be heard by the emperor.[39]

None of these priestly Jerusalemite aristocrats had been personally involved in any of these incidents of violence. By virtue of their social and political position, however, Rome held them accountable nonetheless. This pattern, clearly articulated by Josephus, frames their response, as Jerusalem's *protoi*, to the popular messianic acclaim around Jesus of Nazareth. Pilate would have learned of the crowds' restiveness in any case: he certainly had "ears on the ground," a network of informants. But the priests, frequenting the temple precincts themselves, would have been much more immediately aware of the level of popular agitation. Those themes sounded decades later by the evangelists in their depictions of Jesus' triumphal entry—Jesus' acclamation in messianic terms—would on this Passover around the year 30 only have increased in volume as the holiday approached. God's Kingdom was at hand. Jesus, God's messiah, would himself inaugurate its establishment—perhaps, indeed, from the Temple Mount itself. This destabilizing popular enthusiasm, the *protoi* confirmed, centered on the person of Jesus.

Again, both Pilate and the priests, familiar with the tone of Jesus' mission and message, anticipated no armed rebellion or violent insurrection. But the crowds themselves were unpredictable. Whether energized by anticipation or angered by disappointment, they might riot, an event for which Antioch and Rome would hold the prefect and the priests accountable. This was the prospect that dictated the subsequent course of events. Away from the crowds in the temple's courts, at night, in secret, a contingent of temple police and Roman soldiers arrested Jesus—and Jesus alone. His close circle of Galilean followers was permitted to flee. They were not part of the problem. Thus, they were irrelevant to its solution.

Did the arresting party then lead Jesus to Annas, so that he could be questioned "about his disciples and his teaching," as John says? Letting go of the date of 14 Nisan for these events, and locating them instead at some more indeterminate date in advance of the feast, enhances that possibility. Would Jesus then have been passed from the priest's house to the praetorium? That much is likely: Pilate was the ultimate fixer in this situation. No "trial" before Pilate would be necessary, however. And any kind of public hearing would be (again, because of Jesus' destabilizing popularity) out of the question: there never was a "crowd" before Pilate when he ordered Jesus to the cross. The restive pilgrim crowds in the city—enthusiastically celebrating Jesus, proclaiming him the messiah, stirred up especially on *this* Passover by Jesus' naming it as the date of the Kingdom's advent—would have already sealed his fate.[40]

Together with two others accused of rebellion, *lēstai* whose names and offenses are now completely lost to us, Jesus was crucified outside the walls of Jerusalem. "King of the Jews"—Pilate's sardonic nod to the crowds' messianic convictions—proclaimed his offense. What better way to deflate their hopes, and to discredit Jesus' message? With Jesus' voice silenced, and the pilgrims demoralized, thus pacified, the temple court resumed its normal level of holiday activity. Crisis averted. Pilate and the priests could relax, and put another pilgrimage feast behind them.

THREE

From Miracle to Mission

When Jesus and his immediate followers went up to Jerusalem that final Passover, they were expecting an eschatological miracle: the coming of God's Kingdom and, as a part of that, the revelation of his messiah—perhaps, indeed, the revelation of Jesus as his messiah. Instead, their hopes were brutally crushed. Jesus died on a Roman cross, crucified as "King of the Jews." The later gospel accounts all relate that the men following Jesus fled and hid. But then, according to these same sources, shortly after the trauma of Jesus' execution, some among this demoralized group did receive a miracle, one that they had not been expecting. They saw Jesus again, risen from the dead.

RESURRECTION AND REDEMPTION

Why his followers had this experience is an interesting question. After all, many other Jews in this period followed other charismatic, prophetic figures (John the Baptizer comes readily to mind); but none of their movements outlived the death of their founder. Why was this group different?

These postmortem visitations tell us something about Jesus and something about his followers, and the two are linked. "The resurrection" gives us a measure of the degree to which Jesus of Nazareth had successfully forged his followers into a group intensely, indeed singularly, committed to himself and to his prophecy of the coming Kingdom. His death—unexpected, traumatic, bewildering—threw the whole journey to Jerusalem into sudden reverse, inflicting on them a grinding cognitive dissonance: If Jesus were dead, how could his prophecy be true? If Jesus' prophecy were true, how could he be dead? Resurrection both resolved this dissonance, and reinforced the prophecy. If Jesus were raised, then the Kingdom truly must be at hand.

Who had these postcrucifixion visions of Jesus? When and where did these visions come to them? What did these witnesses see, or think that they saw? And what, finally, did they take them to mean?

To all of these fundamental questions, our sources—the four gospels, Acts, Paul's letters, and (in a way, as we will see) Josephus—offer differing answers. Mark, our (probably) earliest narrative of Jesus' mission, ends with an account of the empty tomb. Jesus had predicted his own passion and resurrection at three earlier points in Mark's story, but his followers never seem to register the information, since his arrest and his empty tomb both seem to come as a total surprise. "And he [Jesus] began to teach them [his disciples] that the son of man must suffer many things, and be rejected by the elders and the chief priests and the scribes, and be killed, and after three days rise again. And he said this plainly."[1]

Mark repeats this prediction twice more, the last time adding that, once Jesus is in Jerusalem, his Jewish adversaries will hand him over "to the gentiles, and they will mock him and spit on him and whip him and kill him; and after three days he will rise."

Nonetheless, when the women come to the tomb on Sunday morning—"Mary Magdalene, Mary the mother of James, and Salome"—they are amazed and frightened to be told by a young man in a white robe inside the tomb that Jesus "has risen; he is not here. But go, tell his disciples and Peter that he is going before you to the Galilee. There you will see him, as he told you." The gospel ends with the frightened women saying "nothing to any one."[2]

Matthew continues his story from this point where Mark ended his, narrating Jesus' appearance in the Galilee. Only two women—"Mary Magdalene and the other Mary"—go to the tomb Sunday morning, where they witness a spectacular intervention with a radiant angel and fainting guards. The angel directs the Marys (who, though fearful, also feel "great joy") to tell the disciples to go to the Galilee. The women then see the risen Jesus themselves, who repeats the angel's instructions. Thereafter, on a mountain in the Galilee, the risen Jesus subsequently appears to the (now) eleven disciples. (Judas Iscariot, one of the original twelve, has hanged himself.) It is only at this point that the risen Jesus commissions this group to extend their mission to pagans/gentiles/nations. (The Greek word in this text, *ethnē*, can be translated by all these words. We will see shortly why these choices in translation matter.) Matthew then closes, offering no further description of what the disciples see.[3]

Luke elaborates and expands on Jesus' postcrucifixion appearances, which bridge the final chapter of his gospel and the first chapter of Acts. A much larger group of women goes to the tomb—"Mary Magdalene and Joanna and Mary the mother of James and the other women." Unlike Matthew's women, these female followers see no angelic spectacle. Two men in shining white robes, however, remind them that Jesus had already spoken about his resurrection. These women, unlike the corresponding characters in Matthew, do not see Jesus raised.[4]

Meanwhile, back in Jerusalem, Peter has some sort of (offstage) encounter with the risen Jesus, while two other apostles meet Jesus near the village of Emmaus. Rushing back to Jerusalem, these two inform "the eleven" when, suddenly, Jesus appears before all of them. To dispel the thought that he might be a spirit, Luke's Jesus emphasizes his physicality: he is in his fleshly body. "See my hands and my feet, that it is I myself. Handle me, and see, for a spirit has not flesh and bone as you see that I have." Acts opens with the risen Jesus presenting "many proofs" that he was alive to his (eleven) apostles. These appearances continue in Jerusalem and end on the Mount of Olives, just outside, whence Jesus ascends bodily on a cloud.[5]

John's resurrection stories are different still. Mary Magdalene alone goes to the tomb early on Sunday. Finding it open and empty, she runs back to the city and tells Peter and the beloved disciple that the body has been moved. They and "the other disciples" rush back to see the empty tomb, and then return to "their own homes" in Jerusalem. Weeping Mary, left alone outside the tomb, next encounters two angels, then the risen Jesus himself. Later on that day, in the evening, Jesus appears to his disciples (only ten? Thomas is missing). Like Luke, John emphasizes the risen Jesus' physicality: he shows his disciples his wounds and, eight days later, commands the doubting Thomas to touch them. The following chapter concludes the gospel with yet more appearances, before a smaller group of the disciples, in the Galilee. "This was now the third time that Jesus was revealed to the disciples after he was raised from the dead." Jesus did "many more things," says the fourth evangelist, too many to recount, and on that note his story ends. The point to mark in this quick review is simply that all of these gospel accounts differ significantly between themselves.[6]

Finally, in terms of our New Testament sources, we have an important passage in Paul's letter to his gentile congregation in Corinth, 1 Corinthians 15.3–8. Berating them for their confusion about Jesus' resurrection and its implications for their own impending transformation, Paul recalls what he had told them earlier, based on a tradition that he himself had received, namely:

> [3] that Christ died for our sins in accordance with the scriptures,
> [4] that he was buried, that he was raised on the third day in ac-
> cordance with the scriptures, [5] and that he was seen by Cephas
> [Peter], then by the twelve. [6] Then he was seen by more than five
> hundred brethren, most of whom are still alive . . . [7] Then he
> was seen by James, then by all the apostles. [8] Last of all . . . he
> was seen by me . . .

No female witnesses, no mention of an empty tomb (though a later verse in Paul's chapter might imply it), no mention of where—Jerusalem? the Galilee?—these visions occurred. Paul affirms Peter's priority (as will Luke; Matthew and John say otherwise), and the subsequent sighting by "the twelve." (Does Paul not know the story of Judas?) Where was James, Jesus' brother—mentioned only by Paul as a witness—and at what point had he become a follower? Paul does not say. The number of early witnesses, further, swells: whereas Luke in Acts 1.15 will speak of an original community of "about one hundred and twenty persons," Paul gives "more than five hundred." And Paul concludes this list with himself ("he was seen by me"). When? Where? In Corinthians, again, Paul does not say. Referring to this event in his letter to the Galatians, though, he implies that the vision of the risen Jesus came to him in the Diaspora, in distant Damascus.[7]

The identities of the witnesses to the raised Jesus, the sequence of Jesus' appearances, and the places where they occurred all vary widely between these five different sources. Interestingly, however, all assert that these appearances began very shortly after Jesus' execution; indeed, within days of his death. And while Mark does not depict Jesus' resurrection, Matthew features a single appearance, at the climax of his gospel. But John, Luke/Acts, and Paul, by comparison, all present a series of epiphanies of various duration and in different locations. No unitary tradition binds these accounts together.

Over how long a period of time, then, did his followers continue to experience the risen Jesus? John's time frame seems indefinite. Chapter 20—perhaps originally the final chapter of this gospel—names a little over a week, but chapter 21, which uniquely depicts a third, Galilean manifestation after the ones in Jerusalem, is very vague, saying only "after this," meaning after the appearance to Thomas. Acts, by contrast, specifies forty days, which frames this initial section of Luke's story between the two spring pilgrimage festivals, Passover and, fifty days later, Shavuot, "Pentecost" in Luke's Greek (Acts 2.1).

Later in Acts, Luke reintroduces the risen Jesus, heard but *not* seen by the miraculously blinded Saul/Paul, who is traveling from Jerusalem to Damascus. Paul himself, contra Acts, seems to name Damascus as his home base (he "returns" there, Galatians 1.17), and he emphasizes, precisely, seeing. As he asks in 1 Corinthians, "Have I not seen Jesus our lord?" Paul's vision occurred only after he had engaged in "persecuting the assembly of God," presumably the group of Christ followers that had formed within Paul's synagogue community in Damascus. Allowing time for the original disciples in Jerusalem to consolidate, then to conceive the idea of a mission, and then to reach into the Diaspora as far as Damascus in Syria, we must suppose that Paul's experience occurred several years after Jesus' crucifixion. The period of the resurrection appearances, in other words, was exactly that: an extended period of time, years in fact, though we cannot from our disparate sources say exactly how long.[8]

To the confusion of these New Testament sources we can add, as well, the so-called *Testimonium Flavianum*, the famous passage in Josephus' *Antiquities of the Jews* 18.63–64. It is a problematic piece of evidence, and most (though not all) scholars assume that Josephus' originally brief notice on Jesus has been partially rewritten by later Christian scribes. In this passage, Joseph states that Jesus was a wise man who worked "startling deeds, a teacher of people who receive the truth with pleasure. And he gained a following both among many Jews and among many of Greek origin." Does Josephus' report relate any material that stems from the lifetime of Jesus?

Josephus wrote his *Antiquities* in Rome toward the end of the first century. He is the only one of our early sources to name gentiles (those "of Greek origin") as among Jesus' original followers. No New Testament source corroborates this claim, though it is not historically impossible: non-Jews visited Herod's famous temple, and they would have been present in its outermost courtyard, where Jesus himself is depicted as teaching. But, for reasons that we will explore further on, the movement that formed after Jesus' death seems to have involved gentiles only eventually and tangentially, and not from its very initial stages. Josephus' report, in this regard, is out of synch with the gospel narratives, which depict an exclusively Jewish following for Jesus during his lifetime and immediately thereafter.

We do know certainly, from Paul's letter to the Romans, that a gentile Christ-following assembly existed in that city already by the mid-first century, if not earlier. And after the first Jewish revolt, having ingratiated himself to Vespasian, Josephus too lived in Rome. In my view, then, this passage in the *Antiquities* most likely represents an unknowing projection on Josephus' part. He retrojected the composition of the current Christian community in Rome contemporary with himself, in the 90s C.E., back onto the original group around Jesus circa 30, the subject of the *Testimonium Flavianum*. Non-Jews do join this movement early on, as we will see; but their presence will demand an adjustment of the gospel message. Thus, they were not part of Jesus of Nazareth's original following.

The identities of the initial witnesses to the risen Jesus also vary, as we have seen, according to which source we consult. So, too, the location of the initial appearances: gospel traditions toggle between the Galilee and Jerusalem. Independently, Paul and the evangelists specify a brief period of time, "on the third day" (or, in Mark, "after three days") between the crucifixion and the first vision, to whoever that may have been (Mary Magdalene, the two Marys, or Peter). This very particular time period may itself have been generated by biblical interpretation. Hosea 6.2, for instance, prophesies that "after two days [God] will revive us; and on the third day he will raise us up, that we may live before him." Even if so, however, the mobilization of the prophet's verse points to a very brief interregnum between Jesus' death and his original followers' experience of his resurrection.

What, finally, did these people—whoever, wherever, whenever—think that they saw when they saw Jesus risen? And, more importantly, how did they interpret this event? Why, and of what, was it significant?

Both confirming and colliding with each other, our New Testament sources again offer different answers. Mark, we have noted, relates no resurrection scene; Matthew, who does, gives no details, apart from identifying Jesus. The evangelists all foreshadow Jesus' resurrection with their respective stories about the empty tomb—clearly, they thereby say, the body was no longer there. The gospels of Luke and John, each in its own way, underscore the continuing physicality of the resurrected Jesus. The witnesses see someone or something that is physically continuous with Jesus' body before his death: for that reason, both gospels emphasize the visibility (and the tangibility) of Jesus' wounds, inflicted during the crucifixion.

Still, each evangelist also insists on some special quality to Jesus' postmortem physical self. Luke's raised Jesus is not immediately recognizable to the disciples in Emmaus, and he materializes abruptly in front of the startled disciples back in Jerusalem. The body of John's raised Jesus may be fleshly, but nonetheless, he is not initially recognizable to Mary Magdalene, and he is able to walk—twice—through closed doors.[9]

Paul's account of the raised Jesus differs significantly from these later stories about Jesus. Alone of our New Testament writers, Paul is a contemporary of the original disciples. He personally knew some of them; and he is in a direct line of transmission of traditions from them. Also, he claims eyewitness status for himself. Further, Paul's discussion of the transformation of the believer's mortal body obliquely obliges the later evangelists' stories of the empty tomb: regular human flesh, Paul teaches, is changed, not shed, at resurrection.[10]

But Paul's vision of the risen Jesus also contradicts the gospels' accounts. Jesus' raised body, Paul heatedly maintains, was precisely *not* flesh and blood. The "perishable" body is "sown," but what is raised, he insists, is a "spiritual body." "I tell you this, brethren: flesh and blood cannot inherit the Kingdom of God, nor does the perishable inherit the imperishable." Some forty years later, Luke's risen Jesus, exhorting his frightened disciples to touch him, will declare, "A spirit has not flesh and bones as you see that I have." Nonsense, Paul would have thundered; the raised body is (re)made precisely of spirit.[11]

Paul's clear statement in 1 Corinthians 15.50—"flesh and blood cannot inherit the Kingdom of God"—will cause no end of trouble in the fourth century, by which time, for the imperially sponsored church, raised *flesh* was a matter of orthodox doctrine. Arguing against Manichaean heretics who derogated flesh as a medium of cosmic evil, Augustine wrestled with this Pauline verse. He formulated a solution: by "flesh" and "spirit," Augustine maintained, Paul intended moral categories, not material substances. A "fleshly body" meant a body directed by fleshly appetites; a "spiritual body" meant one directed by "spiritual"—that is, by morally good—principles. The raised body will be composed of the same flesh as it was during a person's lifetime, urged Augustine. The transformative difference would be moral, since in heaven this solid, raised flesh will be under the total control of spirit.[12]

It is an ingenious interpretation; but this is not, three centuries earlier, what Paul had said. Paul begins this passage of his letter with a kind of cosmic tour. For Paul as for nearly all western people up until Copernicus in the mid-sixteenth century, the earth stood at the center of the universe, where the heaviest matter had sunk. The sun, moon, and five planets—"up" from and higher than the earth—marked out zones of ascending perfection, beauty, and stability. Beyond them, the stars, themselves embodied intelligences—eternal, luminous, fixed—were the height (literally) of visible perfection. Paul and his hearers live within this cosmic organization; and Paul's remarks on different types of flesh in this chapter of Corinthians orient us within it.

In this geocentric universe, matter expresses and even regulates the different strata of reality. Gradations of earthly life are expressed through different "grades" of flesh, as Paul explains. Humans have one type of flesh; animals, another; birds, yet another; fish flesh is different and particular yet again. Further, all earthly bodies are different from all heavenly bodies, which are made of a different medium. And heavenly bodies also vary between themselves: sun from moon, moon from stars, and stars even from other stars. Different categories of beings are composed of different material media: "Not all flesh is alike."[13]

"So it is with the resurrection of the dead," Paul continues. Like a kernel that, once planted, transforms into grain, so also with the flesh-and-blood human body of this life. Resurrected flesh is made of spirit, and it has a completely other, incorruptible glory. That is the kind of body that Paul implies he saw when he saw the raised Jesus. And that is the kind of body, he says, that people whether living or dead will attain when they transform once Christ returns. Paul expects to undergo such a transformation himself, because he expects to live to see the glorious second coming of Christ.[14]

This last point, Paul's condensed time frame, brings us to our fourth and final question regarding Jesus' resurrection. Whatever it was that Peter, the female followers, and however many other original disciples saw, what did they interpret this vision to mean?

The resurrection of the dead was but one of any number of miraculous events that Jewish biblical and postbiblical traditions anticipated as marking the Endtimes, and the establishment of God's Kingdom. Not only would life be restored to the dead; the ten tribes of Israel, "lost" to the Assyrian conquest in the eighth century B.C.E., would also be restored to the nation, "gathered in" with the exiles of Israel. In the final battle between good and evil, the forces of good—led by an archangel, or perhaps by a warrior of King David's house, the messiah—would definitively prevail. The righteous would be vindicated, the wicked punished. The false gods of the nations, subdued in their turn, would themselves acknowledge the god of Israel. Their peoples and former worshipers, the pagan nations, would themselves stream to Jerusalem, to worship together with Israel on God's holy mountain. God would pour out divine spirit upon eschatological humanity. And the mother city of the wide-flung Jewish nation, Jerusalem, restored and resplendent, would shine in the End as the place of God's presence, the seat of his Kingdom.[15]

This catalog of ardent wishes, expectations, and hopes describes the contours of late Second Temple Jewish apocalyptic eschatology: events that would occur at or as the end of time. Jesus had evoked these hopes when he, like John the Baptizer before him and like Paul after him, had announced the impending advent of God's Kingdom. His followers' experiences of Jesus raised—whatever it is that they thought they saw; however we interpret their experience now—point irrefutably to this movement's rootedness in these apocalyptic convictions and commitments. The resurrection of the dead and the vindication of the righteous are two prominent tropes in these traditions, each representing God's opportunity to finally put right all the things that, in the course of normal history, had gone wrong.

His followers' experience of seeing the raised Jesus cohered with these hopes and reaffirmed them. But it also deviated significantly from them, in at least two crucial ways. In biblical and postbiblical traditions, the resurrection of the dead was supposed to be both a communal event and an eschatological one. That is, the raised dead would be a group—"the whole house of Israel," as Ezekiel had prophesied. Or perhaps all humanity, raised for final judgment, as Daniel had foreseen. Or perhaps, said other prophets, only the righteous. And the dead would rise only at or as the end of time.[16]

Herein lay the anomalies of the disciples' experience. Jesus, according to his followers' own visions, had alone been raised. And in the meanwhile, normal time manifestly continued to continue. What sense, then, could be made of these unanticipated—and, for a while, serial—appearances of their risen leader?

Later Christian theologies, adjusted or adjusting to the Kingdom's delay, will interpret Jesus' resurrection as an event significant in and of itself, and as a necessary prelude to their own present circumstances, howsoever they constructed them. For Mark, who seems to be writing in the immediate aftermath of the Jewish War, Jesus' crucifixion and resurrection together comprised an elaborately coded message about the temple's destruction and, following from that event, the second coming of Jesus, the son of man, to be witnessed by Mark's own generation. For Matthew and for John—both, perhaps at least two generations removed from Jesus of Nazareth's mission, and at least one generation after the Roman destruction of Jerusalem—the resurrection established Jesus' identity as messiah and as divine son. For Luke, perhaps early second century, the resurrection of Jesus was the key to interpreting Jewish scriptures, to understanding the meanings of "messiah," and to establishing the mixed-ethnic (that is, both Jewish and gentile) church.[17]

But the original community could only interpret this event—that is, their experiences of Jesus' resurrection—within their own temporal and cultural context, late Second Temple Judaism, circa 30 C.E. For them, the resurrection validated and vindicated both Jesus' message of the coming Kingdom together with his *timetable*: The Kingdom truly *was* at hand. Jesus' own resurrection was for them meaningful as the first of a cascade of anticipated Endtime events. It signaled and signified just how close the general resurrection of all the dead—and, thus, the establishment of God's Kingdom—truly was. The point of his particular resurrection, in other words, was not to express Jesus' special status as such. It was to vindicate his prophecy. "The times are fulfilled, and the Kingdom of God is at hand! Repent, and trust in the good news!" Jesus' resurrection meant that final redemption hovered close to hand.

Decades thereafter, in the words of Paul, who had never met Jesus, we can still catch the urgency of this conviction. Paul asserts strongly to his gentile assembly in Corinth that Christ's resurrection either means the impending Endtime with the general (and bodily, though not fleshly) resurrection, or it means nothing at all. "Now if Christ is preached as raised from the dead, how can some of you say that there is no resurrection of the dead? If there is no resurrection of the dead, then Christ has not been raised . . . and your faith is in vain." Christ's resurrection is significant, insists Paul, only if it indicates the coming general resurrection, to which it is necessarily linked. "Christ has been raised, the first fruits of those who have died," Paul explains; the rest of the dead will be raised, and the living transformed, "each in his own order." Christ was raised first; all others will be raised at Christ's second coming.[18]

Paul in this passage of his letter goes on to sketch further the outline of Endtime events. Once Jesus triumphantly returns, "then comes the End, when he delivers the Kingdom to God the father, after destroying every rule and every authority and every power," including death itself. Once these wicked cosmic powers are "destroyed" and overcome, flesh itself will be changed. The bodies of both the quick and the dead will transmute into bodies of spirit.

"The form of this world," Paul had already warned his listeners earlier, "is passing away." Even when the Kingdom is already some twenty years late, in brief, Paul nonetheless insists that Christ's individual resurrection affirms the original prophecy and the timetable ("Soon!") of Jesus of Nazareth.[19]

KINGDOM AND COMMUNITY

Receiving "the gospel"—Jesus' prophecy of the coming Kingdom—was one thing. Proclaiming it after his death, and in a sense in his stead, however, was something else. How did the original community come to this decision? Why should their conviction that Jesus had been raised have spurred them to inaugurate a new phase, the apostolic mission?

All the gospels depict Jesus as deputizing some of his followers to spread his message of the coming Kingdom in his own lifetime. In Mark, Jesus appoints "the twelve" both as companions and as messengers: they are called to "be with him" and to "be sent out." The twelve, or some subgroup or companions thereof, often serve an obvious literary function in Mark's story: the straight men for Jesus' parables and a kind of chorus, they provide opportunities for Mark's Jesus to expound various teachings. At one point, this group occasions instruction on purifying hands before eating. At another point, they attend to Jesus' sotto voce revelation of his messianic identity. Peter, James, and John witness the Transfiguration; later on, James and John request precedence in the Kingdom and get instructed in humility. In short, though the disciples are also sent out on the road, the gospels all focus much more on their time spent with Jesus as his special companions.[20]

Commissioning this group of twelve to proclaim his message, Jesus also endows them with charismatic powers. They, like their leader, can command "unclean spirits" and "demons," work exorcisms and effect cures. Matthew's Jesus increases their powers to curing "every disease and every sickness," raising the dead, cleansing lepers (a purification as well as a cure), prophesying, exorcising demons, and doing "acts of power." He also explicitly restricts their mission field: his disciples are to proclaim the Kingdom only to other Jews. "Go nowhere among the gentiles, and enter no town of the Samaritans; but go rather to the lost sheep of the house of Israel," as indeed does Matthew's Jesus himself.[21]

Luke's Jesus empowers and commissions not only "the twelve," who heal and preach, but also a larger group, "the seventy," whom he sends out two-by-two as an advance party to villages where he himself is about to go. "Heal the sick in it and say to them, 'The Kingdom of God has come near to you.'" They work exorcisms as well. John, uniquely, depicts "the disciples" as immersing hearers in the vicinity of John the Baptizer and his followers, in Judea. Jesus' hearers, too, in this gospel are designated as "disciples," though "the twelve" are nonetheless distinguished as a special group. Clearly in the synoptic tradition, less clearly in John, these are the men privileged to share Jesus' last meal in Jerusalem.[22]

And, of course, according both to Paul and, variously, to all four canonical gospels, this core group—adjusted occasionally for Judas—receives an early vision of Jesus, raised from the dead. In this same passage in 1 Corinthians 15, however, Paul distinguishes between "the twelve" and "all the apostles." Reciting his list of witnesses, Paul asserts that the risen Jesus "was seen by Cephas, then by *the twelve*. Then he was seen by more than five hundred *brethren*, . . . then by all the *apostles*." Mark, by contrast, a generation after Paul, designates "the twelve" both as "apostles" and as "disciples." In Paul, however, "the twelve" and "the apostles" seem to be two different groups; the "five hundred brethren," yet another—or, perhaps, the number encompasses "the twelve" and "the apostles," too.[23]

Why do all these details matter? Because Paul's list, backlit by impressions from the later evangelists, affords us a glimpse of the size and the structure of the committed community that Jesus had formed around himself and his prophecy during his lifetime. "The twelve" are Jesus' most intimate followers, wandering with him, their number perhaps symbolizing the expected eschatological miracle of the ingathering of the twelve tribes of Israel. Paul anticipates the same miracle: "All Israel"—that is, all twelve tribes—"will be saved," he asserts. The "apostles," by contrast, are explicitly those who take the message on the road, throughout the network of villages in the Galilee and in Judea—perhaps, as Luke suggests, to prepare and "warm up" those villages for Jesus' own arrival. Paul's final group designation in his list of witnesses, the "brethren," grammatically a masculine plural, can denote a mixed group of both women and men. These followers might correspond to those members of the movement resident in villages (and, for all we know, also in Jerusalem) who tended to those others who traveled from place to place. Martha, for example, receives some itinerants together with Jesus in her own home, when they arrive in her village.[24]

If Jesus, as I have speculated, had designated his final Passover as the date when he expected the Kingdom to arrive, then this whole assembly of several hundred, I also imagine, accompanied him to Jerusalem. They may have comprised some of the pilgrims who hailed Jesus in messianic terms as he entered the city. Luke specifically identifies this cheering crowd as "the whole multitude of the disciples." Perhaps, then, everyone—not only the twelve—was in Jerusalem in the days leading up to and following the crucifixion. Perhaps, then, it was in Jerusalem that this earliest core community—disciples, apostles, and brethren: some five hundred persons in all, as Paul says?—experienced the risen Jesus.[25]

What happened next? Mark implies and Matthew and John both state that the disciples returned to the Galilee, to have or to continue to have resurrection appearances there. Luke's disciples, by contrast, on the Sunday following the crucifixion, move between villages close to Jerusalem, and then return to and remain in the city, where they were "continually blessing God in the temple." The risen Christ in the first chapter of Acts explicitly orders them not to leave Jerusalem, "but to wait for the promise of the Father." Paul's letter to the Galatians suggests, too, that the original community was already established in Jerusalem by the time—within two years or so of the crucifixion?—that he received his own apostolic call in Damascus. By early midcentury, this was certainly the case, because at that time Paul goes to confer with the leaders there. In short: Whatever scattering of Jesus' followers may have occurred in the immediate wake of Jesus' arrest and execution, once members of this group began to have visions of Jesus raised, they renounced their Galilean roots and resettled in the holy city.[26]

In any practical way, economically or politically, this relocation made no sense. Many of these people—the twelve in particular—left their livelihoods, perhaps even their families, to move to a place where they had none. And given the brutality of their own leader's very recent execution, their moving back into the sphere of the (hostile?) prefect and high priest—within weeks of Jesus' crucifixion—can be seen, at the very least, as incautious, if not downright reckless.

This band of brothers evidently thought otherwise. Their conviction that Jesus had been raised from the dead, and their interpretation of their visions as reaffirming his prophecy, meant that these people were not concerned with such consequences: the

Kingdom was coming soon. And as Jesus himself had enacted as well as taught, sounding the great scriptural themes about this moment when the Kingdom came, events would unfold from Jerusalem. This is another bedrock belief that Paul's letter to the Romans corroborates: all Israel will be saved once "the Deliverer will come from Zion." In deploying this verse from Isaiah, Paul might intend either God the father himself, or he might be applying the term to the returning, victorious messiah. The point to note here, however, is location: Everything begins, and events unfurl, from Zion, that is, from God's "holy mountain," Jerusalem.[27]

Further: it would be *to* Jerusalem that all the families of man, at the Endtime, would flow. Biblical tradition had long distinguished the human family as comprised of two groups. The first, by far the smallest, was Israel, the descendants of Abraham, Isaac, and Jacob. Their plenum number, at the End, corresponding to Jacob's twelve sons and grandsons, would be all twelve tribes. "The nations," by far the larger group, were themselves divided into seventy "families" or "peoples," the biblical number derived from the total count of descent-groups from the three sons of Noah in Genesis 10. These seventy nations are distinguished from each other according to their kinship groups, their lands, and their languages. All humanity, in brief, is summed up in this eschatological arithmetic: the twelve tribes of Israel and the seventy nations.[28]

"I am coming to gather up all nations and tongues," proclaims Isaiah's god, describing the Endtime while echoing traditions from the Table of Nations in Genesis 10. "And they shall come and shall see my glory. . . . They shall declare my glory among the nations. And they shall bring all of your brethren from among the nations as an offering to the Lord, . . . to my holy mountain, Jerusalem." For Jesus' followers in these heady weeks of serial resurrection appearances, time now balanced on the very edge of the End. To be any place other than Jerusalem simply made no sense.[29]

Acts, which purports to describe this moment of the movement, was probably written in the early years of the second century. Its author, Luke, in both parts of his two-volume work, the gospel and Acts, consistently tamps down and reshapes the vibrant apocalyptic traditions that originally shaped what he had inherited. His Jesus, in stark contrast to Mark's, teaches *against* the idea of an impending Kingdom ("He proceeded to tell them a parable, because he was near to Jerusalem, and because they supposed that the Kingdom of God was to appear immediately"). No need to wait for the Endtime, teaches Luke's Jesus: the Kingdom is already arrived, available as a present reality.[30]

> 20 Being asked by the Pharisees when the Kingdom of God was coming, he answered them, "The Kingdom of God is not coming with signs to be observed; 21 nor will they say, 'Lo, here it is!' or 'There it is!' Behold, the *Kingdom of God is within you.*" 22 And he said to the disciples, "The days are coming when you will want to see one of the days of the son of man, *and you will not see it.* 23 And they will say to you, 'Lo, there!' or 'Lo, here!' *Do not go, do not follow them.*"
>
> (Luke 17.20–23; my emphases)

Luke continues to de-emphasize Endtime traditions throughout Acts. We see this especially clearly when we compare this author with Paul on the issue of "language" or "tongues." In Corinth, midcentury, Paul had praised his congregation for their various charismatic abilities, enabled by their reception of divine spirit, among which was speaking in "various kinds of tongues," as well as being able to interpret these tongues. The tongues-speaker needs an interpreter because the language itself sounded the speech of angels. Energetically unintelligible, "tongue-speech" required someone else, not in the same state of high spirit possession, to make meaningful the speaker's charismatic soundburst.[31]

In Acts 2, as holy spirit descends upon the apostles, they too begin to speak in "tongues." But there the word means not angelic speech but foreign languages—"*other* tongues," as Luke specifies—the better to facilitate the coming world mission. It is still a nice miracle; but it is not charismatic in the way that Paul's mid-first-century community's tongue-speech had been.[32]

Luke's more mundane rendering of "tongues" as "foreign languages" also has a tranquilizing effect on his quotation of an Endtime prophecy from the prophet Joel. Spirit is indeed "poured forth," but its prime function in Acts is ecclesiastical, not revelatory or eschatological. Spirit does not mark the approach of the End for Luke. Rather, spirit builds up the church and guides the gospel out from Jerusalem to the gentiles. That process of international expansion is the story that Luke wants to relate.[33]

And yet, beneath the calm surface of his narrative, Luke recounts behaviors that belie his depiction of the smooth and self-conscious founding of an institution. These behaviors point in quite a different direction, away from institutional formation and toward, instead, the bonds of charismatic community. Our knowledge of Paul's assemblies from his own letters (a good half-century earlier than Luke), our familiarity with Mark (at least one generation earlier, possibly two), and our acquaintance with Essene community structures at Qumran, together provide us with a kind of historical motion-detector. Reading Acts with them in mind, we can better see the agitated improvisations of the year 30 that pulse and surge beneath Luke's becalmed early second-century representations.

For example, the apostles' abandonment of their homes in the Galilee to remain in Jerusalem, as we have already noted, gives us one index of their time frame. The Kingdom was *at hand*, and they wanted to be at the heart of its manifestation. If each of the twelve, as Jesus had averred, was to judge one of the (miraculously ingathered) tribes of Israel, and if Israel was to be gathered in to Jerusalem, then their remaining in Jerusalem kept everyone *à point*. They were ready, focused and waiting, in the right place at the right time.

For a protracted period, too, this group continued to have visions of Jesus. To what end? As Luke relates it, Jesus "presented himself alive to them after his passion with many proofs, appearing to them during forty days, and speaking about the Kingdom of God." But Luke shapes this scene so that it reinforces his own program of decoupling the Kingdom from vivid apocalyptic expectation. Here, Luke's Jesus goes on to tell the apostles that they cannot know God's timetable for final events. More to the point, he charges them to start a world mission: "You shall be my witnesses in Jerusalem and in all Judea and Samaria and to the ends of the earth." This commission in and of itself pries Jesus' resurrection apart from any expectation of the Kingdom's proximate advent. Global enterprises take time.[34]

Luke's readjusted Endtime notwithstanding, however, even he does not entirely decouple the risen Jesus from revelations concerning God's Kingdom. If we trace this idea "backward" to the time of the first generation—which, thanks to Paul's letters, we can do—we can see how Jesus' postmortem appearances and his prior prophecy of the Kingdom would have mutually reinforced each other. Jesus' resurrection, for his reassembled community, was proof of the closeness of the general resurrection, thus the establishment of the Kingdom; and the Kingdom's proximity, in turn, explained and interpreted the resurrection visions, which were themselves the measure of that proximity. These visions and Jesus' prophecy together fortified the apostles' convictions about what else was soon to follow.

In 1 Corinthians 15, half a century before Luke, Paul had surveyed the torrent of final events expected to flow in consequence of Jesus' resurrection appearances: the general resurrection of the dead in Christ; the defeat and destruction of hostile cosmic forces, the pagans' gods (more on this later); the transformation of the fleshly bodies of the living into spiritual bodies. And finally, Paul concludes this letter by summoning the risen Christ.

This closing invocation remains as a rare Aramaic outcropping in Paul's Greek: "*Marana tha!* Our lord, come!" Surviving as it does in the vernacular of the original community, this summons again gives us a glimpse of these people's apocalyptic mind-set. Imagining ourselves back into the weeks following Jesus' execution, when his apostles repeatedly experienced him as raised and present, we can still catch a sense of their focused anticipation in the urgent query that remains in Luke's mannered narrative: "So when they had all come together, they asked him, 'Lord'—addressed to the risen Christ—'will you at this time restore the kingdom to Israel?'" The imminent restoration of Israel, soon, that defining eschatological event, was for his community the original significance of Jesus' resurrection.[35]

What, while experiencing these Christophanies, did this small company in Jerusalem *do?* Acts relates that they gathered together daily. Jesus' followers prayed together and took their meals together. More radically still, they communalized all property. Some of these descriptions fall at the end of Acts 2, where, thanks to Peter's astonishing success at Pentecost, fifty days after Passover, the number of believers in Jerusalem committed to the gospel message, in the course of a single day, rockets from around 120 to over 3,000. Clearly this many people could not "gather together daily" except in the temple's outermost court, the city's largest public space. Acts 2.46 suggests that this was indeed the case, for these people were "attending the temple daily and breaking bread in their homes." Where and how the apostles could possibly have immersed ("baptized") 3,000 people in dry, high Jerusalem—the city is neither on a riverbank nor by the seacoast—is another factual awkwardness in Luke's story. The communalization of goods also suggests that many of these new recruits were not pilgrims—despite the story's setting at the pilgrimage holiday of Shavuot/Pentecost—but rather were locals, with property close to hand.[36]

Idealizations and exaggerations aside, this portrait of principled communalism resonates with the economic organization of another first-century apocalyptic Judean group: the Essenes by the Dead Sea. The Qumran covenanters, like the earliest assembly of Christ-followers resident in Jerusalem, not only practiced community of goods: they also held on to a fierce expectation of an imminent end of days (and did so for over two centuries). Luke, by contrast, suppresses any reminiscence of overt apocalyptic fervor in the traditions that he refracts, and so preserves, in Acts. Writing generations after the period that he purports to relate, Luke's interpretation of Jesus' prophecy has shifted, to make room for the development ultimately of the gentile church. But this detail about the social and economic organization of the earliest postcrucifixion Jerusalem community may indeed preserve a genuine historical tradition that attests to the same apocalyptic commitment and communal sensibility as that of the Essenes.

Paul's letters, mid-first century, support this aspect of Luke's early second-century portrait from a different direction. Paul solicited funds from his gentile assemblies in the Diaspora to send back to Jerusalem, to support "the poor" there. His enthused agreement to contribute to the community in Jerusalem, he reports in Galatians, brought his meeting there with James, Peter, and John to an amicable conclusion. "They would have us remember the poor, which very thing I was eager to do." He gives a fund-raising nudge to his group in Corinth. He frames his appeal to the Romans, a community with which he is still personally unacquainted, with the grand themes of bringing an offering to Jerusalem's temple. "I am now going to Jerusalem to care for the holy ones," he says as he winds up that letter. "Macedonia and Archaia have been pleased to make a contribution for the poor among the holy ones in Jerusalem." The Romans, he implies, should certainly in the same way feel pleased to share in this privilege.[37]

In the 50s, then, Paul's letters provide evidence that at least some portion of the Jerusalem community was still subsisting on communalized charity. Members for the most part were not working for wages and settled into jobs. Displaced, perhaps—as were the Galilean twelve—from their means of production, they depended upon the kindness of strangers, for whose generosity Paul served as one conduit. The intrinsic instability of this sort of economic arrangement again gives us the measure of the original community's time frame, which Paul shared. There was no reason to prepare for the long run. There would be no long run.

So: sometime around the year 30, some days or weeks after Jesus' crucifixion, a gathering of a few hundred disciples, apostles, and brethren regrouped in Jerusalem. They continued to experience the presence of Jesus, which renewed their confidence in his original proclamation of the good news. They met together, ate together, prayed together, worshiped in the temple together, and pooled together whatever resources they had. Always anticipating Jesus' next and definitive manifestation, appealing to heaven, perhaps, for it—"*Marana tha!* Lord, come!"—they together awaited the Kingdom.

THE PAROUSIA THAT FAILED

How long did this excited waiting period last? And what brought it to an end? Luke presents a forty-day gap between the resurrection of Jesus and the end of his subsequent appearances, when Jesus bodily ascends to heaven in a cloud from the Mount of Olives. We might well be skeptical about Luke's precision in naming this time period—it seems dictated by the Jewish liturgical year—but, still, we should attend to the point that his account makes. Appearances of the raised Jesus, whether to the whole community in Jerusalem or only to some members of it, began to taper off; and then, finally, they stopped.

The eventual but lengthening absence of the raised Jesus, despite the continuing charismata of community members, would have begun to force them to reassess the significance of these posthumous appearances. Clearly the raised Jesus was not about to inaugurate the Endtime, because the Endtime, bafflingly, continued not to come.

This combination of the decreasing frequency and, finally, the cessation of Jesus' posthumous appearances, together with the persistent nonarrival of the Kingdom, might have ended the movement then and there. The fact that it did not points, I think, to four interrelated factors that enabled the community to find positive meaning in their confusing circumstances and, thus, to continue.

The first was that these people, or perhaps only certain ones among them, continued to experience and to enact those charismata that had characterized their time together with Jesus during his mission: healing, prophesying, exorcizing demons, perhaps also speaking in tongues. This would further attest to the intensity of the bonds between members. Such bonds, in turn, worked to reinforce these behaviors. Even absent Jesus, they discovered, these followers of Jesus still seemed—and felt themselves to be—

empowered by spirit. *Community experienced charismata; charismata validated community.* The net social and psychological gain was mutual reinforcement.

The second factor, which attests to the social range within the group, was their intensified turn to Jewish scriptures. This would have required that some of these people (more likely and specifically men) would have some degree of education and literacy, itself an index of higher social status. Such people were probably involved with the movement almost from its beginning. And the "secondary literacy" of aural/oral scriptural familiarity of those of lower social status and lesser education in literacy (like Jesus himself, and many of the original twelve apostles) also means that biblical tropes, ideas, and images had always shaped the movement's message. The point is that, from this time onward—the period after the raised Jesus ceased to appear—scripture increasingly provided a matrix of meanings available to those who sought to make sense of their new circumstances. *Indeed, their creative and urgent readings of scripture would have begun to shape and to create new meanings.*

The community thus directed its efforts to reframe and to interpret its recent past experiences and present situation by searching the scriptures. Both Jesus' death and his resurrection "on the third day," which had shocked those who had witnessed them, came to be seen as occurring "according to the scriptures." The gospel message grew increasingly—and increasingly creatively—scripturally articulate. In consequence, *the gospel message gained new content,* which helped to lessen the cognitive dissonance inflicted by recent events. After all, if these events had happened "according to the scriptures," then they had happened according to a divine plan.

This interpretive activity touches upon the third factor that allowed the community, absent continuing appearances from the resurrected Jesus, to perdure. *Biblical interpretation began to express and to refine ideas about "messiah," and the ways that Jesus fulfilled, or would fulfill, that role.* In other words, the more that biblical verses were pressed into this service, the more articulate the shape of Jesus' awaited future appearance grew.

And with these new or newly amplified messianic interpretations of Jesus, fourth and finally, the community was able, eventually, to formulate a plan of action, something to do other than passively wait for the Kingdom. *They themselves would continue Jesus' mission to prepare Israel*—because clearly, in light of the Kingdom's delay, all Israel had yet to be reached. But now, new content about the messenger would begin to inform the original prophetic message. The Kingdom was still imminent. Jesus would still inaugurate it. But to do so, he would have to come back.

In other words, the expression of Jesus' (increasingly) biblically validated status as messiah came coupled together with two other novel ideas, one pertaining to the messiah, and the other pertaining to his community. *The novel messianic idea was that the messiah had to come not once, but twice. The novel social idea was that the community, even absent Jesus, should continue his proclamation.* In other words, this group's evolving interpretation of Jesus as the Endtime messiah eventually propelled them to mount missions. At first, they confined their efforts to Jerusalem itself. Later—a big step forward, and outward—they would take the message beyond the holy city, back on the road, this time to outlying Jewish communities in Judea and in the Diaspora. But they still worked, they were convinced, within a brief period, that tick of time between Jesus' resurrection and his definitive, final return.

The resurrection appearances, as the community interpreted them once they had stopped, clearly did not signal an *immediate*

End. They signaled, rather, an *impending* End. It was within that gap between Jesus' resurrection and his definitive, final, triumphant appearance at and as the End—his victorious Parousia or Second Coming—that the community now lived.

We see this more clearly if we consider Paul together with our other New Testament sources, the gospels and Acts. Read through the lens of almost two millennia of Christian theology, these texts seem to support a bewildering array of Christological titles, multiple ways of speaking about Jesus' unique divine sonship: "lord"; "son of God"; "son of David"; and, in the gospel traditions, "son of man." Indeed, these theologically laden titles for Jesus provided the interpretive means through which Jewish scriptures would eventually transmute, centuries later, into Christianity's Old Testament.

First Corinthians 15.3–4, as we have already noted, gives us one example of this process of meaning making. The shock both of Jesus' death and of his resurrection appearances was soothingly bracketed with positive significance, and an aura of inevitability, by appeal to ancient writings. "Christ died for our sins *according to the scriptures* . . . he was buried . . . and raised on the third day *according to the scriptures,*" Paul insists. No surprises here, his words imply. Nothing novel (much less scandalous), if one understood how to hear the scriptures aright. This interpretive move marks the early community's progress in its domestication—initially for internal consumption—of events in and around Jesus' final Passover. The cross did not disconfirm the messianic status of the Kingdom's messenger. Quite the contrary: the true messiah, as they believed the Bible taught, was and could only be the crucified and raised messiah. Jesus' startling—and distressing, and unanticipated—crucifixion, like the no less startling visions of Jesus resurrected, became confirmation—a confirmation both of the messenger and of his message. Cognitive dissonance in this way ceded to scriptural affirmation.

It is a well-known truism of New Testament scholarship that the idea of a crucified and raised messiah was in fact the original contribution of this small messianic sect to the variety of messiahs evinced in and by late Second Temple Judaism. This novel definition was generated by the circumstances and experiences specific to these sectarians—most specifically, by the incidents surrounding Jesus' death. But by retrofitting these biographical incidents to themes, images, and prophecies in traditional scriptures, his earliest followers grounded Jesus' mission and message in sacred history. And at the same time and by these same means, they also "eschatologized" those scriptures. All Israel had always been awaiting such a messiah, they proclaimed. Moses and the prophets together witnessed to the significance of Jesus as the messiah, the christ. Finally, finally, and in their own days, these prophecies had already been—and would soon be—fulfilled.

The closing chapter of Luke's gospel gives a pellucid example of this process. The interpreter featured there is not a member of the community, but the risen Christ himself. Berating two followers outside of Emmaus for not understanding the meaning of the empty tomb, the incognito savior says, "'O foolish men, and slow of heart to trust all that the prophets have spoken! Was it not necessary that the messiah should suffer these things and enter into his glory?' And beginning with Moses and all the prophets, he interpreted to them in all the scriptures the things concerning himself."[38]

Later, in Acts, Luke offers premier examples of this mode of interpretation in the *bel canto* Christological arias sung by his chief protagonists. "Peter" at Shavuot/Pentecost, for example, introduces the pilgrim crowd to the gospel message and messenger by quoting the prophet Joel. Peter next cites the authority of "David" by invoking Psalms. The prophet Isaiah is thereafter similarly deployed. "Peter"—or, rather, Luke—mobilizes all of these verses in service of his main point, namely, to testify that Jesus' death and resurrection occurred "according to the definite plan and foreknowledge of God." Again, there are no surprises, if one reads the scriptures aright.[39]

Luke's other protagonists—such as Stephen and, later, Paul—burst into similarly scripture-studded sermons. Stephen, for instance, reviews all of Israel's history, from the calling of Abraham in Genesis 12.1, through the entire Exodus narrative, to Isaiah, sprinting thereafter through various traditions and assertions about Jesus to bring that history up to the circumstances of his "current" narrative audience, circa 35 C.E.—or, rather, to that of Luke's actual Greek hearers, circa 110 C.E. Further along in Acts, depicting attempts to persuade Jews in Thessalonika, Luke recounts that "Paul . . . for three weeks argued with them from the scriptures, explaining and proving that *it was necessary* for the messiah to suffer and to rise from the dead."[40]

Luke's scriptural performances in Acts represent inspired—and inspiring—exegesis. They also reflect his interpretation, by the early second century, of inherited Christ-traditions, as well as his idealizations of his community's increasingly distant past. How can we measure the gap between these two different sensibilities, the incandescent apocalyptic expectations of the original community circa 30 C.E., and the calmer, de-eschatologized perspective of Luke, circa 110 C.E., who provides our only "history" of this moment of that community?

For this problem, two different sources come to our aid: Paul's letters, written mid-first century, and Mark's gospel, written sometime shortly after the Roman destruction of Jerusalem in 70 C.E.

(thus, perhaps, c. 75 C.E.). By reading them together with Luke/Acts, we can trace the germination of that peculiarly Christian idea generative for the whole movement. This idea—the kernel of the kerygma ("message")—was that the messiah had to come not once, but twice: once in weakness, hence Jesus' suffering on the cross; once in glory, hence his triumphant messianic return. Jesus the messiah would indeed establish God's Kingdom, but only at his Parousia or Second Coming.

Paul, our earliest author, already presumes this two-stroke messianic manifestation on the part of Jesus. Jesus' first messianic entrance, his crucifixion (accompanied, but only for chosen insiders, by his resurrection) was obviously dictated, first, by a remembered and transmitted biographical fact: Jesus of Nazareth had died on a Roman cross. Seeing the crucifixion *as* a messianic event, however, depended upon the convictions of the earliest community around Jesus, reinforced by Paul's own personal experience: all of these people were convinced that Jesus had been raised from the dead. Minus this conviction, as Paul observed, the message of a crucified messiah was "a stumbling block to Jews and folly to the pagans."[41]

These resurrection appearances of Jesus should have "counted" as his second, messianic revelation in glory. For a brief period, I have argued, the community probably did interpret these appearances in this way. Time disabused them of that interpretation, however, especially once the appearances ceased. Why? Because nothing else changed. The resurrected Jesus did not, after all, establish the Kingdom. But establishing the Kingdom—especially in light of the kernel of Jesus of Nazareth's gospel ("The Kingdom of God is at hand!")—was one of the messianic acts expected, indeed, eagerly anticipated, by this community. This group then made a crucial interpretive adjustment. Jesus' resurrection, they asserted, was indeed an eschatological event. However, they now reasoned, it indicated not the arrival of final redemption, but rather its proximity. To fully achieve that redemption, the risen Jesus as messiah would have to come back.

Eventually, as the years stretched on, evolving traditions would de-eschatologize the meaning of Jesus' resurrection. It shifted from being a time-indicator ("Jesus is raised, therefore the Kingdom must be coming soon!") to being a status-indicator ("Jesus is raised, therefore, he must be the messiah!"). We will shortly see how this shift affects even modern, authorized translations of Paul's letters. Already by the early second century, as we saw just above, the resurrection was used to undergird the messianic interpretation of the cross: only a crucified and raised messiah is the true messiah. But the resurrection itself, later tradition will assert, says nothing about what time it is on God's clock.

In short, the expectation of Jesus' second and public manifestation as messiah was dictated by the failed Parousia of his initial resurrection appearances. The sundry "private" resurrection appearances to his own followers had turned out not to be definitive. But Jesus' concluding eschatological manifestation to close history, to transform the quick and the dead, and to establish God's Kingdom, his followers maintained, would happen soon. And this second, spectacular appearance would be public, indeed cosmic, its results unquestionable.

The tenor of that second, definitive eschatological manifestation, however—what Jesus, once he came back, was going to do—was dictated by much older and more scriptural allegiances. It was at and to this point, their using scriptures to make meaningful their current circumstances, that the earliest community turned to biblical and postbiblical traditions about David, Israel's anointed king and thus God's "son." Their efforts had a simultaneous double effect upon the ways that the community thought about and expressed its "good news." The figure of Jesus was draped in the antique robes of Davidic traditions; and those traditions were thereby "updated" by being conformed to the figure of Jesus—his death as "King of the Jews" and his postresurrection anticipated return.

It is through this process that Jesus became "Christ."

FOUR

Beginning from Jerusalem

Late Second Temple Jews held more than one idea about "messiah." In the Hebrew Bible, the participle *mashiach*, "anointed," occurs only thirty-nine times, and it can refer to various positions and personages. To assume office, priests, and especially the high priest, were anointed. Kings, too, were anointed: they were thus designated as "the Lord's *mashiach*" in Hebrew, "the Lord's *christos*" in its Greek translation, the Septuagint.

In their *Rule of the Congregation*, the Dead Sea Scroll community at Qumran expressed their expectation of both types of messiah, one priestly and, subordinate to him, one royal, "in the last days." Elsewhere, the Scrolls seem to speak of an elusive "heavenly" messiah as well. Less frequently, the Bible designates prophets, too, as "anointed." In the Greek of Habukkuk 3.12–13, "anointed" refers to the entire people of Israel. And, famously, Isaiah depicts the god of Israel addressing a foreign pagan king, the Persian Cyrus, as his "anointed," God's "messiah" (Hebrew) or "christ" (Greek). In postbiblical literature, the term displayed—and would continue to display—impressive interpretive flexibility. Indeed, its eventual application to the figure of Jesus demonstrates precisely that flexibility.[1]

THE MEANINGS OF "MESSIAH"

Despite this variety of applications and attributions, however, it was the biblical figure of David that predominated in later, and especially in Christian, traditions. David the son of Jesse, the warrior-king and singer of psalms; David the father of Solomon, who built the first temple; David who fought off the Philistines and who united the tribes: David *ha-mashiach* had an especially high profile, both in the Hebrew Bible and in some of the various apocalyptic writings that proliferated in the late Second Temple and early Roman period.[2]

In the Bible, David's accomplishments trace back to the special relationship that he shares with God. They love each other, and God promises David that he will continue to love the sons of David's line. Upon this foundation, each promises to build for the other a "house."[3]

The building up of God's "house," that is, the temple in Jerusalem, and of David's "house," that is, the royal dynasty through Solomon his son, were roughly coincident in biblical history. We see the merger of all these ideas—family love, temple, dynasty, and, most significantly for later Christianity, sonship—in an important prophetic passage from 2 Samuel. In this passage, God through the prophet Nathan promises David that sons of his line will always rule the nation.

> 11 The Lord declares to you [David] that the Lord *will make you
> *a house.* 12 When your days are fulfilled and you lie down with
> your ancestors, I will raise up your offspring after you . . . and I
> will establish his kingdom. 13 *He shall build a house for my name,*
> and I will establish the throne of his kingdom forever. 14 *I will be
> *a father to him, and he will be my son.* . . . I will not take *my
> *steadfast love* away from him. . . . 16 And your house and your

> kingdom shall be made sure forever before me. *Your throne will be established forever.*
>
> (2 Samuel 7.11–16; my emphases)

This passage sounds several key themes that will shape in fundamental ways both the proclamations of the postresurrection community in Jerusalem and, later, the assertions of Christian theology. The first is the concept of divine sonship. Like "messiah," "son of God" has multiple referents in Jewish scripture, wherein God has any number of "sons." Genesis 6 introduces the "sons of God" who mate with human women: they themselves are superhuman forces, eventually interpreted as members of the heavenly court, or as angels. Elsewhere, God designates the whole people of Israel, as he frees them from bondage in Egypt, as his son, indeed, as his "first-born"; and he affirms this close relationship in other biblical writings. Paul in Romans repeats this biblical commonplace: when listing the divine privileges and prerogatives of his kinsmen, Israel, Paul pointedly lifts up Israel's "sonship."[4]

Nonetheless, and in a special way, God binds himself to the kings of David's line as their divine father, as the quotation from 2 Samuel 7 states above: "I will be a father to him, and he will be my son." "You are my son: today I have begotten you," God says to a Davidic king upon his coronation, that is, his anointing into office. "I have found David my servant. With my holy oil I have anointed him; . . . He shall cry to me, 'You are my father,' " another psalm sings. Because of this particular dignity, and in this specific way, a "son of David" was also a son of God—another idea that Paul repeats in Romans when speaking of Jesus.[5]

In light of the ways that some later Christian thinkers will interpret verses such as these, it is important to note what these lines about David and his descendants do *not* say. These Davidic rulers, by virtue of their elevated status as messiah/christ/anointed, are thereby also "sons of God." The phrase denotes their special relationship with the deity, not a special metaphysical or "divine" quality on their own part. In other words, David together with the sons of his line, are fully and normally human.

This means, too, that these messiahs are mortal. What then is the significance in 2 Samuel of God's promising to David an eternal throne: "Your throne will be established forever"? "Eternity" here is not an attribute of the individual king. Davidic kings die. It is the line of these kings that is "eternal." "David will never lack a man to sit on the throne of the house of Israel" foresees the prophet Jeremiah. It was in this way that the genealogical-biological house of David, each king in his own generation after the last, anointed with oil, was invested with and designated as the divinely acknowledged rightful political power in the land, and specifically in Jerusalem. Eternal succession expressed the biblical idea of divine, eternal sonship.[6]

In some of the Jewish apocalyptic writings that bloom particularly in the period between the Maccabees and the Mishnah (roughly two centuries to either side of Jesus' lifetime), this idea of the Davidic messiah was variously repurposed. The historical Davidic dynasty had ended with Babylon's destruction of Jerusalem in 586 B.C.E. Mitigated sovereignty of Judea passed from the (notionally) Zadokite high priesthood, yoked to different imperial governors (variously Persians, then Ptolemies or Seleucids), to the conquering Hasmonean family, and ultimately to Herod and his heirs. By Jesus' period, the house of David was long gone, swallowed by time.

It is in this late Second Temple period and for a century thereafter that the qualifications for messiah seem to diverge. Some groups emphasized the supreme importance of *lineage:* the messiah had to be a man of Davidic descent. Others emphasized, instead, *function:* the messiah had to be a mighty warrior, fighting to establish the sovereignty of Israel. We will consider this second, social, here-and-now, not-quite-apocalyptic category—the "political" or "military" warrior-messiah—especially when we look at Josephus and at the turbulence in Judea during the lifetime of Jerusalem's Jesus-following community, in chapter 5. It was the first, apocalyptic category, the messiah of David's lineage who brings about the establishment of God's Kingdom at the End of Days, that particularly excited visionary imagination.[7]

The majority of our extant intertestamental apocalyptic writings do not mention a messiah. And even the Dead Sea Scroll library, in which we find prophecies of coming Endtime messiahs (such as in the *Rule of Community*), we also find descriptions of the final battle between Good and Evil (the scenario described in *The War Scroll*) that contain no mention of a messiah. As one historian of the period has noted, "Just as there are messiahs without Ends"—that would be our second category, the "political and military" messiah—"so there are Ends without messiahs."[8]

But when an apocalyptic messiah does show up in Endtime texts, he is a son of David. We see this already in the classical prophets. "A shoot will come forth from the root of Jesse," proclaims Isaiah: Jesse was David's father. This foreseen Davidic figure will slay the wicked, assemble the ten "lost" tribes of Israel, preside over peace even among animals, and see that "the earth shall be full of the knowledge of the Lord." His rule will extend over even the pagan nations. "The days are surely coming," says God to Jeremiah, "when I will cause a righteous branch to spring up for David." And in the extracanonical *Psalms of Solomon,* the "son of David"—his appearance no less an eschatological miracle than the reassembled ten lost tribes—will arise to rule Israel, "and there shall be no injustice in his days."[9]

Ends without messiahs; messiahs without Ends. The earliest community around Jesus, both pre- and postcrucifixion, had expected the imminent End. That conviction had bound them together as a community. The preaching of Jesus of Nazareth had primed and prepared them for it. Whether or not these followers, in Jesus' lifetime, had thought of their leader as the Kingdom's messiah, the intense and unanticipated highs and lows of their final Passover sojourn in Jerusalem—triumphal entry, then crucifixion, then resurrection, then the outpouring of charismatic acts—compelled them there. Jesus, by Rome's hand, had died "King of the Jews." If he were raised—to no discernible difference in normal time—then surely he must be returning soon as the King of the Jews. Then the Kingdom would come.[10]

The Kingdom's persistent (and baffling) nonarrival, coupled with the falling away of the resurrection appearances, rendered Jesus' *second* coming a necessity. This necessary reappearance, especially in light of Jesus' death as Israel's king, in turn tapped into Davidic traditions. And the apocalyptic, and specifically Davidic messiah in its turn drew upon those traditions that shaped ancient biblical texts.

Some things fit without needing to be adjusted. The David of the Bible, like the historical Jesus himself, had expressed a Jerusalem-centered piety. And God, designating David's "house" and the sons of his line as God's own sons, established between them a special bond of intimate affection. Perhaps Jesus, again, through prayer and praise, had modeled the same kind of piety.[11]

But David the king was also, even preeminently, David the warrior. He fought and overwhelmed his people's enemies. He smashed the Philistines. He prevailed through martial power. His piety went hand in hand with his prowess.

These warrior traditions fit poorly with the actual mission of the historical Jesus of Nazareth. Jesus' family was not Jerusalemite royalty. (And any claim to Davidic lineage by anybody, by the first century C.E., was mythical thinking.) Jesus' activities conformed most closely to those of a prophet, as traditions lingering in the gospel materials still tell us. More to the point: Jesus had taught an ethic of passive nonresistance, of turning the other cheek, of responding to aggression by walking the extra mile. (Even the pugnacious Paul endorses these same behaviors, which suggests that they correspond to earlier, thus inherited, teachings.) The wicked would get their come-uppance, Jesus taught, but God, not man, would be the one to square the accounts.[12]

How could the image of David the warrior be fit back into memories of Jesus' actual mission? The short answer is: it could not be. But the figure of David *could* be used to describe the lineaments of Jesus' future role and behavior at his deferred, definitive second coming. In the early decades of the first century C.E., then, these Davidic, thus military, traditions began to fill out the expectations of the earliest community. Jesus' military messianic future, when he returned, in a sense would compensate for his irenic, non-Davidic earthly mission. And the weight of Jesus' Davidic—or "Davidized"—future in turn began to shape proclamations "backward," affecting and effecting new traditions about Jesus himself. If Jesus would soon reappear as a Davidic messiah, then he must have been descended from the lineage of David, too.

The double appropriation of this aspect of the David-traditions happened quickly, within two-plus decades of Jesus' death. Already by the late 50s of the first century, on the evidence of Paul's letter to Rome, the association of Jesus with David, both past and future, was firm. Paul uses it as the springboard for his own self-introduction:

> [1] Paul, slave of Jesus Christ, called to be his messenger, set apart for God's good news— [2] promised beforehand through his prophets in the sacred scriptures— [3] the good news concerning his *son, from the seed of David according to the flesh,* [4] and declared *son of God in power according to the spirit of holiness by the resurrection of the dead:* Jesus Christ our lord, [5] through whom we have received grace and apostleship in order to bring the obedience of faithfulness on behalf of his name to all the nations/gentiles/pagans, [6] including to you.
>
> (Romans 1.1–6; my translation)

Paul simply asserts Jesus' Davidic lineage here. He does not argue it, but ties it immediately to Jesus' impending apocalyptic reappearance, when the dead would be raised. The claim of Jesus' past Davidic descent, in other words (and for all the interest that Paul shows in it here), seems "caused" by expectations about Jesus' future eschatological performance.

Two-plus generations after Paul, Matthew and Luke will labor over various Septuagint texts in order to fill in the details of such a descent. They will each construct two Davidic, biographical backstories for Jesus. Whereas Paul's earlier declaration of Jesus' Davidic status was focused almost exclusively on Jesus' coming performance in the near future—Jesus' Davidic lineage is mentioned, by comparison, only in passing—Matthew's and Luke's gospels emphatically introduce their main narrative character by constructing for Jesus, through appeals to the Septuagint, an unimpeachably Davidic past.

Their efforts are especially showcased in their birth stories. Christmas Nativity plays seamlessly blend these two gospels, but their respective narratives are in fact mutually exclusive. In Matthew's story, Joseph and Mary are natives of Bethlehem, David's ancestral village; and Joseph is himself of David's line. After Jesus' birth, to avoid a murderous Herod, they flee to Egypt. Only once an angel sounds the "all clear"—around 4 B.C.E., the year of Herod's death—does the holy family return. They avoid Bethlehem, because Judea is now ruled by one of Herod's sons (Archelaus). Instead, they settle in Nazareth in the Galilee—which, the evangelist neglects to mention, is also ruled by one of Herod's sons (Herod Antipas). In this way, Matthew's Jesus, imbued with a Davidic birthplace, can go on to grow up in Nazareth, the town by which he was known.[13]

Luke, reading the Septuagint evidently with these same concerns in mind, generates different biographical "facts." Luke situates Mary and Joseph in Nazareth. Then, because of a tax ordered by the Syrian legate Quirinius—thus in 6 C.E., as we know from Josephus—they journey to Bethlehem, because "Joseph was of the house and lineage of David" (Luke 2.4). The gravid Mary then gives birth to Jesus in the correct messianic town. Sometime thereafter, after a stop in Jerusalem, the holy family returns back home to Nazareth.[14]

These two narratives, despite being mutually exclusive, evince the same late first-century or early second-century concern: how to outfit Jesus of Nazareth with a Davidic messianic biography. The gap in time between their authors and the original generation around Jesus contributed crucially to their opportunity: who was there to challenge them? And, despite their simple differences—like the ten-year gap in chronology (4 B.C.E., the date of Herod's death; 6 C.E., the date of the Roman tax); like the assignment of Mary and Joseph's native village (Bethlehem? Nazareth?)—each evangelist was drawn as well, and for reasons that we do not know, to the Greek text of Isaiah 7.14: "A virgin will conceive and bear a son."[15]

Their appeal to this Septuagintal passage gives us a valuable measure of the degree to which western ideas about Jesus of

Nazareth, by the late first or early second century, were evolving in post-Aramaic contexts. The female who gives birth to a son in Isaiah 7.14 is a "virgin" *only* in the Greek text of the scriptures. In the Hebrew—the tradition that Jesus and his original followers would have known—that female is a young girl or "maiden." And in its original context, this verse had nothing to do with messiahs. It was simply a very odd way of measuring time during the rule of King Ahaz. But this verse becomes "messianized" in the two independent birth narratives of Matthew and Luke, when the evangelists apply it to Jesus' nativity. Thereafter, and for their communities, the mother of the messiah was a virgin.[16]

These two very different yet similar birth narratives also give us the measure of these evangelists' literary freedom. This is an extremely important point to bear in mind. It holds true for all of our narrative New Testament texts, both for all four of our gospels and certainly for Acts. These writers were not doing history, certainly not as our modern discipline, born in the Renaissance, is conceived. They were not consulting archives that preserved historical records of Jesus' birth. None existed. They were not critically assessing various materials and interviewing different people in search of a plausible reconstruction of what might have actually happened.

Quite the opposite: These authors were unconstrained by any historical knowledge. They were therefore free to allow the scriptures to generate the biographical "data" on Jesus that they needed. Their purpose in writing was not to preserve "memories" or to relate a plausible history: It was to persuade their hearers about the messianic identity of their protagonist. The gospels first of all are proclamations, not histories. The evangelists' only constraint was biblical tradition itself: David the king had come from Bethlehem. Therefore, somehow, Jesus had to come from Bethlehem, too.

And so they each wrote up a story, deferring to select biblical passages that conformed Jesus' past to their own current convictions about him.[17]

The first generation, by contrast, focused most intently on Jesus' Davidic, messianic future. When Jesus returns, says Paul, the dead will rise. Jesus' staccato resurrection epiphanies had functioned as a kind of charismatic down payment toward his future, definitive reappearance: on merit of these visions, his followers became convinced that Jesus would shortly return. At that point, he would establish the Kingdom of his "father," the god of Israel. In this way, at his second coming, Jesus would be publicly known to the cosmos—as he was known "now," privately, to the small community gathered around his mission and message—as the eschatological messiah and, thus, as David's "son." And in this way, this messianic attribution, according to the language of Psalms and of Samuel, Jesus as David's "son" was God's "son" too.

Most authorized translations of the opening of Paul's letter to Rome mute Paul's linkage of Jesus' Davidic sonship to these Endtime events. These translations obscure this important passage of Paul's letter by *mis*translating it. And these mistranslations occur for good reason: the ever-expanding lag between Jesus' first coming and his second one.

But Paul, in the mid-first century, wrote in innocence of this long pause in history's sweep. He expected the general resurrection soon—in his own lifetime, in fact. And he expected that event to declare in public, before the universe, what Jesus' own resurrection appearances had earlier declared to select insiders: the Kingdom was at hand.

The standard English misrendering of these lines of Paul's attests, instead, to the pressures of the passage of time. Instead of reading "designated son of God in power *by the resurrection of the dead*," which is what Paul's Greek says, the Revised Standard Version gives "designated son of God in power by *his* resurrection *from* the dead." But that is not what Paul says. He states, rather, that Jesus will be known as "son of God"—that is, as the Davidic messiah—not by his own resurrection from the dead, but by the (general) resurrection of (all of?) the dead. This is a distinction with a difference.[18]

The RSV's mistranslation erases the gap between first-century proclamation and later, postapocalyptic interpretations of it. The RSV puts all the emphasis on Jesus' *individual* resurrection. It thereby decouples Jesus' resurrection from what it was necessarily and immediately linked to, as Paul elsewhere insisted: the final transformation of both the dead and the living at Christ's return, when, as Paul said elsewhere, "he delivers the Kingdom to God the Father." The glow of the impending Kingdom, for Paul as for the earliest community, already brightly backlit Jesus' unexpected, individual resurrection.[19]

This opening passage of Romans in English also seems to distinguish between the human Jesus, a fleshly descendant and thus a "son of David," and the divine Christ, the "son of God" declared as such, according to the RSV, by his individual resurrection. But in the sort of messianic biblical interpretation that Paul's opening statement to the assembly at Rome presupposes, "son of David" and "son of God" are synonyms. The associations are tight, but distinguishable. If Jesus is returning as a warrior to establish God's Kingdom, then he is the messiah. If he is the messiah, then he must be descended from David's house. At the Eschaton—and its signature Endtime miracle, the resurrection of the dead—these messianic identifications will be made universally clear. In the meanwhile, the faithful, in advance of the Kingdom's arrival, knew Jesus to be "the christ."

But again: Jesus of Nazareth was no warrior. Whence this association with David? David's behavior as a conqueror in biblical texts in a sense dictated Jesus' behavior at his definitive Endtime appearance. *Jesus, the second time around, comes as a cosmic warrior.*

Paul had described this public David-style debut already in his earliest letter, 1 Thessalonians. The assembly in Thessalonika, perhaps sometime in the late 40s C.E., was growing concerned: members of their community had died before the return of Christ. The very fact that this unnerved them reveals their time frame: they were expecting the Parousia very soon, and certainly within their own lifetimes. Paul writes to reassure them that things are on track. And in doing so, he provides a quick sketch of the oncoming final events:

> [13] We would not have you ignorant, brothers, concerning those who sleep, so that you might not grieve as others do who have no hope. [14] For since we trust that Jesus died and rose again, even so, through Jesus, God will bring with him those who have fallen asleep. [15] For this we declare to you by the word of the Lord, that *we who are alive, who are left* until the *coming of the Lord,* will not precede those who have fallen asleep. [16] For the *Lord himself* will descend from heaven *with a cry of command, with the archangel's call, and with the sound of the trumpet of God.* And the dead in Christ will rise first; [17] then we who are alive . . . shall be caught up in the clouds to meet the Lord in the air.
>
> (1 Thessalonians 4.13–17; my emphases)

Paul develops this scenario of cosmic battle further in other letters. To the Corinthians, Paul describes Christ's second coming in the language of royal and martial engagement. At the End, he says, Christ will deliver the Kingdom to the Father "after destroying every rule and every authority and every power. For he must reign until he has put all his enemies under his feet." When Christ returns, Paul explains to the assembly in Philippi, "he will change our lowly body to be like his glorious body, by the power that enables him even to subject all things to himself."[20]

Further: the messiah's triumphant return, Paul asserts, will cause the reassembly of the scattered tribes of Israel. This is another Endtime miracle: ten of these twelve tribes had disappeared after Assyria's conquest of the Galilee in the eighth century B.C.E. The Kingdom over which Christ will rule, in other words, would conform to the kingdom of David (c. 1000 B.C.E.): all twelve tribes. And more: Christ will rule over foreign nations and peoples as well. "The root of Jesse shall come," asserts Paul, rounding into the end of Romans, quoting Isaiah, "he who rises *to rule the nations.* In him shall the nations hope"—hope, that is, that they too will be, thanks to Jesus, included in God's Kingdom.[21]

In short, at his eschatological second coming, proclaims Paul, Jesus will arrive the way that a Davidic messiah was supposed to arrive: trumpets sounding, in command, conquering foreign gods and subduing foreign nations, victorious, in power.

Davidic tropes of triumphant kingship shaped expectations about the returning Jesus. And those expectations, already in Paul's letters, began to reshape Jesus' past: such a warrior messiah must be descended from David. Further, and finally, this early appropriation of Davidic themes also accounts for the early community's evolving speculations about what Jesus was doing in the present, before his return. *Where was Jesus during this moment between his resurrection and his Parousia?* Where was he, while his people awaited his return?

David's psalms gave them the answer: Jesus was enthroned at God's right hand.

This image of the postcrucifixion, raised Jesus seated at the right hand of God most likely draws upon Psalm 110, an "enthronement" psalm and a "psalm of David." Mark's Jesus quotes this verse in Greek—"The Lord said to my Lord, sit at my right hand, until I put your enemies under your feet"—to teach that the eschatological messiah (that is, himself) is David's superior. Later, in a moment of highest drama, the trial before the Sanhedrin, Jesus confronts the high priest. For the first and only time in Mark, Jesus acknowledges his own messianic status. "'Are you the messiah, the son of the Blessed [that is, God]?' 'I am, and you will see the son of man [Jesus] seated at the right hand of power.'"[22]

We will explore Mark's odd locution for Jesus, "son of man," further on, when we look at decisions taken in Rome that affected Jerusalem in the year 39–40 C.E. The point here is that Mark's gospel, like Paul's letters a generation earlier, points to the original postresurrection community's "Davidization" of Jesus. These earliest followers provided Jesus not only with a classically messianic future, but also with a regal meanwhile. Raised to and enthroned at God's right hand, Jesus would soon return, making his enemies his footstool. This idea of enemies underfoot, mentioned both by Paul (1 Corinthians 15.25, 27, in the mid-50s C.E.) and by Mark (Mark 12.36, post-70 C.E.), most likely draws from David's songbook, Psalm 110.1. And this derivation in turn reflects the community's postresurrection searching of Jewish scriptures, the better to locate themselves—and the risen Jesus—in their unprecedented, confusing present circumstances.

In other words, Jesus' heightened affiliation with, or assimilation to, Davidic traditions, stimulated by his pre-Passover procession into Jerusalem and by his death as "King of the Jews," occurred as his first followers speculated about his future. Circumstances—namely, the resurrection appearances and then, just as definitely, the *cessation* of these resurrection appearances—compelled this community's conjectures. Ancient scriptures then provided them with their interpretive building blocks to generate new, confirming traditions about Jesus' life, death, resurrection, and second coming. All of these creative revisions were already in place when Paul wrote to Rome.

And eventually—in the later synoptic gospels, especially—Jesus' "Davidization" evolved even further, growing increasingly in "biographical" detail. These tied Jesus' birth to David's ancestral village, Bethlehem. Long patrilineal genealogies, generated backward, likewise tethered Jesus to the correct ancestors. Clearly, the virgin birth stories and the Davidic lineages traced through Joseph evolved independently of each other since, read together, Mary's virginity moots Joseph's lineage. Later church fathers will smooth out this messianic awkwardness, too: Mary herself will also become descended from the house and lineage of David.[23]

THE WHOLE HOUSE OF ISRAEL

Worshiping in the temple, gathering together daily, prophesying and praying, supporting each other financially as well as emotionally: this was the charismatic context within which the community in Jerusalem generated its new biblical understandings of what they had just lived through. And these newer understandings melded with their proclamations of the gospel. But when did they decide to take their evolving message to Jews outside of their immediate community? What, now, would that message be? And how would they broadcast it?

Luke depicts this transition, we saw above, as another miracle: The spirit descends on Shavuot/Pentecost, and gives to those gathered together after Jesus' ascension the power to speak foreign languages. This story also foregrounds Peter as the spokesman of the group. He gives a long Christological address, winding up by citing Psalm 110, the enthronement psalm. Jesus, says Peter, was "delivered up according to the definite plan and foreknowledge of God" to be crucified by "you"—that is, by the crowd of Jews celebrating this pilgrimage holiday. "Let all the house of Israel therefore know assuredly that God has made him both Lord and messiah, this Jesus whom you crucified."[24]

Several things should be noted about this passage. First, and remarkably, Pilate has dropped from view in "Peter's" early second-century retelling of Jesus' passion. The guilty parties are now the "you" of his narrative Jerusalemite audience in the year 30. Historically, however, the setting of another pilgrimage holiday would mean that Pilate and his troops would once again be up in Jerusalem. Luke's characters in Acts seem unconcerned about this.

Second, this shift of responsibility from Rome to Jerusalem in turn entails a modification of the earlier gospel message. The crowd is still exhorted to "repent" but, in context, their "sin" in crucifying Jesus seems to be added to whatever else they are supposed to repent of.[25]

Third, Luke's Peter—in high contrast to what we have seen from Paul a half-century earlier—says nothing about Jesus' expected return. No Endtime looms in this first public address, continuing Jesus' mission: Jesus goes up to heaven and the spirit comes down. We have noted Luke's deemphasizing the final days before, a characteristic of his gospel as well as of Acts. We see here his own careful adjustment of the vivid Endtime expectations that characterized the community that he purports to describe.

Fourth and finally, the enormous size of the crowd ("about three thousand souls") would require that Peter speak in a large public space. In Jerusalem, this would be the outermost court of the temple complex—just where a pilgrim crowd would be gathered.[26]

What can we derive from this chapter of Acts that helps us to construct a more historically sturdy impression of the earliest community's crucial transition from agitated vigil to active outreach?

The launch of the public mission to other Jews on the occasion of a pilgrimage holiday—not necessarily the first one following Jesus' death around Passover—would indeed make good sense. Being in Jerusalem for a festival and preaching within the temple's largest court maximizes the number of Jewish hearers. This is probably what Jesus himself had done. In this instance, those of his followers proclaiming the coming Kingdom from within the temple's court would be following his lead.

The public proclamation of a coming messiah from the temple courts during a crowded holiday, mobilizing some three thousand people: if anything like this, with any numbers even approaching these, had actually occurred, why would Pilate at this time—and for his remaining six years in office—do nothing? In light of what had just happened a scant two months previously, according to the gospels, Acts' "Peter" exhibits truly striking apostolic sangfroid. Would the actual historical community really have been so nonchalant?

But on this point, if only obliquely, Luke *may* relate important historical information about this conspicuously missing person, Pilate. The prefect, I have argued, had known for years that this group around Jesus presented no serious political or military threat. He had never acted against them before that Passover when he struck Jesus down. This group's current proclamation of a coming messiah whom Pilate knew perfectly well was dead doubtless seemed to him to be less than threatening.

Indeed, Rome's continuing indifference to this community—especially as the decades until the War filled with other noisily apocalyptic movements and *living* charismatic leaders—is what allowed it to establish itself back in Jerusalem. The staggering number of Luke's recruits, however, seems conjured for rhetorical effect: he wants to present a thriving movement miraculously going from strength to strength. (So too at Acts 4.4: five thousand sign on.) Three thousand people in Jerusalem suddenly communalizing all property, healing and exorcising and prophesying and preaching the coming End of Days during a festival from the temple, would inevitably have registered on Pilate's radar as a serious disruption—as indeed it would have been.

Did the early community, once the apostles began their proclamations, begin to grow? Doubtless. By such huge numbers? For the reason named above—Pilate's initial and continuing lack of concern—probably not.

What about Luke's generalized inculpation of Jerusalem's Jews? "Peter" enlarges this indictment—again, from the temple precincts—in Acts 3. After miraculously healing a lame man, Peter speaks to the amazed crowd about "Jesus, whom you delivered up and denied before Pilate, when he had decided to release him." Peter then undergirds his narration of Jesus' death and resurrection with the claim that events conformed to "what God foretold by the mouth of all the prophets, that his *christos* should suffer." Luke then nods gently in the direction of an eventual second coming. Heaven, he says, must receive Jesus "until the time for establishing all that God spoke by the mouth of his holy prophets from of old." This oration, too, ends with a call to repentance, including, it would seem, for the "sin" of Jesus' crucifixion.[27]

What seems historically plausible in all this? The call to repentance in preparation for the coming Kingdom, continuous from the days of Jesus' mentor John the Baptizer, seems to me historical bedrock. Acts' global inculpation of Jerusalem's Jews, however, and the corresponding exculpation of Pilate, is a strong and increasingly developed motif in all of the gospels as well as in Acts. This pattern is better explained by the trauma of the year 70.

Why would the almighty god of the universe allow a foreign power to destroy his temple and his city? Later generations, scouring the scriptures after Rome's destruction of Jerusalem, came up with an answer similar to the one that Israel's prophets had developed to account for other confounding historical tragedies: the collapse of the north before the Assyrian invasion, and the destruction of the First Temple by Babylon. The god of the Bible is good; he is merciful; he is just; he controls history. Thus, if something bad happens to his people, it must be for a good reason. God has not broken his covenant with Israel. Rather, he uses these large-scale traumata to call Israel to repentance. Therefore Israel must have sinned.[28]

So too in this first-century instance with Rome. The flames of Jerusalem in the year 70 backlight the later evangelists' passion narratives, and the speeches that Luke gives to "Peter" and to others in Acts. These New Testament writers explain the fall of the city and of its temple by moving the priests, representatives of the now defunct temple, and the city's residents into their narratives' foreground. Their explanation for the catastrophe is brief and, from their perspective, powerful: Jerusalem fell because Jerusalem rejected Jesus. By the time they write, postdestruction, there is no community in Jerusalem left to complicate or to challenge their view.

We see this especially clearly when Luke's Jesus weeps over the city that he is about to enter for Passover: "Would that even today you knew the things that make for peace! . . . For the days shall come upon you, when your enemies will cast up a bank around you and surround you, and hem you in on every side, and dash you to the ground . . . and they will not leave one stone upon another in you, because you did not know the time of your visitation." Such passages move some scholars to think that Luke had been reading Josephus.[29]

Jesus' followers in the year 30, however, innocent of the future—of *this* future—were not burdened by the need to explain the temple's destruction in 70. They never saw it coming. The trauma that compelled them, rather, was the crucifixion of their beloved leader. Their experiences of Jesus raised—which eventually blended into their evolving expectations for Jesus' second, public debut as the eschatological warrior-messiah—was their response. They too scoured scriptures, as would the evangelists long after them. They modified Jesus' prophecy of the coming Kingdom by linking its arrival to his *second* coming. That revamped message provided the core of the good news that they began to proclaim to holiday crowds in Jerusalem: the Kingdom was coming, and Jesus was coming back. Pilate, unimpressed and undisturbed, continued to go about his business.

The priests were a different story. The temple and its tranquil operation were their particular responsibility; but the temple, according to Acts, was also where the apostles particularly liked to hold forth. Early on in his story, Luke depicts "the priests and the captain of the temple and the Sadducees," annoyed by Peter's and John's proclaiming Jesus' resurrection in the temple precincts, simply asking them to stop. The apostles decline their request. In chapter 5, jealous of the apostles, Luke explains, because of their popularity in doing signs and wonders and healing the sick, the priests and the Sadducees throw the lot of them in prison. An angel frees them to go back to the temple and teach. Gamaliel the

Pharisee, a member of "the council," finally advises the priests to just let the matter drop. Agreeing, the priests discipline the apostles and then release them.[30]

Shortly thereafter, however, in a narrative reprise of Jesus' trial scene, Stephen, one of the "Hellenists" or Greek-speaking members of the apostolic community, will be questioned by the high priest and the council and subsequently stoned by a mob. Why? "This man never ceases to speak words against this holy place and the law; for we have heard him say that this Jesus of Nazareth will destroy this place, and will change the customs that Moses delivered to us" (a charge that Luke signals is a lie, since it is tendered by "false witnesses"). Immediately following from this incident, Luke continues, a "great persecution arose against the assembly in Jerusalem; and they were all scattered throughout the region of Judea and Samaria, *except for the apostles*." With this, the priests and the Sadducees fade from view, until Luke reintroduces them when presenting Paul's travails during his final sojourn in Jerusalem.[31]

It is hard to know what to do with this material. Luke's various dramatizations are all highly stylized. This is especially true of Stephen's trial, in the course of which Stephen gives a leisurely lecture to the Sanhedrin on the history of Israel from Abraham to Christ, and utters one of Jesus' own lines from Luke's gospel trial scene. Historically, it is unlikely that such charges—disavowed by Luke as false, in any case—would have prompted any sort of legal action. After all, just southeast of Jerusalem, at Qumran, an entire community was busy producing their own biblical commentaries, developing their own halakhic practices, disdaining the current temple, reviling its priesthood, and anticipating the Endtime arrival of an entirely new temple, which at least implied the destruction of the current one. Against them the Jerusalem priesthood never so much as lifted a finger. Also, finally, Luke depicts the Jesus-community in Jerusalem as observing the law and regularly worshiping in the temple, as it does Paul when he later returns to the city. Temple piety, both during Jesus' lifetime and thereafter, seems to have characterized this movement.

As Josephus reveals, things were not always smooth between these two groups. In 62 C.E., Ananus the high priest will have James, Jesus' brother, stoned, an incident we will return to further on. But was the relationship between the early community and Jerusalem's priests a tale of unending harassments and persecutions? Again, even on the evidence of Luke, the answer is no. What he does present in Acts 3 to 5 are several cycles of Peter and others "teaching and preaching Jesus as the messiah" daily in the temple, and the priests trying to get them to stop. It is hard to avoid the conclusion that, after an initial burst of anxious attention, the Jerusalem priesthood, too, for the most part left the earliest community alone.

What, then, about "the persecution" that supposedly befell the community upon Stephen's death? Why were "the apostles," too, not "persecuted," especially if they were the ones best known to the populace and to the priests? Luke does not bother to clear up the confusions of his presentation. Instead, he uses this episode of persecution (by whom and how, exactly?) to begin to relate the spread of the movement outside of Jerusalem, to Samaria, to Gaza and Joppa and Caesarea on the coast, to Cyprus and to Antioch. But Luke also seems at pains to say that these spreading missions took care to remain coordinated with the "mother" community in Jerusalem—which means that the community was still there, and that these other "brethren" were free to come and go. Some seventy years earlier, Paul—albeit through gritted teeth, at the same moment as he strenuously asserts his independence—

also gives evidence of this same effort at coordination. He confers at least twice with the apostles back in Jerusalem about his own mission.[32]

Luke uses "the persecution" to move his story along in two important ways. First, Stephen's death and the subsequent persecution introduce us to Saul/Paul. (Luke extends the high priest's authority, fantastically, as far as Damascus. As noted above, that authority did not extend even as far as Qumran.) And, second, this hostility begins, and explains, the spread of the mission outside of Jerusalem. Further on down the road—literally—Antioch represents a narrative and a demographical tipping point in Luke's story: from here on, the "brethren" take the good news not just to other Jews, but also to "the Greeks" (that is, to gentiles, who would be pagans). Before pursuing these apostles into the Diaspora, however, I want to return to Jerusalem, to the earliest years of the post-crucifixion community there. What finally prompted their decision to continue Jesus' mission to Israel? And how did they organize themselves in order to be able to do so?[33]

◆◆◆

It is harder to wait and do nothing than it is to wait and do something. Jesus was raised. He was enthroned at God's right hand. Still, no Kingdom came. The period of Jesus' resurrection appearances gave way to an ever-lengthening period of no resurrection appearances. Still the Kingdom did not, would not come. Some members of the community—a few hundred people in total?—eventually took advantage of the pilgrim-swollen city during a festival. They proclaimed the coming Kingdom, now to be inaugurated by their returning messiah, to the holiday crowds. They reinforced their message with their charismatic gifts: working cures and exorcisms, urgently interpreting the meaning of the times by appeals to ancient scriptures. Word spread. Others joined.

The priests, apprehensive as ever about disorder during the holidays, initially attempted to curtail this behavior, and failed; some priests, perhaps, even joined the movement. ("The number of the disciples multiplied greatly in Jerusalem, and a great many of the priests were obedient to the faith"; Acts 6.7.) Now, even after the festival, this commune of Jesus' followers continued to witness in the city.

And yet the Kingdom did not come. Something was wrong. With the prophecy? Impossible. Then the problem must be with them. What could they do to further prepare? Remaining in Jerusalem—waiting, expecting, witnessing—while declaring the coming Kingdom from the Temple Mount had added momentum to the movement and the validation of increase (both in terms of new members and in the properties that they pooled). But what else could they do?

Belief that the world is imminently to end has been, paradoxically, one of the longest-lived convictions of Christian culture. It has endured for two millennia, the designated date of the End calculated variously, from Roman antiquity on into the western Middle Ages, swelling especially around the year 1000. Indeed, anxieties surrounding the year 2000, with its timely hysteria about widespread computer failures ("Y2K"), rested on a long and continuous history.[34]

The approach of the End has been repeatedly proclaimed by inspired millenarian movements, which especially flourished in nineteenth-century America. In the 1950s, a group of U.S. scholars had the opportunity to observe and to interview a Christian group that foretold the world's end for a certain December 21. The named date came and went. Time did not end. The world continued—but so did this group. In their study, *When Prophecy Fails: A Social and Psychological Study of a Modern Group That Predicted the Destruction of the World*, the scholars explained how.[35]

The group's prophecy was absolutely disconfirmed; and yet, members of the group were convinced that the prophecy was true. The sociologists described the members' situation as one of extreme "cognitive dissonance," that mental gear-grinding caused when a vital belief is at the same time both firmly held and yet also, unambiguously, disconfirmed. Intriguingly, the group responded to its disappointment by *increasing* its outreach efforts. Why? The better, conjectured these scholars, to reduce the "cognitive dissonance." How so? The more you talk and convince others that you are right despite all evidence to the contrary, these scholars suggested, the better, the more validated, you feel. The initial prophecy—disconfirmed but never discredited, retrieved and revived through reinterpretation—can thus continue to survive.

It is tempting to frame the Jesus movement's first generation—which thought that they would be history's last generation—with these modern sociological studies. Despite the seriatim setbacks at its very origins—Jesus' death and, thereafter, the diminishing of his resurrection appearances, the continuing delay of his return, and the ever-extending wait for the Kingdom—the movement endured. As one historian of ancient Christianity, thinking with these modern sociological studies, has put it, this movement succeeded precisely as its central prophecy failed.[36]

This first generation in Jerusalem evidently did *not* think that Jesus' prophecy had failed. They seem to have assumed, rather, that they had misunderstood its prerequisites, and therefore misconstrued what they themselves were supposed to do to contribute to its fulfillment. The delay itself becomes variously explained and accounted for, which led to many internal disagreements. When we consider the letter to the Galatians in the next chapter, we shall try to chart out these different first-century solutions to the problem of the Kingdom's delay.

Paul's letter to the Romans, in the late 50s of the first century, gives us a glimpse of this process of rationalizing the delay of the Kingdom. In this epistle, Paul accounts for the Kingdom's evident deferral, both to himself and to the gentile community in Rome.

The eighth chapter of Romans might have seemed like a good place to end the letter. Paul had brought the themes of the preceding chapters to a rousing crescendo. The sin of idolatry had plunged the pagan world into moral chaos; Jewish law could not help gentiles to resist sin and to reform. Through Christ, however, gentiles now had a path to righteousness. Exhorting and encouraging the spirit-filled ex-pagan pagans of the Roman assembly, Paul pointed ahead to their fast-approaching final redemption. God has adopted them as his sons. They now—intimately—could call God by his Jewish name, "Abba." As God's newly adopted sons, they too, along with Israel, could—and soon would—inherit the Kingdom.[37]

But Paul continues on from there. Abruptly, in chapters 9 through 11, he shifts topic, talking passionately about his "kinsmen according to the flesh," that is, ethnic Israel. They are already God's "sons," quite apart from any relationship to Christ. God has granted them defining privileges: his presence (RSV: "glory"); his covenants; the Torah; the temple cult (RSV: "worship"); the promises of redemption; and the "blood" relation to the messiah, who is "of their race." So why are more Jews not signing up for this messianic movement that Paul champions? After all, God does not go back on his word: his gifts and his promises, once given, are "irrevocable." If God is about to include adopted gentile sons in his Kingdom, he certainly was not going to exclude his prior "sons," Paul's own kinsmen. In fact, Paul strenuously asserts, God will certainly redeem all Israel. So why then, apart from "a remnant chosen by grace" (among whom, Paul) was Israel currently, persistently indifferent to the gospel?

Paul's answer midcentury—more than twenty-five years after Jesus' initial prophecy—is that God was delaying final events to give more time for the gentile mission. Pagans must first be turned to Israel's god—to the exclusion of their own gods—before the End could begin. Paul feels that he has already fulfilled his own apostolic commitments, as he sees them. He has proclaimed the gospel to nations "from Jerusalem as far around as Illyricum," that portion of the Mediterranean world arcing from Jerusalem through Asia Minor (modern Turkey) to Rome and, perhaps, Spain, that encompassed Greek speakers, hence, "Greeks." In his own view, and to his own satisfaction, Paul has covered one-third of the known world.[38]

In Jewish tradition, Greeks had descended from Japhet, one of the three sons of Noah who had repopulated the world after the flood (Genesis 10). Together with the offspring of the other sons, Shem and Ham, the global number of "peoples" or "nations"—individuated by land, language, and kinship-group—reached seventy. When Paul speaks of the "fullness of the gentiles" coming to the gospel in Romans 11, this is the biblical number that he has in mind: all seventy gentile nations, or perhaps representative numbers from each of those nations. And Paul expects all of this to happen soon. One reads Romans 11 with the sound of wind rushing past: the End is closing in.

Paul's premier sense of self was as "apostle to the pagans." Only his letters from midcentury survive. By that time, he would have had to explain to his own ex-pagan congregations, as well as to himself, why the Kingdom was already "late"—some twenty-five years after Jesus' resurrection—and why many other Jews were not persuaded by this messianic reading of their ancient scriptures. In

Romans, Paul lays out his two-phase explanation. Israel would have received the gospel, had God wanted them to. But instead, God was currently and deliberately *preventing* most of Israel from so doing, for strategic reasons: to give Paul (and other apostles) more time to reach out to the pagan nations. Once the "full number" of gentiles came over, God would cease this strategic hardening of Israel, and *then* history's finale could begin. At that point, "a Deliverer will come from Zion / he will banish ungodliness from Jacob."[39] It was the outreach to the gentiles—the time it was taking to turn pagans from their gods to Paul's god—that was holding things up.

Mid-first century, Paul's message represents his adjustment to the Kingdom's several-decades-long delay. In the years immediately following Jesus' execution, however—that period from which we have no texts—the earliest community faced no such lengthy lag, nor could they or would they have anticipated it. And they had two other explanatory sources to draw on to account for the Parousia's evident tarrying. One was their personal experience of Jesus' own mission. The other, the ancient traditions about the End of Days expressed in sacred scriptures, which had inspired Jesus himself.

Jesus' mission had focused on fellow Jews. And ancient prophetic scriptures had prioritized Israel's ingathering, to be followed by the turning of the nations. This was also a two-stage model of redemption, similar to Paul's later one. But by holding on to the ancient prophetic traditions, the Jerusalem community held on as well to the older sequence of saved ethnic groups. God first redeems Israel; then the nations, renouncing their idolatry, would be redeemed as well.[40]

Matthew's gospel expresses this view with particular clarity, as we have seen. Not only does his Jesus go "nowhere among the pagans"; Matthew's Jesus orders his apostles to follow suit. In Matthew, the mission to pagans is authorized only by the risen Christ, at some point after Jesus' death: "Go, and make disciples of all nations." Israel first; "nations" or "pagans" or "gentiles" after.

Matthew's Jesus states forthrightly what the other gospels narratively depict. While Jesus shows up routinely at synagogue gatherings on the Sabbath (the synoptic tradition) and especially in the temple precincts during holy days (John), he interacts only rarely with non-Jews. And he preaches the gospel—"The Kingdom of God is at hand; repent!"—to none of them. The most important gentile whom Jesus speaks with at any length, in all these stories, is Pilate. Jesus does not announce the good news to him.

The community's sending apostles from Jerusalem, its decision to resume the mission, taking the message out on the road, thus did not require a persecution to get going, though that is what Luke would later devise. It only required a decision to continue the pattern that Jesus himself had inaugurated, when he commissioned his followers—the twelve and, in Luke's gospel, the seventy as well—to spread the good news. This means that, as before, when Jesus was alive, so now too: the apostles would wander between areas of Jewish (and Samaritan) settlement, meeting with villagers and townspeople often on the Sabbath, when their audiences would be already assembled for their weekly instruction in ancestral laws. These apostles would interpret scriptures together with those gathered, demonstrating their own empowerment by spirit through exorcising demons, through giving prophecy, and through healing. They would call their Jewish hearers to repentance, and they would proclaim the approach of God's Kingdom.

To this core evangel of the Kingdom's coming will have been added some specifically postcrucifixion proclamations. That Jesus had been crucified as King of the Jews. That he had been raised "on the third day," and appeared before his disciples and his community. That he was about to return, conquering and glorious. That to prepare for this event, Israel should repent of their sins. That when Jesus did return, then the dead would rise, the twelve tribes would reassemble in Jerusalem, and the whole world would acknowledge Israel's god. The apostles would be announcing that the prophets' ancient promises had been put on fast-forward. Events—on the evidence of Jesus' own resurrection—were moving quickly.[41]

According to the synoptic traditions, Jesus had purposefully sent out his apostles poorly prepared for long-term travel. Journey without food; teach for free; depend on those you teach to feed you. Bring with you only the clothes on your back. Take no money. Go barefoot. Leave bag and staff behind. Again, these arrangements—or rather the almost total lack thereof—measure the movement's commitment to the Kingdom's closeness. To the obvious question—how long could such itinerate poverty be maintained?—the apostles could respond with the obvious answer: not long. That, of course, was the point: not much time remained.[42]

"You will not have gone through all the towns of Israel," Matthew's Jesus teaches the twelve as he sends them on their way, "before the Son of Man comes." Within the context of this gospel, Matthew's Jesus predicts his own second coming. But might this teaching reflect something stretching back, behind Matthew's Greek, to the apostles' Aramaic, and even to Jesus himself?[43]

We cannot know, of course, any better than probably Matthew could have. If some version of this saying qua prediction of the Parousia does trace back to the postcrucifixion apostolic mission, it could represent what these apostles were telling their listeners. How short is the time? Jesus will return before we can reach every place of Jewish settlement. If some version of this saying qua prophecy of the coming Kingdom traces back to Jesus himself, it might represent what he had been telling his listeners. How short is the time? Very short. Not all Israel will have the chance to repent that I give to you now.

"All the towns of Israel" is the phrase to focus on here, because it helps to explain what the apostles thought they were doing, and why, after the resurrection appearances fell off, they decided to resume their itinerate practices. Why had Jesus not yet returned? Why is the Kingdom taking so long? Because all of the "towns of Israel" had yet to be reached.

The first phase of their movement's mission, during Jesus' lifetime, had been to Jewish villages in the Galilee and Judea, and to Jerusalem. The second phase of their mission, after the onset and then the cessation of the resurrection appearances, had been to proclaim the coming Kingdom, linked with Jesus' triumphant future return, from the largest court of Jerusalem's temple. "All the towns of Israel," then, would be the next, that is the third, phase of their mission.

Did they still travel so austerely? Did they continue to get on the road while making no provision for the morrow? The much greater distances that they now prepared to travel, well outside of their old network, suggest that they had to make adjustments. (Luke's Jesus actually suggests this change.) So these apostles wandered not only into villages, but—for the first time—into major pagan cities as well, cities like Caesarea, Damascus, Antioch. "All the towns of Israel," they realized, did not mean all the Jewish towns of Herod the Great's territories. It meant all the towns where Israel dwells. Some of these lay within Herod's old kingdom. More lay outside, ringing the Mediterranean, in the Diaspora. They had to prepare for longer journeys now.[44]

And it was then and there, in this later phase of the mission, in the synagogues of these mixed cities within and without Jewish territories, that the apostles discovered something that, in rural Galilee, had been outside of their experience. These urban synagogue communities held more than just Jews. They also held pagans.

Thus began, unintended, the mission to the gentiles.

ISRAEL AND THE NATIONS

Just as pagans could be found visiting with Israel's god in his temple's precincts, they also could be found, variously affiliated, in the synagogues of western diaspora cities. There they could listen to biblical traditions sung out in their own vernacular, Greek, becoming acquainted with a powerful god without having to journey to Jerusalem. Synagogue inscriptions gratefully acknowledged the donations of generous pagan benefactors. A priestess of the imperial cult funded the construction of a synagogue building. Alexandrian pagans joined with Jews to feast together annually in celebration of the scriptures' translation into Greek. Gentile town councilors involved themselves in synagogue activities and projects. One pagan city even minted coins bearing an image of Noah's ark.[45]

Sometimes an interested outsider might choose to come over entirely to a Jewish way of life, making an exclusive commitment to Israel's god and for men, momentously, receiving circumcision. Such behavior occasioned sharp comment and vivid resentment from pagan critics, who viewed it as a form of cultural and religious treason. It was also potentially dangerous. Gods presided over the ancient city. Deserting local gods for an exclusive allegiance to a distant foreign god destabilized relations between heaven and earth. Lack of respect made gods angry, and angry gods acted out. Plague, earthquake, famine, flood; disrupted seasons or invading armies: all these figured in the repertoire of divine anger. Why tempt heaven with flagrant disloyalty?[46]

Much more common, however, was the "both/and" model of association, showing respect to Israel's god and adopting some Jewish practices—Sabbath observance gets frequent mention—while also continuing with the worship of native gods. The centurion Cornelius in Acts 10, for instance, represents such a person: he prays to the Jewish god while, as an army officer, he would also and necessarily be involved with Roman gods as well. Diaspora Jewish communities evidently had no problem with such arrangements, and they obviously benefited from good relations with their immediate pagan neighbors. And, as long as such "Judaizing" or "god-fearing" (two ancient terms for this sort of sympathetic "outsider" behavior) did not lead to conversion, most pagans had no problem with it either.

Jesus had had no "gentile policy." Given his preaching ambit—for the most part small Jewish villages, whether in the Galilee or in Judea—he would not have routinely encountered many. The great exception to this observation is, of course, Jerusalem, which attracted numerous pagan visitors, especially during the grand holidays. When there, Jesus taught in the temple's outermost court, where pagans, too, could have heard him. The low pagan profile in traditions about Jesus' mission, however, could very well reflect his own principled decision. At the End of Days, according to prophetic paradigm, Israel's redemption anticipates the universal turning of pagans to Israel's god. Jesus, following in the footsteps of his great mentor, John, was called to prepare Israel. God would take care of the nations himself.[47]

The Judaized pagans of these urban synagogues thus presented the apostles with a startling new opportunity. Once the apostles brought their testimony to the synagogue, they not only persuaded some of its Jews to repent and to immerse in Jesus' name in preparation for the coming of the Kingdom. They also persuaded some of its associated pagans, who likewise wanted to commit to this charismatic assembly. But how should these gentiles be integrated into the movement? Jesus himself had left no teachings on this matter.

The apostles needed to improvise, and that is what they did. They drew upon that same prophetic paradigm within which the movement had always functioned: the expectation that, in the End, the nations too would renounce their false gods and worship the one true god alongside of Israel. Thus, apostles welcomed these pagans into their new assemblies too.

But there was one major proviso: these gentiles absolutely could not worship their own gods or sacrifice before their images anymore. By immersing in Jesus' name, by receiving holy spirit, by being empowered to prophesy, to receive visions, to exorcise demons, to heal, these ex-pagan pagans had to shut the door on the old age and step into the new. Just as the original community back in Jerusalem represented a beachhead of the Kingdom, so too did these new non-Jewish members. By committing to Israel's god alone, they were no longer pagans—and, thus, no longer god-fearers: they were *eschatological gentiles*. What greater confirmation that the times were fulfilled, that the Kingdom of God truly was at hand?[48]

These ex-pagan pagans were walking into absolutely uncharted social territory. *Like* proselytes, they made an exclusive commitment to Israel's god; *unlike* proselytes, they did not assume the bulk of Jewish tradition. *Gentile men were not required to circumcise.* They remained gentiles, which was precisely the point: God's Kingdom was to encompass all humanity, Israel and the nations. *Like* god-fearers, these gentiles were still gentiles, that is, they retained their native ethnic status as non-Jews. *Unlike* god-fearers, they could no longer worship their native gods.

It was a brilliant solution to what could have been a confounding problem. And the phenomenon itself represented a profound validation of the mission's message:

> 2 It will come to pass in the latter days that the mountain of the house of the Lord
> Shall be established as the highest of the mountains
> And shall be raised above the hills;
> And all the nations shall flow to it,
> 3 And many people shall come, and say:
> "Come, let us go up to the mountain of the Lord,
> To the house of the god of Jacob;
> That he may teach us his ways and that we may walk in his paths."
> Out of Zion his teaching [Hebrew: *torah*] will go forth,
> And the word of the Lord from Jerusalem.
>
> (Isaiah 2.2–3 RSV, modified)

Into a synagogue in Damascus, then, within a few years of Jesus' crucifixion, came apostles in his name, proclaiming the gospel. They witnessed; they interpreted scripture; they performed deeds of power; they prophesied and they healed. They drew both Jews and also gentile god-fearers into their tiny new assembly, which formed within the penumbra of the Jewish community.

And it was there that they encountered Paul the persecutor.

FIVE

THE ENDS OF THE AGES

What was it about these apostles, coming into his Damascus synagogue, that so roused Paul's ire? And what exactly did Paul do when, in his own words, he "persecuted" the new movement?

Some sixty years later, when Acts reprises this theme of Paul-as-persecutor, Luke provides an answer. "Persecution" for Luke meant "execution." Acts depicts Paul as witnessing Stephen's stoning and approving of Stephen's death. Thereafter, "breathing threats and murder," the Paul of Acts, coordinating his actions with the high priest, leaves Jerusalem to extend the persecution to the synagogues of Damascus. Luke gives little direction to his reader in terms of explaining what it was about the early movement that Paul so objected to: his characters all seem to move through a field charged with muscular anti-Christian aggression. This impression from Acts in turn seems to inform the RSV translation of Paul's own statement in Galatians. The RSV depicts Paul as persecuting "violently"; and what he persecuted was "the church."[1]

Paul's own letters, however, offer us a different, and a more plausible, interpretation. In another letter, 2 Corinthians, Paul reviews a list of the woes, those "persecutions" that he himself has suffered as an apostle of Christ:

> [24] Five times I have received at the hands of the Jews forty lashes
> less one. [25] Three times I have been beaten with rods; once I was
> stoned. Three times I have been shipwrecked, a night and a
> day I have been adrift at sea; [26] on frequent journeys, in danger
> from rivers, danger from robbers, danger from my own people
> and danger from pagans, danger in the city, in the wilderness,
> and at sea; danger from false brethren, [27] in toil and hardship.
>
> (2 Corinthians 11.24–27 RSV, modified)

Further:

> For the sake of Christ, I am content with weaknesses, insults, hardships, persecutions and calamities.
>
> (2 Corinthians 12.10 RSV)

In this passage, Paul complains that everyone is ganging up on him. No fewer than five times, Paul's fellow Jews subject him to a community discipline, thirty-nine lashes. Magistrates beat him with "rods" (a Roman judicial punishment). He is "stoned," presumably by irate urban gangs. He feels endangered by other diaspora Jews, whom he calls "my own people." "False brethren," Paul's characteristic label for other members of the Jesus movement with whom he disagreed, also frustrate his progress and dog his steps. Finally, Paul is buffeted by the elements—wind, rain, and water—the domain of the lower gods.

We will look at all of these agents of Paul's sorrows momentarily. For now, I will focus on the specifically intra-Jewish "persecution" that he highlights, "the thirty-nine lashes." First of all—a fact easy for modern readers not to realize—the member of the Jewish community subject to such lashing would have had to consent to receive it. Jews in the Diaspora belonged to their communities voluntarily. Strong dissent could mean simple departure: the person to be flogged, if he did not choose to acknowledge (or to grant) the community's authority over him, could always walk away. Further, the flogging itself, administered to Jews by other Jews, was disciplinary, therefore inclusive: its aim was to spur the offender to change his behavior. In other words, the social goal of the thirty-nine lashes was rehabilitation. It was meant to whip the offending party back into behaving acceptably. Josephus implies the same, when he comments that violating the laws of charitable giving might well earn the stingy offender this treatment.[2]

Perhaps, then, if this penalty is the "persecution" that Paul the apostle received no fewer than five times, it was also the one that he gave, earlier on, to those other apostles who walked into his synagogue community in Damascus. Perhaps, also, he extended this discipline as well even to those members of his own synagogue who had joined with the apostles, together forming the Jewish core of this new assembly. In so doing, Paul would not have acted alone: his synagogue's authorities would also have had to share his negative assessment of the new movement, and to mandate this disciplinary action. He, Paul, would perhaps have acted as their agent; but the social context of such lashing was the wider Jewish community, within which this Christ-following assembly would have gathered as a smaller subgroup.

The RSV's translation of Galatians 1.3—"I persecuted the church of God violently, and tried to destroy it"—is thus misleading on two counts. First, "church" sounds like a religious institution other than, even in competition with, "synagogue." "Church" rests on the Greek word *ekklēsia*, which means "assembly." That is the term that I have used for this word throughout this book. There was no such thing as a "church" in the early decades of the first century. Members of the Christ-following assembly would have formed within, and thus considered themselves part of, the host synagogue community. For this reason, Jewish members of this assembly submitted themselves to disciplinary lashing. And the synagogue also would have considered these Christ-following Jews part of their own community, or else it would not have subjected them to this penalty. "*Punishment implies inclusion.*"[3]

The second misleading element of the RSV translation is "violently," a word choice influenced, I have suggested, by the lurid aggression depicted in Acts. A more accurate translation of the Greek word—*hyperbolēn*, like our own word "hyperbole"—would be something like "to the utmost" or "to the maximum" or "extravagantly." "I persecuted the assembly of God to the utmost, and tried to destroy it." Paul oversaw or perhaps even personally administered these lashings, extending his reach to as many Jewish members of the assembly as he arguably could. Note, too: non-Jewish Christ-followers would have been spared. The synagogue had no authority over voluntary gentile affiliates.

Still, what would have convinced both Paul and the other authorities of his synagogue community that visiting apostles of the Jesus movement, and perhaps those synagogue members who joined with them, merited disciplinary lashing? To answer this question, we have to refer back again to Paul's woes listed in 2 Corinthians 11. More than only synagogue authorities harassed Paul. Roman magistrates also "persecuted" him. So did the "false brethren," those other members of the Christ movement with whom he disagreed. So too did urban mobs, other diaspora Jews, and "pagans," meaning perhaps pagans other than Romans. And as he hints at in this passage and says forthrightly elsewhere, Paul was beleaguered as well by pagan gods.

THE BATTLE OF THE GODS

The pagan gods of the New Testament easily become invisible to modern readers. Most readers, if theist, are monotheist, convinced that only one god exists. But in antiquity, even for ancient "monotheists," all gods existed. Look at Exodus, for example, or Psalms, or Jeremiah. Even in his own book, God was not the only god.[4]

What distinguished ancient monotheists, be they pagan, Jewish, or eventually Christian, from their nonmonotheist contemporaries was their conviction that a single god stood supreme over all the other, lower gods. Heaven, even for "monotheists," remained highly populated. Its power structure is what defined ancient monotheism: one single god was on top. But a lot of other, lesser deities—for Jews too, as well as for pagans and, eventually, for Christians—ranged beneath.

Paul has already introduced us to some of these gods, back in 1 Corinthians 15, when he talked about stars and planets, the sun and the moon, all of which, in antiquity, encircled the earth. And in that same chapter he also mentioned those astral agents—the rulers and authorities and powers—whom the victorious returning Christ would overwhelm. Pagans conceived of these cosmic elements and forces as forms of intelligent life, immortal and in that sense divine. Jews agreed. As Philo of Alexandria, Paul's elder contemporary, said in his learned commentary on Genesis, the firmament of heaven is "the most holy dwelling place of the manifest and visible gods." For Philo no less than for his pagan neighbors, stars and planets were gods. We still call these stars and planets by their ancient divine names: Mercury, Venus, Jupiter, Saturn. Closer to earth lived more gods still. Psalm 95.5 in Greek had dismissed these proximate deities as "godlings"; "The gods of the pagans are demons"—*daimonia*, little gods, that is—still divine powers, but also subordinate, in the Psalmist's view, to his own god, the god of Israel.[5]

Gods not only populated the ranks of heaven: they also, and importantly, presided over the Greco-Roman city. Sacrifices and public ceremonies honoring these deities pleased them and inclined them to be gracious. A lot of urban culture—its calendar of holy days, its athletic and rhetorical competitions, its convening of city councils, its theatrical performances and horse races—revolved around the unending project of keeping the gods in a good mood: all of these activities were dedicated to their honor. Greco-Roman cities were not secular spaces. They were pagan religious institutions.

Diaspora Jews had lived for centuries within these pagan religious institutions, showing respect to the gods of their cities (and, thus, to their gentile worshipers) while drawing the line at performing urban cult acts or public sacrifices. Some pagan critics complained of this as the Jews' "impiety," meaning precisely their avoidance of public pagan cult. But pagans seem to have understood and accepted this idiosyncrasy of Jewish religious culture, and for the most part were prepared to respect it, because Jewish practices were known to be ancestral and ancient. Some pagans, as we have seen, even became "god-fearers," mingling with Jews in their synagogue assemblies and adding the Jews' god to their own native pantheons.[6]

Problems came not when everything was running well. Problems came when things broke down. An earthquake, a flood, a famine, a plague: these were not religiously neutral events. They registered divine discontent. Happy gods made for happy humans, which is why cities spent so much time honoring their gods. Unhappy gods, however, made for unhappy humans. Careful attention to proper ritual—the ancient definition of "piety"—might again secure heaven's goodwill. Simple prudence, however, advised that it was smarter not to put the city at risk to begin with. Keeping up displays of respect to heaven, humans hoped that heaven would in turn look after the city. Gods, in other words, were not just immortal powers; they were powerful social agents, very sensitive to slights—as could be the people who worshiped them.

Into this carefully maintained urban religious ecosystem, working their way via the network of diaspora synagogue communities, walked the apostles of the early Jesus movement. What these apostles urged on their Jewish hearers would have required no huge adjustment religiously so much as an altered perspective. The god of Israel, they proclaimed, was about to end history. Some of the behaviors that they consequently encouraged—focused repentance, immersion for sin in Jesus' name, reception of divine spirit—were indeed new. But diaspora Jews attracted to the Jesus movement still prayed to the same god as before; they still read the same scriptures as before; they still kept the same calendar as before; and their traditional practices, domestic and liturgical, were all the same as before. Jews joining the Jesus movement, in short, did not "convert" so much as make a lateral move within Judaism, similar to a decision to move from being a Sadducee to becoming a Pharisee, as Josephus, in his own life, had done. To an outside observer, it would all have seemed like some version of Jewish business as usual.[7]

But the god-fearers, those pagans affiliated with the diaspora synagogue, were in an utterly different situation. As pagans, they had been born into their obligations to their gods—as, indeed, Jews were born into their obligations to theirs. If these pagans were baptized into the Jesus movement, however, they could no longer worship their native gods, the gods of their families and of their cities. They had to commit exclusively, these apostles taught, to the worship of the god of Israel.

Male god-fearers, the apostles also taught, did not need to be circumcised. Why would they? The point made by the ancient prophets was that the nations, once redeemed, should join in Israel's worship *as* gentiles, representatives of those seventy families descended from Noah's sons (Genesis 10).

But by assuming that single most socially obvious of Jewish behaviors—refusal to engage in public cult—these gentiles were acting as if they had "become" Jews, when in fact they had not. Allegiance to the Jesus-assembly for the pagan god-fearer, in other words, required a much more radical form of Judaizing than the synagogue had ever requested, much less required. These ex-pagan pagans and their apostolic mentors may not have been too worried: after all, the nations' turning to Israel's god was yet another sign of the nearness of the End. But everyone outside of this new movement, whether pagan or Jew, had good reason to be worried. What if the gods, insulted and angry, struck back? And what if pagan neighbors, anxious and angry, struck at the synagogue, the obvious source of this disruptive new movement? Alienating the gods put the city at risk. Alienating the city put the synagogue at risk.

This is the highly charged situation that stands behind Paul's behavior as a "persecutor" in Damascus. He worked within his synagogue to discipline fellow Jews, to turn them away from broadcasting such a socially disruptive, perhaps even dangerous message. It was disruptive because Paul's synagogue also held affiliated outsiders, pagan god-fearers. Perhaps, indeed, it was to this already Judaized pagan population that Paul himself, before he joined the Jesus movement, had once "preached circumcision," urging the males among them to fully convert, as he says in Galatians 5.11. But if these synagogue gentiles now received the gospel, they would have begun to act as if they had converted, when in fact they had not. They were thus, in the eyes of the pagan majority, still obligated to their own native cults and gods, those celestial guardians of the city's common weal.

And this is the highly charged situation that stands behind Paul's own manifold persecutions. Once he began to preach the gospel to pagans, to turn them, through Christ, from their gods to his god, the god of Israel, Paul was on the receiving end of what he himself had once dispensed. He was "persecuted" by synagogue authorities, by Roman authorities, by angry pagan crowds, by fellow Jews, by other members of the Christ movement, and, not least, by the gods themselves.

The anger of these lower gods only made Paul more defiant. He complains to the Corinthians that "the god of this age" has blinded the eyes of unbelievers. He scorns as cosmic lightweights the "elements of the universe" that his ex-pagans in Galatia had formerly worshiped. Pagan gods, he tells his Corinthian assembly, are mere *daimonia*, "demons" or "godlings." "We all know that there are many gods and many lords," he remarks to them, "but *for us* there is only one god, the Father, . . . and one lord, Jesus Christ." Besides, Paul and his communities knew something that their unaffiliated pagan and Jewish neighbors did not know: soon, very soon, Christ would return to combat these cosmic forces once and for all. Would these divine cosmic subordinates then be "destroyed"? Or rather, would the returning Christ rehabilitate them, turning these lower divinities, too, to the supreme god, Israel's god, at the End?[8]

These gods, for Paul as for his contemporaries, pagan or Jew, were very real. And they served an absolutely vital role in the story of impending redemption that the earliest community of Jesus' followers, postresurrection, had constructed. No pagan gods, no cosmic battle. No final battle, no Davidic, warrior messiah. Renounced but nonetheless required, the gods of the nations figured crucially in the Jesus movement's drama of apocalyptic redemption. By serving as Jesus' cosmic foes, these gods enabled Jesus' followers to frame his future (re)appearance as the return of an eschatological warrior-messiah. And after conquering and subduing the gods of the nations, raising the dead and transforming the living, the messiah son of David would turn the Kingdom over to his father, Israel's god. The battle loomed in the (near) future. But on the merit of Jesus' resurrection, this small Jewish sect, together with its sprinkling of eschatological gentiles, *knew* how things would finally work out. Victory was assured. "All gods," sang the ancient Psalmist, "bow down before him."[9]

◆◆◆

The god-fearers, those Judaizing pagan adherents of urban synagogues, had presented a wonderful target of opportunity for the early Jesus movement. Because they were already in some sense familiar with Jewish scriptural traditions through their contact with the synagogue, they could understand the significance of terms like "messiah" or "David" or "Jerusalem" or "Kingdom" that articulated the gospel message. Their synagogue context enabled them to listen, to understand, and to respond. And because of its own apocalyptic principles, this Jewish movement saw the incorporation of gentiles as a natural—indeed, as a prophesied and promised—extension of its mission to Israel. In the End, the nations, too, would stream to Jerusalem.

And again because of its apocalyptic principles, these apostles knew what had to be required of these gentiles: no more worship of lower gods. Amazingly, these pagans obliged. This surprisingly positive pagan response to the good news of the fast-approaching Kingdom in fact confirmed the apostles in their apocalyptic convictions. If pagans voluntarily turned from their idols to worship the true god, then surely the Ends of the Ages was at hand, the Kingdom already on its way.

Finally, because of this same prophetic paradigm of Israel's redemption coming coupled together with the turning of "the nations," this apostolic outreach specifically to gentiles, the fourth phase of the Jesus movement's postcrucifixion missions, never required male circumcision. There was no reason to turn, or to want to turn, these gentiles "into" Jews. This means that Paul's so-called "Law-free" gospel was not his own invention. The phrase describes, rather, the movement's mode of operation from its early years, the time when it first admitted "eschatological gentiles" into the fold.[10]

The god-fearers, however, also presented a tremendous liability to the new movement. Their attraction to the gospel fractured the Jesus-community both in the Diaspora and at home, back in Jerusalem. The longer that time continued, the more destabilizing the effects of this gentile-but-not-pagan affiliation grew. Should these people be formally brought within the commonwealth of Israel, assuming responsibility for ancestral Jewish practices including, for men, circumcision? Eventually, by midcentury, some apostles within the movement thought so: Paul rails against them, especially in Galatians. Christ-following gentiles' formal conversion might stabilize the situation in the Diaspora: conversion to Judaism, while hardly a topic of pagan enthusiasm, was a known phenomenon. As Jews of "a peculiar sort," that is, as converts or "proselytes," these people would gain a place to stand both within their local synagogues and within their own cities of residence. Local synagogues would not feel that their own place within their city was being jeopardized. As converts, these people would not be under the same obligations to their old gods. Their own place within their city would be regained and divine anger, perhaps, averted. A pro-circumcision "policy" in the movement's new diaspora setting had advantages.

Against this idea, however, stood centuries of prophetic traditions. In the End, as Isaiah had foreseen, the gentiles were to join *with* Israel, but they would not *join* Israel. Their place in the

Kingdom was to be *as* gentiles, now free from their enchainment to idol worship. "The root of Jesse shall come," prophesied Isaiah, "he who rises to rule the gentiles. In him shall the gentiles hope." Paul repeated this verse from Isaiah when summarizing his own view of final redemption in his letter to the Romans. Gentile Endtime inclusion did not mean an Endtime "conversion." A policy of circumcision, of turning these gentiles "into" Jews, would undermine the very same positive sign of the times that they themselves embodied.[11]

Luke, writing his version of Jesus' birth narrative in the late first or early second century, had "foreshadowed" this turning of the gentiles through the gospel mission to the god of Israel. When Mary and Joseph, with the infant Jesus, encounter the aged Simeon in the temple, Simeon breaks into a canticle of praise. Holding the infant, whom Simeon intuits to be the Lord's *christos*, he sings out:

> Lord, now let your servant depart, according to your word.
> For mine eyes have seen your salvation, which you have prepared
> in the presence of all peoples.
> A light of revelation to the gentiles,
> And for glory to your people, Israel.
>
> (Luke 2.29–32)

Nevertheless, the outreach to Judaized gentiles, even as portrayed in Acts, was a while in coming. To effect the movement's transition out from Jerusalem to other areas, Luke mobilizes his (incoherent) persecution against the assembly in Jerusalem, when everyone except the apostles has to flee the city. Even still, it takes divine prompting to get things going. An angel tells Philip to head toward Gaza, where he encounters an Ethiopian eunuch. The eunuch is evidently a god-fearer who had come to Jerusalem. By good luck, he "happens" to be reading one of the prophet Isaiah's passages about God's suffering servant. Taking advantage of this opportunity, Philip explains that these verses actually relate to and describe Jesus. Convinced, the eunuch requests baptism. Philip obliges, but then is whisked away by the Lord's spirit, eventually finding his way to Caesarea.[12]

For the righteous Roman centurion Cornelius, two chapters later, even more divine interventions are required. Angels appear in order to relay heavenly directives. Peter, falling into a trance state, experiences a mysterious vision of "unclean" animals, and a voice from heaven orders him to "arise and eat." The reluctant apostle continues to be frozen by indecision, or simple bafflement. In short, Peter requires a lot of celestial prompting before he consents to baptize the pious god-fearing centurion along with his household. Divine spirit needs to push things along.[13]

Acts describes how the numbers of gentile adherents increase the further into the Diaspora that the movement spreads. After both sets of these episodes of outreach, however, Peter's in Caesarea and the other apostles' in the Diaspora, Luke relates troubled discussion back in Jerusalem over the issue of proselyte circumcision. Are these (male) gentiles to join the community of Jesus' followers as ex-pagan gentiles, or should they be required to formally convert and, thus, to be circumcised? What seems to settle the issue for Luke is that these gentile members, whose previous active paganism up to their encounter with the gospel he delicately foregoes mentioning, also seem to possess the Spirit. Christ-following gentiles, like their Jewish compatriots, can work charismatic acts. Charismata validate their status.[14]

As Acts pushes the movement ever further into the Diaspora, things change back in Jerusalem, Luke hints. Leadership of the home community passes from Peter, who goes out on the road, to James,

Jesus' brother. Unlike Peter, James (apparently) always remains in Jerusalem. Paul's letters, much earlier than Acts, might also hint at this shift from Peter's leadership in the mid-30s C.E. to James's in the 40s. In Galatians 1.18–19, Paul names Peter before he names James; but for his second trip to Jerusalem, narrated briefly in Galatians 2.9, Paul first gives James when naming the home community's "pillars."

These shifts and changes notwithstanding, the Jerusalem community itself seems to have remained a nerve center of the movement. Whether it had the authority to impose a decision on the Diaspora's various missionary efforts seems, however, on the evidence of Paul's letters alone, very unlikely. Different and contesting missions characterized the movement by midcentury, especially—as we know from Galatians—over the issue of whether to circumcise male gentile adherents.

Paul complains bitterly against those apostolic colleagues whose views on gentile participation differ from his own. In various places he reviles them as "false brothers" or as "hypocrites." They are "dogs," "evil-workers," and "mutilators of the flesh." Paul calls them out as "super-apostles" (said with swingeing sarcasm) and as "boasters," "false apostles," "deceitful workers," and "ministers of Satan." In brief, the mid-first century diaspora mission, specifically on the issue of gentile incorporation, would have been much less fractured and factious had Jerusalem actually had the authority to impose some kind of order. The calm council that Luke depicts in Acts 15 represents a narrative form of wishful thinking.[15]

Paul seems to refer to some version of this same council in Galatians 2 when, "fourteen years" after his first trip, he again returned to Jerusalem to consult with James, Peter, and John. Alas, he says only that he went up prompted by "revelation." What was revealed? Why the consultation? We have no idea. Hovering around the edges of Paul's description of this earlier meeting, however, which took place perhaps around 49 or 50 C.E., is his current problem: whether the ex-pagan gentile men in Galatia, now members of the movement—that is, in the early to mid-50s—should receive proselyte circumcision. That is the immediate occasion of Paul's letter: his gentiles in Galatia were turning to "another gospel"—that is, they were listening to Christ-missionaries other than Paul, missionaries who did urge such circumcision. Paul says "now" that the "three pillars" had supported him then, back in the day, in Jerusalem, despite the dissent voiced at that meeting by "false brothers."

We have to infer what this dissent before the pillars was about, because again Paul does not say. And sometime after that meeting in Jerusalem, Paul describes an argument between himself and Peter in Antioch. The smoke of heated rhetoric beclouds the issues. In Antioch, disagreement seems to have been about eating in community. Should the assembly meet only in Jewish houses, or in gentile houses as well? Paul's framing of this episode, however, makes it seem like the question of gentile circumcision was in play somehow in Antioch, too. Paul's main focus then swims into view: the main objects of his anger in this letter are his current, less-than-loyal gentile assemblies in Galatia.[16]

So powerful is Paul's toxic rhetoric in Galatians that it still effects, and even distorts, modern critical reconstructions of the beginning decades of what will eventually be Christianity. Freedom, grace, Spirit, life: these describe Paul's "law-free" mission and message, and Christianity in general. Slavery, works, flesh, death, the Law: these describe the "Judaizing" message of Paul's circumcising opponents and, by extension, Judaism in general. But, as we have already seen, the outreach to gentiles had never required circumcision. In this regard, it was "Law-free" from the beginning. And, again as we have already seen, the outreach to gentiles had always required exclusive worship of the god of Israel, and foregoing sacrifices before images of other divinities. In this regard, it was a "Judaizing" gospel from the beginning, insisting on a public behavior that Paul himself demands of his gentiles as well. No other gods and no images—the first two of Judaism's Ten Commandments—were always the sine qua non for any and all gentiles joining this movement. In this regard, even Paul's own gospel was never "Law-free."

Paul and Acts both converge on one clear point: by the mid-first century, a good twenty years after the birth of the postcrucifixion missions, the question whether to formally convert ex-pagan pagans to Judaism had become a contentious issue for the Jesus-communities, both in Jerusalem and most especially in the Diaspora, where the question had immediate social consequences. Why did it become an issue? Because of the mounting social instability that "eschatological gentiles" occasioned for their cities, and for the synagogues within them. Gods easily grew angry. The presence in these diaspora cities of pagans who were ex-pagans, gentiles refusing to show respect to their own gods, was readily perceived as a standing provocation, both by other pagans as well as, it was feared, by the gods themselves.

Was this roiled social context in the Diaspora the single most pressing problem that the Christ-communities faced? Yes and no. The biggest single problem was that the End, stubbornly, continued not to come. All of these other problems—the mounting and contentious diversity within the movement, the social instability of communities in the Diaspora, the bitter infighting between these various missions—flowed from that single, essential, irrefutable problem. All these complexities and confrontations were the varied symptoms of the delay of the End.[17]

Luke's later presentation in Acts 15 smooths over all of these problems. If we did not have Paul's own letters, we would not know how divisive things had actually become. In this chapter of Acts, Pharisaic members of the community propose that Jesus-following gentiles be required to convert to Judaism. Apostles and elders convene to ponder the matter. Peter then presents himself as the apostle to the gentiles par excellence: he argues strenuously against the Pharisaic position. James next takes the floor. Quoting from an assortment of prophetic authorities—Amos, Jeremiah, and Isaiah—James affirms and even amplifies Peter's position. He then suggests that the council write to Christ-following gentiles advising them "to abstain from the pollutions of idols and from fornication and from what is strangled and from blood." The encyclical communication duly goes forth, advising diaspora communities of the council's policy decision. This smooth humming of Luke's ecclesiastical bureaucracy stands in sharp contrast to the discord so evident in Paul's own letters. As Paul's vivid anger and his intemperate name calling energetically evince, in the mid-first century no single "gentile policy" ever existed, much less prevailed.

What historical sense, then, can be made of Luke's other descriptions of the Jerusalem community? Chapter 6 of Acts presents an organized group of widows supported by daily distributions from the community, and seven Greek-speaking Jews, headed by Stephen, who function as what we would call deacons. Acts 15.2 suddenly introduces "elders," who take a role in framing ecclesiastical policy, and in communicating it widely. All of these forms of stable institutionalization—widows, "deacons," authoritative elders, coordinated policies—seem drawn from Luke's own period in the early second century, when, as we know from other sources, some diaspora communities were indeed organizing along such lines. For the woolly, charismatic early decades of the Jerusalem community, these stable social formations seem anachronistic.[18]

So too, for different reasons, Luke's report of some kind of split between the Greek-speaking Jews in Jerusalem (the "Hellenists"), represented first of all by Stephen, and the Aramaic speakers (the "Hebrews") is difficult to assess. The split cryptically prefaces the "great persecution," where the Greek-speaking Christ-followers are run out of town but the Aramaic speakers stay put. And this "persecution" itself serves Luke as his springboard for the next phase of the movement, its mission to diaspora Jews and, by extension, also to diaspora pagans. Does Luke transmit inherited, thus perhaps historical, information? Or are these episodes and events merely his own plot devices, deployed to move his story along? Different commentaries offer different answers. I do not know.[19]

What we do know, from a Greek first-century synagogue inscription found in Jerusalem, is that Greek-speaking diaspora Jews did relocate to the city and formed a community there. Perhaps Jesus' followers resident in Jerusalem drew members from this population too. And already within a very few years of the crucifixion, some apostles had established an assembly within the synagogue community in Damascus: Paul "persecuted" it, before receiving his call to join (perhaps around 33 C.E.?). And three years thereafter he went up to Jerusalem, though only for the first time (contra Acts), to see Peter and James. Unfortunately for us, peering at Paul's prose in order to understand the meaning of all these comings and goings, Paul does not say what he, Peter, and James talked about.[20]

What is clear from Galatians is the fact that people within this movement were traveling outside of Jerusalem from very early on, within a few years of the crucifixion; and they ranged widely. Emissaries of the prime community already penetrated the Diaspora. The assembly in Jerusalem has some kind of special status and, thus, a notional authority. But we should not exaggerate their authority: after all, Paul was in no special hurry to get there. After receiving his apostolic call, he first went off into Roman Arabia and then subsequently returned to Damascus, only getting around to visiting with Peter and James "after three years."[21]

The new Roman Empire, meanwhile, was itself slowly consolidating. After Octavian's successful struggle in the civil war against Antony and Cleopatra in 31 B.C.E., the Julio-Claudian dynasty began its reign. Blessed with administrative genius as well as political prudence and good health, Octavian, now "Augustus," enjoyed an astonishingly long rule of four decades. His adopted son Tiberius succeeded him in 14 C.E., reigning until 37. He, in turn, was succeeded by a Julio-Claudian of the next generation, Gaius, also known as "Caligula." Power had pooled, politics stabilized, around this imperial family. A certain calm—the Pax Romana—settled over the Mediterranean.

But not for long. Gaius had neither the shrewdness nor the mental stability of his imperial predecessors. The dynastic succession, which seemed to promise the regular and regulated exercise of power, instead, due to the contingencies of Caligula's character, threatened to cause chaos—specifically in Jerusalem. Jesus' followers thus had a ringside seat, in 39–40 C.E., for a totally unanticipated confrontation, a battle of the gods. The divine emperor Caligula challenged the power of YHWH. Foreign cult, the emperor mandated, would be introduced in Jerusalem's temple. The apocalyptic abomination of desolation was speeding its way down from Antioch, along the coast road, to God's holy mountain.

THE IMAGE OF GOD AND THE SON OF MAN

The normal polytheism of ancient "monotheism" can be a difficult concept for moderns to grasp. A no less difficult idea is antiquity's evident comfort in designating special human beings—and, emphatically, Roman emperors—as "gods."

Sometimes the case for human divinity could be made by invoking divine lineage. Greek and Roman gods were known to have sexual relations with human partners, from whose progeny important political dynasties might spring. Alexander the Great claimed to descend from Heracles, as did the family of his successor-general, Ptolemy. The Seleucids, that family of Alexander's general who ruled in Syria, claimed descent from the god Apollo. Julius Caesar and the Julii, through Aeneas, famously enjoyed a connection to the goddess Venus, a connection that would contribute to Caesar's ultimate divinization. Caesar's divinity in turn burnished the status of his adopted son Octavian, later Caesar Augustus, proclaimed in inscriptions throughout the empire as "god, the son of god."[22]

Sometimes the case for human divinity was made by invoking intrinsic divine power, which Romans called *numen*. This idea was connected to devotion to family cult, and the ways that the presiding spirit or "genius" of the family—in Latin, the *gens*—was concentrated particularly in and on the family father. By positioning himself as the "father" of the empire, Augustus encouraged a new cultic etiquette, both private and public. He would accept cultic honors, themselves a marker of divinity, that his subjects would offer to his imperial *numen*. And while he could not be everywhere, his image was. Portrait busts and larger-than-life statues of Augustus proliferated throughout the empire. Offerings were made before them. Like temples, they established places of asylum and were invested with numinous power. To oppose the emperor was to commit a religious offense, not a crime but a sacrilege. The living emperor, through Augustus's adaptation and adoption of such family cult practices as dedicated images, incense, offerings, festal days, and liturgies, had become a god.

Builder of Jerusalem's beautiful temple, Herod the Great also erected temples to the imperial god Augustus, though not in his Jewish areas. Caesarea held one such temple; Sebaste, in Samaria, another; Caesarea Philippi, another. It made good political sense. Rome did not mandate imperial cult in its provinces. The provinces, rather, requested directly of the emperor that they be permitted to establish his cult in their own cities. Wealthy local patrons subvened the costs, which were considerable. The local cult of the distant emperor had to fund the temple structure and its endowment. It was responsible for the procurement and maintenance of the imperial images. The imperial priesthood, which presided over the annual cycle of festal days sacred to the Julian family, was filled by local aristocrats, who also sponsored the sacrifices. The noble lady and Paul's contemporary, Julia Severa, who built the synagogue in her town in Asia Minor, had also served as a priestess in the imperial cult.

Initiative had its rewards. The hope was that establishing a cult would ingratiate one's city and province to the emperor. The city worshiped the emperor's divinity; he, in turn, would direct his benevolent gaze toward the city. This was an elaborate and expensive way of establishing or cementing a good client-patron relationship in a classic Mediterranean idiom. By building temples to the god Augustus, Herod ensured and protected the Jewish commonwealth, his own client kingdom. In YHWH's sacred citadel of Jerusalem, meanwhile, prayer and sacrifice were offered *for* the emperor, not *to* him. Augustus, a long-distance god-fearer of a very special sort, endowed these sacrifices himself.[23]

Anti-Jewish riots in Alexandria in 38 C.E., one year into Gaius's reign, unexpectedly upended this nice public display of mutual respect between Rome and Jerusalem. Interethnic hostilities between the Greek and the Jewish residents of the Egyptian city erupted into violence in Alexandria's streets and synagogues. In the wake of that violence, two Jewish delegations, one led by Philo, and a pagan delegation led by Apion, journeyed to the imperial capital to lay their respective cases before the emperor.

Apion got there first. Shrewdly, he goaded Caligula. Everyone in the entire empire worshiped the divine emperor, Apion observed—everyone, that is, except the Jews. The Jews, alone of all the emperor's subjects, refused to honor his divinity in the way that it should be honored, that is, by sacrificing before his image.

The thought obviously gnawed at Caligula. By the time that he finally consented to see Philo, his mind was made up. Shocking the Jewish emissary, the emperor declared that he would correct this intolerable situation himself. Caligula would raise his own cult statue of Zeus-Gaius in Jerusalem, placing it within the temple's very sanctuary. That was where, in any other temple, a cult statue was to be found.[24]

Gaius knew what he was doing. Directing his legate in Syria, Petronius, to install his statue, he also ordered that Petronius take with him half of the Roman fighting force in Antioch, two of his four legions, an escort of some ten to twelve thousand men. The emperor expected Jewish resistance. He was clearly willing to get his way through use of force.

To get from Antioch to Jerusalem, Petronius had to march through the Galilee. By the time that he got there, he found his way blocked by masses of unarmed Jews—tens of thousands, Josephus claims—Judeans as well as Galileans, women and children as well as men. It was a huge act of passive resistance. "Slay us first!" Josephus reports them crying. "Falling on their faces and baring their throats, they declared themselves ready to be slain."[25]

The crowds remained in place for forty days, neglecting their fields and refusing to move. Jewish aristocrats, meanwhile, importuned the beleaguered legate. Finally, Petronius wrote to Caligula, advising him to desist. Caligula returned the message: Petronius, he ordered, should kill himself. Luckily for the legate, however, a second letter reached him first, this one informing him of the emperor's assassination. Twenty-seven days thereafter, Caligula's earlier letter demanding his suicide finally wandered into Petronius's hands. Back in Rome, meanwhile, Gaius's uncle Claudius succeeded him as emperor. Claudius immediately rescinded imperial orders concerning the cult image of Zeus-Gaius. The Jews massed in the Galilee returned to their homes. Relations between Rome and Jerusalem quieted down once again.[26]

Caligula had traumatized Jerusalem. Indeed, the emperor had traumatized the whole Jewish homeland and, for that matter, Jews everywhere. Philo, putting the thought into the head of Petronius, speculated that the wide-flung Jewish nation would erupt in revolt, and that Jews even beyond the eastern edge of the empire, in Babylon, would not hesitate to join in defending Jerusalem's temple against the cult image of the Roman god. Such a threatened desecration, to some Jews, must have seemed like the end of the world.[27]

In fact, we know it did. Our evidence stands in one of Luke's sources: the earliest gospel, Mark. Caligula's attempt to erect his own cult image in Jerusalem's temple inspired some of Jesus' early followers to consult the prophecies in the Book of Daniel.

"Daniel" had spoken of a similar desecration of the temple. This was no accident. Written in the name of a prophet who had lived through the Babylonian destruction of the temple in 586 B.C.E., this book was actually composed during the troubles in Jerusalem under Antiochus IV of Syria (167–164 B.C.E.). It was under Antiochus that Hellenistic cult had been introduced into Jerusalem's temple—in the prophet's view, the "abomination of desolation."[28]

Antiochus's act triggered the Maccabean Revolt, which ultimately succeeded. But "Daniel" wrote during the dark days, when the desolating sacrilege really did seem like the end of the world. Good ultimately would prevail, Daniel knew; the god of Israel would surely triumph. In a vision, Daniel saw God give to one "like a son of man, coming with the clouds of heaven," an everlasting "glory and kingdom," and dominion over all humanity. But, the prophet knew, there was still to be a lot of darkness before the dawn—wars and turmoil and "a time of trouble such as never has been," once the archangel Michael arose to free Daniel's people. But at that point, all battles won, the dead themselves would awaken, the righteous rising to everlasting life, the wicked to perpetual shame. When would these things be fulfilled? the prophet asked his mysterious revealer. The words of the prophecy "are shut up and sealed," counseled this being, "*until the time of the End.*"[29]

This was a brilliant literary device on the part of the second-century author. The very act of knowing Daniel's prophecy would indicate that the book had been unsealed. The reader of the prophecy would "activate" the fulfillment of the prophecy by the very act of reading the prophecy. Through this act of reading, the Endtime would arrive, and would be understood to have arrived.

Sitting in Jerusalem, thinking with Daniel's prophecy; facing the prospect of two Roman legions installing the image of the empire's god in the temple of their god; awaiting the return of their victorious messianic redeemer: the members of Jesus' community, in the winter of 40, were convinced that they knew how matters stood. All the signs converged. Caligula's initiative put matters past doubting. Now was the time of Jesus' return. Soon, his people would see Jesus, the Danielic son of man, coming in clouds with great power and glory, gathering his elect, ruling over the nations, raising the dead, establishing the Kingdom.

Their calculus, it turned out, was wrong. Assassination deflected Caligula's initiative. Time continued to continue. But the community's reading of Daniel gave further shape and detail to their expectations about Jesus' return. We see this clearly in the gospel of Mark. But I think that we can catch the echoing refrains of Daniel's prophecy already in Paul's earliest letter, 1 Thessalonians, written within only a few years of these events. The dead, Paul says there, "awaking from sleep," are soon to be caught up together with the living community, "we who are alive, who are left." All will ascend to meet the returning Lord "in the clouds." Meanwhile, "the archangel"—Michael, perhaps? (Daniel 12.1)—will cry out, to the sounding of the heavenly trumpet. The final battle would be joined.[30]

Paul, it turned out, was wrong. His generation passed away; time continued to continue. But Mark, sometime shortly after the year 70, *did* know with certainty that the End truly was at hand. Writing in the immediate aftermath of the Roman destruction of Jerusalem, Mark visualized the triumphant invading army with its military standards standing where they "should not be"—that is, on the ruined Temple Mount. These standards were used as mobile sites of army cult. The abomination of desolation was back: cult to foreign gods had been performed on and in temple territory. Mark knew how things stood. Once again, all the signs converged.[31]

Mark put his prophecy back into the mouth of Jesus. In the wake of the War of 66–73, the evangelist set his narrative in the year 30, during the week of Jesus' last Passover in Jerusalem. In this passage of Mark's gospel, Jesus sits with several disciples on the Mount of Olives, looking down at the site of the city's future devastation. To a disciple, wondering at the size and grandeur of the temple precincts, Mark's Jesus had responded, "Do you see these great buildings? There will not be left here one stone upon another, that will not be thrown down." "When will this be"—that is, when will the temple be destroyed—"and what will be the sign, when these things are all to be accomplished?" several of the disciples press to know.[32]

Mark's Jesus at this point embarks on his great apocalyptic soliloquy. Predicting wars and rumors of wars, Jesus foresees the advent of "many" who will claim, "I am he!" These various messianic pretenders, he warns, will lead crowds astray. War, earthquake, famine: these catastrophes will cluster, indicating the onset of cosmic labor, the beginning of the birth pangs of the End. Jesus describes the harassments to befall his future followers, who will be beaten in synagogues and hauled before governors. Such confrontations imply a diaspora setting, which Jesus in effect goes on to mandate. "The gospel must first be preached to all nations" before the End can come.[33]

When, then, will the End finally arrive, and how can one know? Mark's Jesus grows more specific still:

> [14] But when you see the *desolating sacrilege set up where it ought*
> *not to be* (let the reader understand), then let those who are in
> Judea flee to the mountains. . . . [19] For in those days there will be
> such tribulation as has not been from the beginning of the cre-
> ation which God created until now, and never will be. [20] And if
> the Lord *had not shortened the days,* no human being would be
> saved; but for the sake of the elect, whom he chose, *he shortened*
> *the days.* [21] And then if any one says to you, 'Look, here is the
> messiah!' or 'Look, there he is!' do not believe it. [22] False messi-
> ahs and false prophets will arise and show signs and wonders, to
> lead astray, if possible, the elect. [23] But take heed; I have told you
> all things beforehand.
>
> (Mark 13.14–23; my emphases)

After and only after this turn of events, a coded description of Rome's triumph over Jerusalem on the ruined Temple Mount, Mark writes, will Jesus return. But return he will, as the glorious and triumphant Son of Man, "coming in clouds with great power and glory" to gather up his elect from all the corners of the world. "Truly, I say to you, this generation will not pass away before all these things take place." Mark's Jesus addresses his prophecy to his narrative audience in the year 30. But the evangelist, speaking through him, addresses his own generation, sometime after 70. It was that second generation who had taken the gospel out into the Diaspora. It was they who had witnessed a terrible famine in the year 47. It was they who had seen the prophets and messianic pretenders who fill Josephus' pages in his descriptions of Judea in the run-up to the War. And it was they who had seen the utter destruction of the city and the temple. Surely, now, the times were fulfilled. The mindful believer had to remain alert. To wait. To watch.[34]

It was Daniel, especially in chapters 7 and 12, who had bequeathed to Mark the image of the victorious Son of Man, cloud-borne, gathering up the saints, whom Mark here casts as Jesus. Mark's apocalyptic aria also showcases his bookishness, as the evangelist breaks the fourth wall with his direct address to his current audience: "Let the reader understand." The "reader" should know that Daniel's prophecy, with the temple's destruction, finally was now being realized. The scroll was unsealed and opened, the words revealed, the Endtime had begun to arrive. Now Mark's generation—the generation that had witnessed the temple's stones cast down and Rome's pagan sacrifices on God's mountain—would see the returning Jesus, the triumphant "Son of Man." When? Unclear, but soon. Indeed, even some of Jesus' own "sinful and adulterous generation" would still be alive to witness these events. Once Roman military might devoured God's temple so that no sacred stone stood upon the other, God's clock had begun to toll midnight.

Rome's army had initiated the apocalypse.

THE MOUNTAIN OF FIRE

Luke, incredibly, breathes not a word about the turmoil and trauma caused by Caligula, even though he sets his story about Jerusalem's community precisely during these middle decades of the first century. Instead, he offers a cautionary tale about Herod Agrippa—ruler of his grandfather Herod's territories from 41 to 44 C.E.—who takes action against "some who belonged to the assembly." Once again, these troubles occur during Passover.[35]

Beheading James the son of Zebedee, Agrippa also had Peter arrested; we are not told why. Once Peter makes a miraculous escape (aided by an angel), Agrippa executes his hapless guards as well. A few verses later, Phoenician subjects of Agrippa's in Caesarea hail him as divine. "The voice of a god, and not of a man!" they proclaim. Agrippa sickens on the spot. Soon after, he dies, smitten by "an angel of the Lord." Agrippa's demise seems like a death styled according to the sins of Caligula. But of the emperor's initiative itself, Luke is absolutely silent.[36]

Acts will occasionally mention God's Kingdom, but not as an impending and dramatic historical and cosmic change. This fits Luke's overall calming effect on the apocalyptic traditions that he had inherited. In his gospel's twenty-first chapter, where he rewrites Mark 13, Luke soothes Mark's expectations of the imminent Endtime, dropping entirely Mark's statement that the Lord had already "shortened the days." After all, Luke, writing in the early second century, knows something that Mark had not known. The temple's destruction in 70 had not been, as Mark had claimed, "the sign when these things are all to be accomplished."[37]

Most pointedly, Luke also drops Mark's reference to Daniel's prophecy about the "abomination of desolation," with its startling cue to "the reader" to understand that the prophet's scroll had been unsealed. Instead, Luke substitutes a description of the Roman military siege—clearly a nod to the city's destruction, but leached of Mark's apocalyptic alarums. Jerusalem's tribulations are social and military, not cosmic and eschatological. For Mark, his troubled age had marked the "birth pangs" of the End. Not so for Luke. He did not see his age as laboring toward history's finale.[38]

To get a better sense, then, of what Jerusalem's community was actually living through in the four decades of life remaining to it—the proliferation of "false" messiahs, "false" prophets, wars, rumors of wars, and persecutions that Mark's Jesus "predicts" for his community—we need to turn to the evangelists' Jerusalemite contemporary, Josephus. And we turn back our own story's clock, returning to the troubled power vacuum that formed after the death of Herod the Great in 4 B.C.E., and to the men who strove to fill it.

◆◆◆

Herod had named his son Archelaus as his heir in Judea. Archelaus had had to leave for Rome shortly after that first, disastrous Passover when he was in charge, to secure his inheritance through imperial ratification. Other ambitious men, remaining local, contested for supreme leadership in his absence. How did they think that they could possibly succeed? Archelaus alone stood a chance of gaining Augustus's approval. The ambitions of these pretenders were deeply unrealistic, yet they acted on them anyway, and they gained significant followings. In preparing to go up against Archelaus, these men also and therefore were preparing to go up against Rome.

Josephus identified several of these challengers, and they spanned a wide social range. One Judas had something of a revolutionary pedigree: he was the son of Ezekias the "arch *lēstēs*," that is, a brigand or insurrectionist. Gathering followers in the Galilee, Judas invaded and sacked Herodian palaces. Meanwhile, Simon, "a slave of King Herod but a handsome man, preeminent thanks to his size and bodily strength," also made his move. He placed the "crown ['diadem'] on his head . . . and was proclaimed king" by those loyal to him.

A rebel; then a slave; and, finally, even a shepherd, a man named Athrognes, stepped into the breach. This Athrognes, sniffs Josephus, was "distinguished neither by his ancestry nor by the virtue of his character." Also renowned for his size and his strength, he together with his four brothers "fought for the crown," which Athronges alone claimed. Josephus' aristocratic snobbism particularly comes out here. Who was this Athronges, a mere shepherd, to claim kingship? To this question a follower might have responded: A new David.[39]

These men and their numerous followers were subdued whether by Roman troops called down from Antioch or by Archelaus himself. Josephus characterizes all of these usurpers as "kings" and their followers as *lēstai*, "brigands" or "revolutionaries"—the same word that showed up so frequently in the gospels' narratives about Jesus' arrest and execution. And Josephus charges all of these strongmen with "seizing the crown" or, as he puts it in Greek, the "diadem," and with "presuming to kingship" and with being recognized as "king" by their followers.[40]

Josephus speaks similarly of those popular Jewish leaders who emerged during the years immediately preceding the war against Rome in the late 60s, that uncertain period at the end of Nero's reign. The last of the Julio-Claudian emperors, Nero had ruled from the death of Claudius in 54 C.E. until his own death in the year 68. Thereafter, with the position of emperor no longer a dynastic legacy, Rome erupted in civil war as various contenders strove to claim supreme power.

Judean strongmen took advantage of these confusions to stake their own, more local claims. Josephus names John of Gishala, who attempted to establish a "monarchy": John, says Josephus, acted as a "tyrant." Another leader, Menachem, was the son of Judah the Galilean, the man who had led the tax revolt against Rome in the year 6 C.E. Menachem assumed royal prerogatives and was greeted in Jerusalem "as a king." But in reality, asserts Josephus, Menachem was nothing but a *lēstēs* and a tyrant. Yet another popular leader, Simon bar Giora, gathered his own partisans, who hailed him as "king." The Romans availed themselves of Simon's ambitions: he survived the siege of Jerusalem in order to be ceremonially executed back in Rome as part of the new Flavian dynasty's celebration of its triumph over Judea.[41]

So why does Josephus nowhere describe or refer to these various "kings of the Jews" as, specifically, messianic pretenders? Seen from our post-Christian historical vantage, the term "messiah"—*christos* in Josephus' Greek—might seem too "religious" an identifier for these eminently political, military, rebellious strongmen. Their actions were pragmatic. They were concerned to seize power—to bring about their own kingdoms, not God's. Opportunity, not scripture, dictated their deeds.

And yet, Josephus does describe and refer to these various "kings of the Jews" as "messiahs." But he does so by transposing Jewish messianic rhetoric into Greco-Roman political idiom. "Putting on a diadem" *functions* in Greek to indicate the assumption of political power, just as "anointing" does in Hebrew. "Tyrant" is a negative moral and political assessment, but it signals monarchical power, just as "messiah" does in the language of scripture. If we translate Josephus' Greek terms back into their native Judean ones, we see more clearly the messianic lineaments of these defeated "kings"—John of Gishala, Menachem son of Judah, and Simon bar Giora. In Greek, Josephus derided these leaders' royal pretensions. To their Judean followers, however, they would have been "messiahs."[42]

Further, scripture did indeed inform the programs of (at least) some of these strongmen, as Josephus notes ruefully toward the end of his history. "What more than all else incited them to war," Josephus writes, "was an ambiguous oracle, likewise found in their sacred scriptures, to the effect that, at that time, one from their own country would become ruler of the world. This they understood to mean someone of their own household, and many of their wise men went astray in their interpretation of it."[43]

Just a decade earlier, Paul, looking to Isaiah, had ventured exactly the very same interpretation that Josephus, shortly after 70, would so pointedly disavow. "The root of Jesse shall come," Paul confidently counseled the assembly in Rome, "he who rises to rule the nations." Paul spoke the "Jewish" Greek of the Septuagint's Isaiah. Had he been speaking the "political" Greek of Josephus' *Bellum*, he too would have used the language of diadems and of kings. Paul was confidently announcing the approaching advent of the king messiah, lord over the gentile nations, the Davidic *christos.*[44]

Awareness of the effects of this messianic prophecy, in the context of the Jews' war with Rome, echoes in the work of two later Roman historians, Tacitus and Suetonius. Writing of the War in the early second century, Tacitus observes of those trapped in Jerusalem that "the majority firmly believed that their ancient priestly writings contained the prophecy that this was the very time when the East would grow strong and that men starting from Judea should possess the world." Tacitus's contemporary, Suetonius, speaks similarly in his description of Vespasian's rise to power. "There had spread all over the East an old and established belief that it was fated at that time for men coming from Judea to rule the world." It was this "old and established belief"—Suetonius's characterization of Jewish prophecy—that had inspired and encouraged the people to rebel.[45]

All three historians, Josephus, Tacitus, and Suetonius, grant that the Jews' prophecy itself was true. It was the popular Jewish interpretation of the prophecy that had been wrong. The world ruler arising from the East "at that time" was not the messiah. He was the new Roman emperor, Vespasian. Vespasian was the general whom Nero had tasked with suppressing the Jews' rebellion, which broke out in 66 C.E. At the end of the Year of the Four Emperors, the turmoil that had followed upon Nero's death in 68, Vespasian emerged the winner. His troops had declared him supreme ruler while he was still in Judea.

The point to note here is "that the rebels, too, had an exegesis by which they justified their undertaking." Josephus, writing the *Bellum* initially in Aramaic, translated more than just his words into Greek. He translated concepts. His literary model was the great classical historian Thucydides. For the purposes of Josephus' project, a Greek who wore a "diadem," the ancient crown of ruling authority, was the functional equivalent of an "anointed" Jew.[46]

The Greek idiom captured the political and military power that is also an aspect of "the anointed one," though "diadem" obviously lacks the scriptural and specifically Davidic resonance. But Josephus' brief notice in his history about this biblical "oracle" unobtrusively restored it. Religious and political motivations—combined with the surprise of encouraging circumstances (the power vacuum after Herod's death; the young empire's deep instability and its crisis of power and politics in the early years of the War)—all went into the mix. Indeed, prophecy and politics, for these messiahs as for their followers, reinforced each other. In short, Jesus' followers in Jerusalem were not the only Jews consulting ancient prophecies in order to understand the signs of the times, the better to learn when the messiah would be on his way—or, in the perspective of the early assembly in Jerusalem, on his way back.

Living prophets—often disavowed by Josephus as "sorcerers" or "impostors"—continued to consult scripture also. In the mid-40s, the inspired leader Theudas took his supporters—"the better part of the masses," says Josephus—out to the Jordan River. He promised them that he would part the waters there. Before he could work the miracle, Roman troops cut them down. The following decade prophets arose, whom Josephus again characterized as "sorcerers and impostors." These men agitated Jerusalem with "revolutionary changes," claiming "falsely" to be divinely inspired. They too attracted large crowds, whom they led out into the desert to receive from God "tokens of deliverance." Another prophet, a Jew from Egypt, around this same time gathered a large following and marched on Jerusalem: the city's walls, he vowed, would collapse on his command. Again, these visionaries failed: Rome's muscular interventions ended their missions. But some of these men made enough of an impression that they found their way into the book of Acts.[47]

Ancient writings scripted these acts of power. All of these promised miracles recalled biblical episodes from Israel's foundational history. Theudas's parting the waters of the Jordan echoed both Moses's leading Israel across the Red Sea and Joshua's leading the twelve tribes across the Jordan on into the promised land. Going into the desert to seek deliverance would recapitulate the liberation from Egypt and the giving of the Torah on Sinai. The miraculous crumbling of Jerusalem's walls recalls the miraculous fall of Jericho, Joshua's point of entry into the Land. Enacting key moments in the birth of the nation, these signs prophets signaled the eschatological nearness of final redemption. Their grounding in biblical miracle also accounts for the size of their popular followings. Scriptural authority undergirded not only their own message; it also supported the hopes and convictions of their followers.[48]

These prophets were not, like the bandit-kings, leading large groups of armed men to attack Roman installations. They spoke to religious hopes, not to dreams of militant insurrection. Their followers—whose numbers Josephus emphasizes—were unarmed. Roman troops nonetheless cut them down. Judea's prefects and procurators did not like the look of masses gathering around charismatic prophets, awaiting miracles. An excited crowd's enthusiasm might too easily spill over into sedition. For that matter, recalling the fate of John the Baptizer, Jewish rulers evidently felt the same way.[49]

At Passover in Jerusalem, back in the year circa 30, Pilate had made the same judgment call about Jesus. No armed insurgents followed the prophet from Nazareth, as Pilate knew full well. It was the size and the enthusiasm of the crowds swarming around him on that particular Passover that had determined Jesus' fate.

◆◆◆

Luke's story in Acts moves out into the Diaspora and stays there, following Paul around from one synagogue community to the next. Luke returns Paul to Jerusalem only in his twenty-first chapter, toward the end of his story. He frames this return with an ominous prophecy: Jews in Jerusalem will bind Paul and deliver him into the hands of the gentiles. Undeterred, Paul presses on from Caesarea, appearing before James "and all the elders."[50]

Pleased with the way that Paul's mission is going, these men also caution him: Law-observant Christ-followers ("many thousands") have heard disturbing rumors that Paul teaches diaspora Jews "to forsake Moses, telling them not to circumcise their children or to observe the customs." To assuage them, Paul undertakes some rites at the temple, where he inadvertently provokes a riot. Other Jews accuse him, falsely, of bringing Greeks into the temple, presumably past the boundary marking their area off from the women's court. Put into protective custody, Paul then moves within the Roman system, to be heard before the procurator Felix and other notables until, finally, he comes to Rome. Luke gives his readers only one last backward glance at the Jerusalem community, when he has one Tertullus refer to it as "the sect of the Nazarenes."[51]

For more on James, we have to turn to Josephus. In the *Antiquities*, he relates briefly that the high priest Ananus—whom Josephus considers both rash and arrogant, as well as harshly Sadducean in his judgments—convened a Sanhedrin. Ananus brought before it "a man called James the brother of Jesus the so-called *christos*, and some others" (unidentified). Accusing them of transgressing the Law, the high priest had them executed by stoning. Other men resident in Jerusalem—"the most fair-minded and who were strict in the observance of the Law," Josephus writes—were offended by the high priest's actions. (Historians often identify this group as Pharisees.) They complained to the Romans, and so brought about Ananus's deposition. These things happened in 62 C.E.[52]

What had James and these others done? Josephus does not say. This incident does reveal, however, that as late as 62 relations between James and other Law-observant Jerusalemites unaffiliated with the Jesus movement were good, so good that these other men sought and secured Ananus's dismissal. How did James's death affect his community? Where was Peter during all this? Did members of the Jesus-assembly also feel threatened? All good questions, for which we have no answers: We have absolutely no information to draw on.

Paul's final letter, to Rome, provides perhaps the slightest glimpse, from a distance, of the Jerusalem assembly just a little before this time. Paul is on his way back to the city, to deliver his collection "to the poor among the saints at Jerusalem." Perhaps this implies that the assembly there was still practicing community of goods. Perhaps (like Qumran's Essenes?) they were especially focused on prayer, worship, and scriptural interpretation, and so needed the material support of others.[53]

This Christ-following community in Jerusalem, and its emissaries abroad, had lived through the "false messiahs" and "false prophets" performing signs and wonders that Mark's Jesus would later "foretell." They knew full well that the good news of the coming Kingdom had been preached to the nations. They had endured trials and tribulations, at home and abroad. So they watched there and waited, still expecting the return of Jesus, his definitive manifestation "from Zion." It was upon them and their generation, after all, that "the ends of the ages have come."[54]

The end that overtook this messianic assembly, and the city, and the temple, however, was delivered not by God's hand, but by Rome's. In 66 C.E., waves of contingencies converged to precipitate the War. Civic disputes broke out between Jews and gentiles in the mixed city of Caesarea, the seat of Roman government in the province. Caesarea's Jews appealed to the procurator Gessius Florus, who proved both heavy-handed and inept. The closing years of Nero's reign, in Judea as elsewhere in the empire, were marred by administrative incompetence, of which Florus was a shining example. Meanwhile, on the popular front, signs prophets such as Theudas and the Egyptian fed the flames of labile religious enthusiasms. And ambiguous messianic "oracles" in sacred scripture fanned other, ultimately destructive hopes. The decisive action issued, significantly, from the temple itself. Eleazar, the son of the high priest, by convincing other priests to cease offering sacrifices for the well-being of the emperor, finally let slip the dogs of war. The country broke into open rebellion.[55]

It is at this point that the young priest Yosef ben Mattityahu, known to us now as Josephus, enters history. Quitting the capital to organize the defense of the north, Josephus faced off against the army of Vespasian and Titus at the Galilean city of Jotapata. It was there, in the wake of Rome's successful siege, that the true meaning of scripture's "ambiguous oracle" came to Josephus: Vespasian, he now understood, not the messiah, was the true subject of the sacred prophecy. Nero might still be emperor, but Vespasian and, following him, his son Titus, would rule thereafter. That prophetic interpretation saved Josephus' life.[56]

The revolt stretched on, profiting from Rome's turmoil after Nero's death. Once Vespasian had secured imperial power, however, Titus could press on with the siege of Jerusalem. The onslaught of his missiles killed the prophet Jesus, son of Ananias. Ever since the holiday of Sukkot seven years before, in 62 C.E., "when the city was enjoying profound peace and prosperity," this Jesus had proclaimed the impending destruction of Jerusalem and of the temple. "During the whole period up to the outbreak of the war . . . he repeated his lament. . . . His cries were the loudest at the festivals." Outside the walls, meanwhile, stood Josephus, pleading fruitlessly with the rebels to surrender.[57]

The end came in August of 70 C.E. Titus's troops, enraged by the rigors of the campaign, poured into the city with iron and fire. Fighting was brutal and bitter. In the course of this bloody confusion, a soldier set the edges of the sanctuary aflame. Ultimately, the whole of the temple compound would be engulfed. Eyewitness to the chaos, Josephus later wrote,

> As the temple burned, anything found was looted and anyone caught was killed. The slaughter was massive—no pity shown for age, no regard for rank: children, old men, laymen, priests were killed indiscriminately, and war extended its grip to encompass people of every class and condition. . . . The roar of the flames mingled with the groans of the dying. . . . And the Temple Mount, one huge mass of fire, appeared to be boiling up from its very roots.
>
> (*BJ* 6.271–75)

And yet, in the midst of this bloody conflagration, Josephus also witnessed the tenacity of hope, and the powerful authority of Jewish prophecies of redemption. Surrounded by frenzied soldiers, with the city in ruins and the temple collapsing before their eyes, a large number of men, women, and children—six thousand of them, according to Josephus—climbed onto the roof of the last standing colonnade in the outer court.

This effort availed them nothing. There would be no escape. Exhausted and enraged, Roman troops fired the colonnade from below, and no one survived. But what had they even been thinking? "Their destruction was due to a false prophet," Josephus recounts, "who that very day had declared to the people in the city that God commanded them to go up into the temple, to receive the signs of their deliverance."[58]

Were some among them James's people?

EPILOGUE

We know nothing about the fate of the original assembly in Jerusalem. We know precious little about James; a little more about Peter; more by far, but still not much, about Paul. From Paul we at least have firsthand evidence, his seven letters, all dictated in a brief period of time several decades after his initial involvement in the movement. From Peter and from James we have nothing—at least, nothing directly. (The letters attributed to them in the New Testament are pseudonymous.) On James's death, we at least have Josephus. On Peter's and Paul's deaths, only later legends.[1]

Tradition abhors a vacuum. Later ecclesiastical writers and, later still, New Testament scholars have rushed to fill in the abundance of gaps in our first-century evidence. With the exception of Paul's letters, however, all of our other ancient sources—the gospels and Acts, and also Josephus—stand to the other side of the destruction of Jerusalem. And all of the modern work on these sources stands centuries after the evolution of Christianity into one of the West's defining institutions—and one of the West's most sustained fonts of anti-Judaism. It's a lot to look through, to try to see what this movement was like in its very first generation, when Christians were Jews.[2]

This book has tried to peer *behind* Acts, to understand what would have preceded the tales that shape Acts' smooth narrative. Appealing to the kinetic apocalyptic convictions that shape Paul's correspondence, as well as to some of the similar traditions available in the Scrolls, I have attempted to reimagine the stages by which the earliest Jesus-community would have first come together again, after the crucifixion. To understand how and why, despite the difficulties, these first followers of Jesus would have resettled in Jerusalem. To reconstruct the steps by which they became in some sense the center of a movement that was already fracturing bitterly within two decades of its founder's death. To see how the seriatim waves of expectation, disappointment, and fresh interpretation would have sustained this astonishing assembly in the long decades framed by Pilate's troops in 30 and Titus's in 70.

By the time that Luke wrote Acts, this movement would have lived through the heightened expectations—and disorienting disappointments—of at least four anticipated Endtimes. The first would have been Jesus' final Passover in Jerusalem circa 30 C.E., when the community accompanied Jesus to Jerusalem, and witnessed the crushing event of his crucifixion. The second would have been both marked and sustained by the resurrection appearances, which eventually tapered off and then, finally, ceased (circa 30–32 C.E.?). The third sprang up with the near-calamity caused by Caligula (39–40 C.E.). The fourth, visible in our second-generation source, Mark's gospel, awaited the End in the wake of the temple's destruction (post-70 C.E.). Luke's calm narrative smooths out these lived peaks of vivid expectation, the valleys of disorienting cognitive dissonance, and the various solutions offered by creative reaffirmations. Luke betrays little of these processes. He speaks, instead, of the founding of the Christian church.

For this reason, throughout this study, I have avoided using the terms "Christian" and "church." These words too readily conjure the later realities of organized institutions, and of a religion separate from, different from, and hostile to Judaism. But in its founding generation—which was committed to the belief that it was history's *final* generation—members of this movement were traditionally observant Jews, Paul included. (And for that matter, reaching back to the period before his crucifixion, so was Jesus.) These people all studied Jewish scriptures. They honored the god of Israel through offering sacrifices at the temple. They came together on the Sabbath. They imagined final redemption, inclusive of eschatological gentiles, as a natural extension of the history of Israel.[3]

Then as now, different Jews interpreted different Jewish ancestral customs differently. Jewishness has never been uniform. In Paul's period, Sadducees disagreed with Pharisees, who quarreled among each other (beit Hillel and beit Shammai) while interpreting scriptures differently from the ways of the Essenes. Some Jews in Alexandria did things one way, others another way. The Diaspora nourished a wide diversity of Jewish practice. Certain elements remained recognizably constant—circumcision for males; avoidance of public cult to foreign gods; Sabbath observance—but diversity prevailed. We have a better sense of how things worked if we imagine the Torah as widely dispersed sheet music: the notes were the notes, but Jews played a lot of improv.[4]

The gospels, too, are a genre of Jewish scriptural improvisation. They "messianize" Jesus' death and they "Davidize" Jesus' life. Daniel's apocalyptic "son of man," foregrounded in part thanks to Caligula, also contributed to shaping traditions about Jesus' Parousia. However the historical Jesus might have spoken the phrase, Mark's gospel anchors it in Jesus' lifetime by presenting the idea in two Christological modalities. Jesus as Mark's suffering Son of Man defines his clearly foretold death; Jesus as Mark's triumphant Son of Man defines his glorious imminent return. Matthew improvises similarly, repeatedly framing Jesus' words and deeds with, "This was done in order to fulfill what was said in the scriptures." So too Luke, with his character's long references to the Law and the prophets, conformed to (and even created some of) the details of Jesus' life, death, resurrection, and (now distant) return. And the fourth evangelist stretches traditions in other directions still. But John's gospel is also dealing, again, with the same biblical sheet music, sounding in its own way these shared scriptural notes.[5]

All of these New Testament texts are often read as antagonistic to Jews and to Judaism. I think that this is due, again, to the long shadow of later Christian anti-Judaism, cast backward. We simply assume that "Judaism" and "Christianity" are two incompatible traditions because that is the way that, in large part, things eventually worked out. So too when reading Paul. He says terrible things about the Law—but he says them with reference to his gentiles, who are listening to other apostles urging them to accept proselyte circumcision. (And Paul says *really* terrible things about these other apostolic colleagues!) Elsewhere, Paul affirms the Law, quoting from the Ten Commandments, urging its observance on his gentile assemblies. "The Law is holy, and the commandment is holy and just and good." And as late as the late 50s, Paul is still praising the cult of sacrifices offered in Jerusalem's temple. The Paul of history stands entirely within Judaism.[6]

His divinization of Christ might seem contrary to this idea. If we place ourselves back within Paul's first-century geocentric universe, however, it may seem less so. For Jews as for their pagan contemporaries, divinity was constructed and construed along a gradient that spanned heaven and earth. The very architecture of the universe—earth at the center, then the moon, then the five planets and the sun, then the realm of the fixed stars—articulated these grades. Special humans were divine. David and his line were in some special way God's sons; Augustus was a god the son of a god (his adoptive father, the deified Julius). On account of his excellence, says Philo, Moses "was named god and king of the whole nation." In the early third century, in his commentary on Paul's letter to the Romans, the great Christian theologian Origen of Alexandria pronounced both David and Paul "gods."[7]

Paul, importantly, never claims that Jesus is a god. The closest he comes is to say that Jesus was "in the *form* of [a] god" before he appeared "in the likeness of men." Capitalizing "God" throughout this passage in Paul's letter, the Revised Standard Version mistranslates it. Paul's world contained both God, the chief biblical deity, and gods, such as those represented by the nonhuman "knees" in this same passage in Philippians 2: they will bend to the victorious returning Christ and to God the Father. Jesus is not "God." He is, however, a divine mediator; a human being (*anthrōpos*), though "from heaven." (What James, Jesus' brother, would have made of such claims I have no idea.) Jesus becomes *radically* divinized—as much god as God the Father—only during the imperially sponsored episcopal councils of the fourth and fifth centuries, a period when the (now Christian) emperor was also (still) considered divine. Back in the mid-first century, when Christians were Jews, Jesus was high on the cosmic gradient, but he was nonetheless human. Our current categories of "humanity" and "divinity" do not stretch in these ways. Theirs did.[8]

Paul fought with Peter in Antioch after men from James arrived there. Oceans of ink have been spilled trying to account for the causes of their fight. Because of one prominent scholarly tradition of interpretation, James and Peter have long been cast as conservative, Law-observant apostles, "Jewish Christians" who wanted Christ-following gentiles to be circumcised. Paul, by contrast, is the "Law-free" radical who insists that gentiles (and, in some readings, Jews too) be unencumbered by Law-observance. And this reconstruction presupposes that Paul, too, had stopped living a Jewish life. He thereby transmutes from being a "Jewish" Christian into a sort of honorary gentile one, as well as the premier defender of and spokesman for a "Law-free" gentile Christianity.[9]

This interpretation misreads all parties. From the beginning—before Paul was even involved—the movement had admitted gentiles without requiring them to be circumcised. James, Peter, and John all affirmed that position, back in Jerusalem. But these gentiles were responsible for maintaining some specifically Jewish behaviors, such as worshiping only Israel's god, and renouncing sacrifices made to idols. All the apostles, Paul included, were agreed on this, and in this sense *no* form of the gospel, for gentiles, was "Law-free." And finally, Paul, as we have seen, worked in concert with James about the collection for the Jerusalem community throughout the rest of his missions. No ideological breach yawned between the two men.

The Diaspora, with its synagogue-going pagans, posed a special and a largely unanticipated challenge to this Galilean-Judean movement, no less than it offered a surprising opportunity. But as long as god-fearing pagans, once immersed "into Christ," took the step to radically Judaize their cultic life, worshiping only Israel's god and shunning their own gods and their former idols, they were "in." It was those apostles of Christ midcentury who wanted to circumcise these gentiles—Paul's "false brethren" and the "mutilators of the flesh" who flicker just beyond the edge of our peripheral vision as we read his letters—who were the true innovators.

Proselyte circumcision was never James's position—in fact, again according to Paul, James disavowed it. The mission to gentiles to turn them into Jews was a midcentury innovation; and it was internal to the Jesus movement.[10]

What then of the Jews in this moment of the movement? On this point, again, the future imposes itself upon the past. Later majoritarian western Christianity was largely gentile, and not Law-observant. By definition, then, a Christian is not Law-observant. Since Paul is the New Testament's preeminent Christian, so goes this argument, he must have dropped Law-observance too.

This contradicts how Paul defined Israel: as God's sons, the recipients of God's presence, his covenants, the Law, the temple cult, the promises; related by blood to the patriarchs and to the messiah. It distorts Paul's view of final redemption: all Israel (all twelve tribes) and all of the nations (all seventy of them). It denies his own pride in and attachment to his ancestral traditions, "the traditions of my fathers," as he says in Galatians. And it thereby cuts off this apostolic generation from the great prophetic sources of its own eschatological vision, Isaiah in particular. When God's last "Put out the light" is spoken, all humanity is redeemed. All humanity comes to Jerusalem. All humanity worships in the temple.

But redeemed humanity gathers in two families: Israel, those twelve tribes descended from Abraham, Isaac, and Jacob; and everyone else, all seventy nations, descended from Noah's three sons. If, for this vision to be realized, gentiles in the Christ movement had to remain gentiles, so too then did Jews have to remain Jews—that people constituted by the family connections and God-given privileges and promises that Paul in Romans chapters 9 through 11, and again in chapter 15, so proudly pronounced. "For the gifts and the calling of God are irrevocable!" The day of that realization verged on arriving, this earliest community was convinced, because their messiah, slain and resurrected, was about to return.[11]

What did happen to this earliest original community of Christ-followers? Did they perish in the flames of Jerusalem? Perhaps some did. A fourth-century church tradition, however, relates that they fled the city just before the Roman siege. Prompted by a prophecy, this story relates, the assembly fled to Pella, on the East Bank of the Jordan. Indeed, explained Eusebius, our source for this tale, the siege could only begin once "those who believed in Christ . . . removed from Jerusalem." Might this tradition relay reliable historical information? Maybe, maybe not: scholarly views, on this as on so many matters, diverge.[12]

For Christian late antiquity, post-Constantine, "Jewish Christians"—Jews who combined Torah observance with belief in Christ—eventually became the measure of heresy. Variously labeled and identified as "Ebionites," or as "Nazoreans," such people, sputtered Jerome, "insofar as they want to be both Jews and Christians, are neither Jews nor Christians!" Jerome's contemporary, the Manichaean Faustus, himself considered a heretic by the fourth-century Roman church, likewise complained. "Such people practice circumcision, they keep the Sabbath, they shun swine's meat and other things like that, all according to the Law. And yet they still claim to be Christians!" By this point, "Ebionites" and "Nazoreans" seem to have transformed into categories to think with, mobilized in order to clearly define "orthodoxy." Traditions of interpretation "against the Jews," by the fourth century—which, thanks to Constantine, was the first Christian century—had become one of the drive-wheels of patristic theology. It is useful to ponder the fact that, by Augustine's period, James, Peter, and Paul would all have been condemned as heretics.[13]

The categories that we think with, of course, matter. They orient us. With historical work, categories determine how you see, which in turn determines what you have to work with. *How* you see is what you get. For this reason, I would dispute my own title. "Christians" is an anachronistic term for this first generation, and therefore a distorting one. "Christianity" conjures images of bishops and doctrines, of creeds, of ordered theology, of monks and virgins and martyrs and (with Constantine) of emperors; the image of an institution comfortably settled within time, not one unstable, vibrant, energetic, conflicted, even impatient, glowing with charismata on time's edge. If we use "Christian" of this first generation, we pull them out of their own context, domesticating them for ours.

We thereby lose an appreciation for the vitality of this community's eschatological commitments, their conviction that God, through Christ, was going to act *soon.* It was that conviction that pushed Jesus' followers to concentrate back in Jerusalem so soon after his crucifixion. It was that conviction that prompted them to proclaim the good news in Jerusalem, and then to take the message out to Israel of the Diaspora. It was that conviction that enabled them to welcome in those "eschatological gentiles" who had left their old gods behind. They worked to prepare their world for the imminent realization of God's promises to Israel; and with the turning of the nations from their gods to Israel's god, these followers of Jesus were confirmed in their beliefs.

In their own eyes, they were history's last generation. It is only in history's eyes that they would become the first generation of the church.

ACKNOWLEDGMENTS

"Why don't you write a book about early Christian origins?" asked my wonderful literary agent, Sandy Dijkstra. "You should call it *When Christians Were Jews.*" What a good idea, I thought; and so I embarked upon a round of research centering on the years between Jesus' crucifixion and the Roman destruction of Jerusalem. That was in 2012.

I should have known it at the time, but I did not: the apostle Paul insisted on commandeering my efforts. I ended up having to deal with him first, before he would let me pay any serious attention to his apostolic cohort—to Peter, to James, and to that entire generation without whom we would have no reason to know about Paul to begin with. Only after I had written *Paul: The Pagans' Apostle* would Paul let me write a book about them. Here it is.

I would like therefore to thank Sandy, for her fecund suggestion, but also my patient editor at Yale, Jennifer Banks. Because of the vicissitudes of my research, Jennifer also had to put up with Paul and, in consequence, with ever-renegotiated deadlines as well. To her and to her (no less patient) editorial lieutenant, Heather Gold, I owe many thanks. My gratitude, too, goes out to

Ann-Marie Imbornoni, production editor *extraordinaire*, for helping transform my typescript into print. Ben Frankel proofread closely, short-stopped errant commas, and helped me to get the index under way: thank you, Ben.

This book was written in Jerusalem. Simply being here, being able to walk to and in the Old City, to stand near the Kotel and, when local politics allowed, to pace the Muslim area built upon the ruins of Herod's magnificent structure, charged my imagination and filled me with sadness and wonder. What a beautiful, blood-soaked, beloved, contested piece of the planet Jerusalem is. In telling the story of Jesus' hope-filled generation, back when Christians were Jews, I have told a part of Jerusalem's story as well.

As the semesters between 2012 and 2018 came and went, students and colleagues at the Hebrew University continually stimulated and challenged me to wrestle with our refractory ancient evidence in every way I could. My deepest thanks go to them, and especially to professors Brouria Bitton-Ashkelony and Oded Irshai, the past and present heads of the university's Center for the Study of Christianity and my dear friends. Brouria and Oded, you are two of the reasons why Jerusalem is one of the best places in the world to work on ancient Christianity.

Every time my confidence failed, every time I was stuck for a word, every time I forgot what time it was, my husband, Fred Tauber, was there. Thank you, Zev, for this and for so much more.

I dedicate this book to our grandchildren. May their times be more peaceful than ours.

TIMELINE

Before the Common Era (B.C.E.)

c. 1000 David consolidates cult in Jerusalem. His son Solomon builds the First Temple.

722 Assyria's conquest of the North (Israel); deportation of ten tribes.

586 Babylon conquers Jerusalem, destroys the temple, and deports population.

530s Persia conquers Babylon. Cyrus permits exiles to return to Judea. Beginning of Second Temple period.

332 Alexander the Great conquers Judea. After his death in 323 B.C.E., Ptolemies in Egypt and Seleucids in Syria rule Judea by turns for the next 150 years.

167 Rivalry between Zadokite brothers for high priesthood. Antiochus IV introduces Greek rites in Jerusalem's temple, which the prophet "Daniel" sees as the "abomination of desolation," a sign of the impending Endtimes.

166 Maccabean Revolt, led by Hasmonean family. Temple rededicated in 164 B.C.E. ("Hanukkah"). Rome extends power into eastern Mediterranean.

152 Jonathan the Hasmonean elevated to high priesthood. The Zadokite "Teacher of Righteousness" quits Jerusalem(?), joins

with Dead Sea sectarians, committed to the belief that they are living in the Endtimes.

141 Simon, Jonathan's brother, rules as both high priest and king; independent Hasmonean monarchy.

63 Rivalry between Hasmonean brothers for high priesthood. Rome intervenes, sending Pompey, who masters Jerusalem and defiles the temple.

37 Herod the Great becomes king. He marries into Hasmonean family, and appoints the high priests himself, controlling their terms of office. Herod rebuilds Jerusalem, greatly expanding the Second Temple precincts.

c. 4 *Birth of Jesus, according to Gospel of Matthew.* Herod dies, dividing his kingdom between his three sons, Archelaus (Judea), Antipas (Galilee, Perea), and Philip (Transjordan). Rebellions break out; Varus the Syrian Legate crucifies 2,000 outside of Jerusalem.

Common Era (C.E.)

6 Augustus deposes Archelaus. Judea becomes a Roman province under a prefect (colonial governor) subordinate to the legate in Antioch. A census to assess taxes for administering the province triggers a revolt led by Judah the Galilean. Various Judean strongmen (Judas, Simon, Athronges) vie with armed followers for Archelaus's throne. Annas serves as high priest; five of his sons will also assume that office. *Birth of Jesus according to the Gospel of Luke.*

18 Caiaphas, Annas's son-in-law, appointed high priest; serves until 36.

26 Pontius Pilate appointed prefect of Judea; serves until 36.

c. 28 Jesus receives purification of John the Baptizer, who is later beheaded by Herod's son Antipas. *Jesus begins his mission, announcing the impending End times and coming Kingdom of God.*

c. 30 *Pilate crucifies Jesus as "King of the Jews" in Jerusalem* around Passover; some of Jesus' followers visually experience the presence of *Jesus raised from the dead.* They settle back in Jerusalem, to prepare for and then to proclaim the message of the fast-approaching Kingdom, now to be inaugurated by God's messiah, the triumphant, returning Jesus.

33(?) Stephen lynched by Jerusalem mob(?).

c. 33/34 Jesus movement spreads in neighboring Diaspora. Unanticipated reception of their message by synagogue-affiliated pagans causes confusion within the movement, and between apostles and their host synagogue communities. *Paul persecutes, then joins, the movement in Damascus.*

c. 36(?) Paul goes to Jerusalem to meet with Peter and James, Jesus' brother.

38/40 Anti-Jewish riots in Alexandria. Antipas deposed as ruler of the Galilee, replaced by Herod's grandson, Agrippa I. Emperor Gaius (Caligula) resolves to put a cultic image of himself within Jerusalem's temple, occasioning a massive protest strike in Galilee and Judea. Some in Judea (among them, Jesus' followers) regard Caligula's intervention in Jerusalem as the prophet Daniel's "abomination of desolation," a signal for the coming Endtimes. Caligula's assassination in January of 41 ends the crisis.

41 Agrippa I assumes control of Judea. His territories revert to Roman administration after his death in 44.

44 Agrippa I executes James son of Zebedee; Peter imprisoned, then escapes from Jerusalem.

c. 45 The prophet Theudas rallies masses of followers; all are cut down by Roman troops.

c. 49 Paul, group meeting of Jesus followers in Jerusalem to try to regularize "policy" for integrating ex-pagan gentiles into the movement.

50s Decade during which Paul writes most of his seven surviving letters. The Egyptian and the various "signs prophets" gather mass followings in Judea, and are pacified by Rome.

57 Paul journeys to Jerusalem for final trip.

62 James, Jesus' brother, executed in Jerusalem by the high priest Ananus.

66 Judea and Galilee revolt against Rome. Josephus put in charge of defense of the Galilee, where he is defeated by Vespasian and Titus at Jotapata (67). Josephus prophesies that Vespasian will become emperor.

68 Roman army destroys the settlement at Qumran. Emperor Nero commits suicide in June of 68, inaugurating the "Year of the Four Emperors," as Roman strongmen contest for imperial power. Vespasian emerges victorious (69); his son Titus presses on with the siege of Jerusalem. Jewish strongmen (John of Gishala, Menachem son of Judah, Simon bar Giora) vie for power within the city.

70 Titus's troops overwhelm Jerusalem, destroying the city and its temple.

73 The rebel stronghold Masada is destroyed, ending the revolt.

c. 75(?) The writer of the *Gospel of Mark* composes his story, seeing the presence of the Roman army's standards on the Temple Mount as the "abomination of desolation" signaling the beginning of the Endtime. Josephus writes his history of the war, the *Bellum Judaicum*.

c. 90–100 *Composition of the gospels of Matthew and of Luke, and possibly of John.* Josephus writes *Antiquities of the Jews.*

c. 110(?) *Composition of Acts of the Apostles.*

135 Following defeat of the Bar Kokhba, the emperor Hadrian erases Jewish Jerusalem, building in its stead a pagan city, Aelia Capitolina.

NOTES

PROLOGUE

1. Mark, generally considered to be the earliest gospel, seems to have been written in the wake of the Jerusalem temple's destruction in 70 C.E. This proclamation of the coming Kingdom defines Jesus' first speech in Mark 1.15. For the translation of *pisteutei* as "trust" rather than as "believe," Paula Fredriksen, *Paul: The Pagans' Apostle*, 36; on the concept more generally in antiquity, Teresa Morgan, *Roman Faith and Christian Faith:* Pistis *and* Fides *in the Early Roman Empire and Early Churches.* Jesus' own apocalyptic convictions were explored in two classics of historical Jesus research, Albert Schweitzer, *The Quest of the Historical Jesus* (original publication, 1906); and, before him, Johannes Weiss, *Jesus' Proclamation of the Kingdom* (original publication, 1892). More recently, Dale Allison, *Jesus of Nazareth: Millenarian Prophet*; and Paula Fredriksen, *Jesus of Nazareth, King of the Jews.*
2. Scholars date 1 Thessalonians to the late 40s of the first century: it is Paul's earliest letter. "We who are left alive" at the Lord's second coming—presumably Paul included—appears at 1 Thessalonians 4.15. On the Lord's proximity, Philippians 4.5. For God's "shortening" of the time until the End, 1 Corinthians 7.29; 10.11; cf. 2 Corinthians 6.2, on salvation as "Now!" Romans 13.11–12, finally, announces the hovering realization of the Endtime (emphasis mine).
3. Paul characterizes the members of the Jerusalem community whose views differ from his own as "false brothers" in Galatians 1.18–19 and 2.4–9. Paul reports going up to Jerusalem to consult with men there in Galatians

1.18–19 and 2.1–2; cf. 1 Corinthians 15.3–7. For his final exhortation to contribute to his fund drive for Jerusalem, Romans 15.26.

Here and throughout this book I will occasionally refer to Paul's assemblies as comprised of "ex-pagan pagans." I have two reasons for doing this. The first is that the word *ethnē* in Greek translates both as "pagan" and as "gentile": Greek does not distinguish between what we consider "ethnicity" and what we consider "religion." To other ancient pagans, a fellow pagan who ceased worshiping the traditional gods without converting to Judaism would still be a pagan who was obligated to those gods. This continuity of peoplehood and pantheons, as we shall see, explains much of the later hostility toward the early Jesus movement once pagans/gentiles began to join. "Ex-pagan pagans" draws attention to this fact: a pagan, in the view of his peers, can never be an "ex-pagan."

4. Steve Mason, *Josephus and the New Testament*, provides a thorough orientation on the ways that Josephus' works enrich historical research into Christian origins.
5. For a concise survey of this history, E. P. Sanders, *Judaism: Practice and Belief, 63 BCE–66 CE*, 3–43.
6. Josephus comments on sedition and holiday crowds in *BJ* 1.88; on the messianic prophecy leading up to the rebellion, *BJ* 6.312–13.

1. UP TO JERUSALEM

1. Jesus' ambit for the most part seems to have been the farming and fishing villages of rural Galilee and villages in Judea. No tradition records his ever journeying either to Tiberias or to Sepphoris, the two major Galilean cities.
2. Zadok the high priest anoints Solomon in 1 Kings 1.34.
3. For God's covenant of circumcision with Abraham, see Genesis 17. For a *parti pris* description of these events between Jerusalem and Antioch, 1 Maccabees 1.12–15; cf. 2 Maccabees 4.11–17; for a succinct overview, Sanders, *Judaism*, 15–21.
4. 1 Maccabees 1.54; on the "abomination of desolation," Daniel 9.27; 11.31; 12.11. Was this conflict "religious persecution," or an administrative blunder? See the considered remarks of John Ma, "Relire les *Institutions des Séleucides* de Bikerman."
5. 1 Maccabees 8 records this alliance between Rome and Jerusalem.
6. This rabbinic appreciation of Herod's architectural genius appears in the fifth- or sixth-century text of the Babylonian Talmud, b. Bava Batra 4a. For more on Herod the master builder, see esp. Peter Richardson, *Building*

Jewish in the Roman East; also, by the same author, *Herod: King of the Jews and Friend of the Romans.* See also the briefer appreciation of Herod—the king everybody loves to hate—by Geza Vermes, *The True Herod.*

7. Sanders provides an excellent architectural and liturgical orientation to Herod's temple, *Judaism*, 55–72, and illustrations, 305–14.
8. On the priests' resolution to arrest Jesus secretly on account of his extreme popularity, Mark 14.2; on the Sanhedrin's (incoherent) blasphemy charge and its two plenum meetings, 14.53 and 15.1. Pilate obliges the priests in chapter 15, crucifying Jesus under the titulus "King of the Jews" at 15.26.
9. For a compare-and-contrast analysis of these two quite different passion narratives, see Paula Fredriksen, "Markan Chronology, the Scene at the Temple, and the Death of Jesus."
10. John 3.22 relates Jesus' Judean mission, having him pass through Samaria in John 4.4 on his way back to the Galilee. Once again in Jerusalem for an unnamed feast in 5.1–2, he goes up for Sukkot in 7.2, 10, and is still there for the "feast of Dedication" (Hannukah) in 10.22. The final trip to Jerusalem begins at 11.55.
11. Paul mentions the assemblies in Judea in connection with his joining the Christ movement in Damascus in Galatians 1.22–24.
12. Jesus replies to Annas at John 18.19–20.
13. Mark 12.29–31 and the parallel verses in Matthew and in Luke relate Jesus' invocation of the Ten Commandments. On the place of the Ten Commandments more generally in the teaching of John the Baptizer, Jesus of Nazareth, and the apostle Paul, see Paula Fredriksen, *Sin: The Early History of an Idea*, 6–49 and notes.
14. Mark 10.19 presents Jesus as reciting these commandments. Josephus claims that they played a central role in the Baptizer's mission, *AJ* 18.116–19 (again, encoded as "piety" and "justice"). On Honi, Hanina, and other charismatic Galilean holy men, see especially Geza Vermes, *Jesus the Jew*, 58–82.
15. John's Jesus states repeatedly (and omnisciently) that "my hour is not yet come," John 2.4; 7.6, 30; 8.20; cf. 12.23. On this gospel's characterization of Jesus, the classic article by Wayne Meeks, "The Stranger from Heaven in Johannine Sectarianism"; also Paula Fredriksen, *From Jesus to Christ*, 19–26.
16. In this connection, the speech that Luke gives to Gallio, the Roman proconsul of Achaia, in Acts 18.12–16 perfectly conveys what any Roman official would have thought about intervening in intra-Jewish religious

disputes: "But when Gallio was proconsul of Achaia, the Jews made a united attack upon Paul and brought him before the tribunal, saying, 'This man is persuading men to worship God contrary to the law.' But when Paul was going to open his mouth, Gallio said to the Jews, 'If it were a matter of wrongdoing or of vicious crime, I should have reason to bear with you, O Jews. But since it is a matter of questions about words and names and your own law, see to it yourselves. I refuse to be a judge in these things.' And he drove them from the tribunal."

17. Mark 11.18. On the progressive exculpation of Pilate in the passion narratives, see too Fredriksen, *From Jesus to Christ*, 116–22. In other first-century sources, Pilate comes off as much less sympathetic than he does in the gospels. Philo of Alexandria characterizes him as a man of "inflexible, stubborn, and cruel disposition," whose tour of duty was marked by his "venality, thefts, assaults, abusive behavior, and his frequent murders of untried prisoners"; *Embassy to Gaius* 38.302. Neither Josephus nor, a generation later, the Roman historian Tacitus describes Pilate any more positively, *BJ* 2.169–75, *AJ* 17.55–59, 87–89; Tacitus, *Histories* 5.9, 3 and 5.10, 1. For a consideration of these sources, see Helen Bond, *Pontius Pilate in History and Interpretation.*
18. For a review of these various positions—which agree, oddly, only on the so-called temple incident—see Paula Fredriksen, "What You See Is What You Get." The argument that priests oppressed the population through coercive purity rules—which Jesus, through his temple gesture, repudiates—utterly fails as explanation, since priests themselves, in light of their work around the altar, were regulated by many more purity rules than was the lay population. Also, this purity legislation was biblical. See also E. P. Sanders, *Jesus and Judaism*, 443, s.v. "purity"; also Sanders, *Jewish Law from Jesus to the Mishnah*; John P. Meier, A *Marginal Jew*, vol. 4, esp. chapter 35, "Jesus and Purity Laws," 342–477.
19. Any New Testament introduction will walk the reader through these issues. For a brief overview on the relations between the canonical gospels, Fredriksen, *Jesus of Nazareth*, 18–34; on the relation of John in particular to the Synoptics, Moody D. Smith, *John among the Gospels.*
20. Acts 22.3 claims that Paul studied under Gamaliel; cf. 7.58 and 8.1, which have Paul in Jerusalem. For Paul's boasting of his own Jewish excellence, Philippians 3.5–6 and Galatians 1.14.
21. Acts 7.58 and 8.1 presents Paul as present at and consenting to Stephen's death. In his own letters, Paul speaks of his past persecutions at Galatians 1.13–14, Philippians 3.6, and 1 Corinthians 15.9–10.

22. Paul leaves Jerusalem and heads to Damascus in Acts 9.1–4. While on the road, he has his encounter with the risen Christ. Briefly witnessing to the gospel in Damascus, he heads back to Jerusalem shortly thereafter, Acts 9.26–28. Galatians 1.15–20, Paul's own letter, has Paul always situated in Damascus and going up to Jerusalem only some three years after his call.
23. Acts depicts the blinded Saul's auditory experience of the risen Christ at 9.3–5, 22.6–11, and 26.9–18. Paul himself emphasizes seeing, 1 Corinthians 15.8; cf. 9.1. Galatians 1.16, more elusive, states that God revealed his son "*in* me."
24. For a reconstruction of Paul's "unknown years"—what he was doing between the time he received his apostolic call and his period in Antioch's Christ-following assembly—that *does* exhibit a robust confidence in Acts, see Martin Hengel and Anna Maria Schwemer's *Paul between Damascus and Antioch: The Unknown Years*, n.b. xi–xiv, for their detailed chronological table.
25. 1 Corinthians 10.18, on partnership with God around Israel's altar in Jerusalem, cf. 9.13 on sacrifices and food sharing at and through the temple.
26. For his whole discussion on sacrifice, food, and divine-human sharing, 1 Corinthians 10.19–22.
27. For this vocabulary, and the mechanics of Levitical sacrifice as present in Paul, see Fredriksen, *Pagans' Apostle*, 317, s.v. "purity" and "separation/sanctification/holiness."
28. For Paul's roaring condemnation of the sorts of vices entailed by idol worship, see esp. Romans 1.18–32. On the separation of pagans who do not know God from those who do, 1 Thessalonians 4.4–5. On Paul's gentile mission as "priestly service" and the gentiles themselves as an altar offering, Romans 15.16 and Philippians 4.18; cf. e.g., Leviticus 1.9, 2.2, 3.5, and frequently.
29. On likening his ex-pagan pagans to the Jerusalem temple—God's spirit rests in both—see 1 Corinthians 3.16, 6.19; 2 Corinthians 6.16.
30. On God's in-dwelling in the Jerusalem temple, Matthew 23.21.
31. For Pliny the Elder on "the solitary tribe of the Essenes," *Natural History* 5.73; Philo, *That Every Good Man Is Free*, 75–80, and *On the Contemplative Life*, 1–3; Josephus, *BJ* 2.119–61, reprised in *AJ* 18.18–22. Geza Vermes provides a convenient English translation, *Dead Sea Scrolls*.
32. On Essene patterns of behavior, see the primary texts cited in the preceding note. On sexual renunciation within Christ-following

communities in light of the impending End, see especially Paul's remarks in 1 Corinthians 7 ("the form of this world is passing away," v. 31b). Matthew's Jesus praises those who become "eunuchs for the sake of the Kingdom of Heaven," Matthew 19.12. That the earliest community in Jerusalem "held all things in common," Acts 4.32–37, a form of social organization that coheres with Paul's collections for "the poor" in Jerusalem. Much later Christian communities, apocalyptic or not, famously engaged in extreme forms of asceticism in antiquity, on which see especially Peter Brown, *Body and Society*.

33. These remarks on the temple's new priesthood appear in Qumran's Commentary on Habakkuk: 1 QpHab 2:2; 5:11; 11:4ff.; alluding to Pompey, 9:4–7; on the Wicked Priest's defilements, 8:8–13.
34. Josephus on Judah and Zadok, "founders" of the disastrous "fourth philosophy" advocating armed resistance to Rome, *AJ* 18.6–8.
35. On this delegation's appeals for *autonomia*, *AJ* 17.295–314.
36. On Judah and Zadok, *AJ* 18.5; cf. *BJ* 2.117–18.
37. *AJ* 17.253–54; cf. *BJ* 2.40–46.
38. Josephus describes John in *AJ* 18.116–19. On John's role as Jesus' mentor, John P. Meier, *Marginal Jews* 2:19–233; much more briefly, Fredriksen, *Jesus of Nazareth*, 184–97; for differences as well as similarities between the two men, Dale Allison, *Constructing Jesus*, 204–20.
39. Jesus sends the purified leper to the priest in Mark 1.40–44.
40. On Jesus-followers and the altar, Matthew 5.23–24.
41. Fredriksen, *Jesus of Nazareth*, 52–65, on purifications.
42. For this reconstruction of Jesus' entry into Jerusalem and Passover purifications, see esp. Sanders, *Historical Figure of Jesus*, 250–52.
43. On the eschatological gathering of the nations to worship Israel's god at the Temple Mount, see Isaiah 2.2–4; 66.18, gathering all nations and tongues; 25.6, the shared feast; 56.7, the temple as a house both of sacrifice and of prayer.
44. Mark 12.14–15 and parallels, on paying the Roman tax.
45. Fredriksen, *Jesus of Nazareth*, 241–59.
46. Unlike his priestly Hasmonean in-laws, Herod could not serve in the temple, since he descended from a family of Idumean converts.
47. On the variety of messianic figures represented in the Scrolls, see esp. John Collins, *The Scepter and the Star: The Messiahs of the Dead Sea Scrolls and Other Ancient Literature*; and, together with Adela Yarbro Collins, *King and Messiah as Son of God*; Magnus Zetterholm, ed., *The Messiah in Early Judaism and Christianity*; and, on the various political

and religious functions of this designation, Matthew Novenson, *The Grammar of Messianism: An Ancient Jewish Political Idiom and Its Users.*

2. GOD'S HOLY MOUNTAIN

1. The temple worship of Jesus' early followers appears at Matthew 5.23–24, Luke 24.53, and Acts 2.46.
2. John 2.19–22.
3. On the temple as a "den of robbers," Mark 11.17 RSV.
4. On his people's commitment to their traditional sacrificial worship, Josephus, *AJ* 15.248. For Joseph and Mary's offering a sacrifice of pigeons after Jesus' birth, Luke 2.22–24.
5. Tobit 14.5.
6. This interpretation of Jesus' action as a prophetic enactment rather than a statement of censure was pioneered by E. P. Sanders in his classic study, *Jesus and Judaism,* esp. 61–90. In *From Jesus to Christ,* I endorsed this reading myself, 111–14. I have since revised my view, as will be made clear in the discussion that follows; see too the introduction to the second edition of *From Jesus to Christ*, xxi–xxiv.

   After Sanders's book, most New Testament scholars were able to shift over to understanding Jesus' gesture as a visual prophetic enactment, but they preserved the older antitemple explanation: the temple would be destroyed because Jesus disapproved of it, for some reason or another. See, for example, most recently, Dale Martin, "Jesus in Jerusalem: Armed and Not Dangerous"; and my reply, Fredriksen, "Arms and the Man."
7. E.g., Luke 24.53: "and they were continually in the temple, blessing God."
8. Jesus predicts the temple's destruction in Mark 13.2; cf. John 2.19. On the temple as the "forsaken house," Matthew 23.38 and Luke 13.35. Luke's Jesus mourns over the city in 19.41–44. Finally, Jesus is accused of threatening to destroy the temple at Mark 14.58, cf. 15.29; so similarly at Stephen's trial, Acts 6.14.
9. On "the word of the Lord" concerning events at the End, 1 Thessalonians 4.15; on Paul's reception of tradition, 1 Corinthians 15.3 and *passim.*
10. I spell out these arguments in *Jesus of Nazareth,* 207–14 and 225–47; see also "Gospel Chronologies" and "Arms and the Man."
11. The synoptic gospels portray these acclamations at Jesus' triumphal entry in Mark 11.10, Matthew 21.9, and Luke 19.38. The priests' anxieties about popular tumult appear in Mark 14.2 and parallels.

12. Mark 14.53–15.1, the hearings before the Sanhedrin; 15.2–15, the hearing before Pilate; 15.26–27, Jesus crucified as "King of the Jews" between two "robbers."
13. Jesus is baptized offstage in John 1.31–34; for the full scene in the temple, including Jesus' prophecy of his own resurrection, 2.13–22; Jesus is next up in the city, without incident, in 5.1.
14. The messianic acclamation at the triumphal entry, John 12.12; the earlier consultation of the Sanhedrin, 11.45–53.
15. The composition of this arresting party differs considerably from the Synoptics' civilian crowd, John 18.1–4. Jesus stands before Annas in 18.13, 19–24. John depicts no Sanhedrin "trial" with Jesus present.
16. The dialogue between Pilate and Jesus is quite drawn out, with the prefect shuttling back and forth between the priests and the mob outside of the praetorium, and Jesus within, John 18.28–19.16. John develops the theme of Pilate's extreme reluctance to carry out the sentence even more than do the Synoptics. Jesus is crucified again under the titulus, again between two others, 19.18. Mary discovers the empty tomb, and subsequently the risen Jesus, in 20.1–18.
17. In a recent article, Fernando Bermejo-Rubio has urged that this conundrum—that Jesus was crucified but that his followers were not—is false. Bermejo-Rubio identifies the two "robbers" hanged with Jesus as two of Jesus' own followers. The gospel accounts make no such claim; Bermejo-Rubio advances it as an inference: "(Why) Was Jesus the Galilean Crucified Alone? Solving a False Conundrum," esp. 144–49. The hypothesis also requires that Jesus and his followers were actively involved in anti-Roman activities, which in turn accounts for their being armed with "swords" in Gethsemane: Bermejo-Rubio, "Between Gethsemane and Golgotha; or, Who Arrested the Galilean(s)? Challenging a Deep-Rooted Assumption in New Testament Research." I address these issues further *infra*.
18. The quotation is E. P. Sanders's observation, *Historical Figure of Jesus*, 254.
19. On this point—the insecurity of both of these positions, prefect or priest, should events in Jerusalem spin out of control—Fredriksen, *Jesus of Nazareth*, 171–73.
20. I find John's depiction of temple police plus Roman soldiers much more plausible as the arresting party: ibid., 235–59.
21. John switches between "the chief priests" and "the Jews" in his version of the scene before Pilate, John 18.28–19.23; I take "the Jews" to indicate a crowd larger than only the priests.

22. Josephus' Passover census appears in *BJ* 6.420–427. For the duties of the priests, and especially the responsibilities of the chief priest during this hectic holiday, see Helen Bond's sympathetic and informed reconstruction, *Caiaphas: Friend of Rome and Judge of Jesus?* esp. 45–49 specifically about Passover.
23. On the theological power of Mark's depiction of Jesus' back-and-forth with Caiaphas at the Sanhedrin trial, and its unlikeliness as history, Fredriksen, *From Jesus to Christ,* 115–20.
24. Perhaps there were two different groups in Jerusalem, one pro-, the other anti-Jesus? This is not impossible. But again, were Jesus so visibly and viscerally repudiated by Jews in Jerusalem in the ways that the gospels depict, Pilate would have had little reason to crucify him.
25. Scholars have long noted the ways in which evangelical passion traditions, as they continue to develop, progressively inculpate "the Jews" and exculpate Pilate, who eventually will become a saint within the Ethiopic church. A classic study of this process is Paul Winter's *On the Trial of Jesus;* see too the remarks of C. K. Barrett, *Jesus and the Gospel Tradition.* For a long and detailed analysis of the trial scenes, Raymond E. Brown, *The Death of the Messiah,* 2 vols.; and an impassioned response by John Dominic Crossan, *Who Killed Jesus? Exposing the Roots of Anti-Semitism in the Gospel Story of the Death of Jesus.*
26. The armed disciple appears at Mark 14.47 and Matthew 26.52. Matthew's arresting "mob" is also armed with "swords" as well as with clubs, 26.47; cf. Luke 22.51 and John 18.10–11. The classic argument for Jesus' actually leading an armed rebellion against Rome was put forward by S. G. F. Brandon, *Jesus and the Zealots;* more recently—and with variations in the details—Martin ("Jesus in Jerusalem: Armed but Not Dangerous") and Bermejo-Rubio ("Between Gethsemane and Golgotha") have put forth similar reconstructions. As my discussion above reveals, I am unpersuaded; see too Fredriksen, "Arms and the Man," for the full argument.
27. For the meanings of *machaira,* see H. G. Liddell and R. Scott, *Greek-English Lexicon* (rev. ed. 1968), p. 1085A. The first definition is "large knife or dirk; carving knife; sacrificial knife." "Short sword" appears only as the second definition.
28. Abraham approaches Isaac with a *machaira* in the Greek text of Genesis 22.6; the Hebrew is *machelet.*
29. The arrest in Gethsemane—and the swooning soldiers—occur in John 18.6.

30. Such belligerence and active militancy also sits oddly with all the other material we have in the gospels and in Paul's letters about the movement's eschatological ethics, its pattern of passive resistance and of obeying civic authorities: see *From Jesus to Christ*, 98–101, for a quick survey of this material.
31. On Jesus' apocalyptic threats to unreceptive villages, Matthew 11.20–24 and Luke 10.13–15; see too Allison, *Constructing Jesus*, 227–30. Josephus' characterization of Jesus appears in *AJ* 18.63–64, the so-called Testimonium Flavianum, on which more *infra*.
32. On Jesus' status as prophet, John 6.14, 7.40, and 9.17. Cf. Matthew 21.11, and Luke 24.19, 21.
33. On the different ways that the evangelists attribute messianic status to Jesus, *From Jesus to Christ*, 18–52 and 177–204. See, for example, Mark 10.47–48, on the blind Bartimaeus; 11.1–10, the Triumphal Entry; 12.35–37, Jesus' disputing that the messiah is David's "son." Allison carefully wades through and weighs in on the inconsistent primary documentation, *Constructing Jesus*, 279–93. On the wide range both of definitions of "messiah" and of the significance of the attribution, see now esp. Novenson, *Grammar of Messianism*.
34. I reconstruct the final days of Jesus' mission with this hypothesis, *Jesus of Nazareth*, 244–59.
35. Thus Luke 19.11, and Acts 1.3, 6.
36. *Declamationes maiores* 274.13.
37. *AJ* 18.64; cf. John 18.13.
38. On Annas and his sons, *AJ* 20.198; see too Bond, *Caiaphas*, 33–56.
39. These events are related in *BJ* 1.651–55 and *AJ* 17.149–67 (Herod), in *AJ* 18.85–86 (on the termination of Pilate's and Caiaphas's positions), and in *BJ* 2.232–44 (the murders in Samaria).
40. For the hearing before Annas, John 18.12–13; before Pilate, 18.28.

3. FROM MIRACLE TO MISSION

1. This first Passion prediction occurs at Mark 8.31–32; cf. 9.1: "He charged them to tell no one . . . until the son of man arose from the dead." On the narrative strategy of these predictions, see my *From Jesus to Christ*, 107–10.
2. Mark's next two Passion predictions occur at 9.31 and again at 10.34–35. The women go to the tomb in 16.1 but are too frightened to speak, 16.5–8. The earliest versions of Mark's gospel end here. As Frank Kermode noted long ago, Mark's "conclusion is either intolerably clumsy; or it is

incredibly subtle"; *The Genesis of Secrecy: On the Interpretation of Narrative*, 68.

3. The women visit the tomb in Matthew 28, seeing the risen Jesus in 28.9–10. Judas's hanging is mentioned in 27.5. The so-called Great Commission from a mountain in the Galilee—"Go and make disciples of all nations"—closes Matthew's story, 28.16–20.
4. Luke 24.4–9. Evidently, these women are Galilean, Luke 23.55. The women at the tomb serve as a prequel to Luke's resurrection stories.
5. Luke mentions Peter's (offstage) visitation at 24.34; the evangelist's attention is trained on the supper at Emmaus, 24.13–35. Once Jesus appears to the disciples in Jerusalem, he reassures them of his physicality by eating a piece of fish: ghosts can't eat, 24.42–43. The gospel ends with the community's following Jesus out to the village of Bethany, then returning to Jerusalem and "continually" blessing God in the temple (24.50–53).
6. The stories by the tomb, and with doubting Thomas, occur in John 20.1–29; the appearances in the Galilee, 21.14, 25.
7. Galatians 1.15–17 implies that Paul received his vision of the raised Jesus in Damascus. At another point in this correspondence, when repeating eucharistic traditions, Paul mentions "the night when [Jesus] *paredidoto*" (1 Corinthians 11.23). The RSV translators, who do know traditions about Judas, render this word as "was betrayed." It could equally well be translated, in the passive voice, as "was handed over." But Greek also has a "middle voice," which indicates verbs with reference to oneself: often, their forms are identical to the passive verbal forms. In that case—were this a middle voice verb—the sentence in English could read "the night that he gave himself up." The main point to bear in mind, especially in light of Paul's invoking "the twelve" at 1 Corinthians 15.5, is that Paul seems not to know traditions about Judas.
8. Acts 9.3–8 speaks of the blinded Saul/Paul. Paul insists on his having seen Christ in 1 Corinthians 9.1, as well as the passage in chapter 15 cited above. On Paul's "persecuting" the Christ-assembly in Damascus, Galatians 1.13; see further on this issue Fredriksen, *Pagans' Apostle*, 77–93.
9. On Luke's disciples not recognizing the raised Jesus, Luke 24.16, 31; Jesus suddenly appears before the disciples in Jerusalem, 24.36–37; Mary's initially not recognizing the raised Jesus, John 20.14; Jesus getting through closed doors, John 20.24, 26.
10. 1 Corinthians 15.3–8 gives Paul's list of witnesses, as he received the tradition, including himself at the end. The transformation of the bodies

of both the quick and the dead is described in 1 Corinthians 15.35–51: the flesh-and-blood body becomes *pneumatikon*, a "spiritual" body.

11. On spiritual body, 1 Corinthians 15.42–44, contra flesh-and-blood bodies, which cannot inherit the Kingdom, 15.50. Luke's flesh-and-blood risen Christ appears at Luke 24.39.
12. The Manichees challenged Augustine to reach for new interpretations of Paul's letters. Against them, Augustine began to frame "flesh" as a moral rather than as a material principle in his work on Romans in the mid-390s, especially in qu. 66 of his *Answers to 83 Questions.* His fullest—and calmest—pronouncement comes decades later, in *City of God* 22.21; see Fredriksen, "Beyond the Body/Soul Dichotomy."
13. 1 Corinthians 15.39–41.
14. 1 Corinthians 15.37–50, cf. vv. 20–26 on transformation of human bodies dead or living. Paul speaks of his own expectation to be among the living for this transformation in 1 Thessalonians 4.15. "Spirit" in Paul is still material; but it is very, very fine matter. For the ways that ancient cosmology corresponds to ideas about humans and their transformation, see Dale Martin, *The Corinthian Body*, esp. chapter 5; more on sidereal bodies and Paul's ideas on resurrection, Matthew Thiessen, *Paul and the Gentile Problem*, 129–60.
15. Sanders, *Jesus and Judaism*, 77–119, provides one survey of these eschatological hopes and traditions; see also, more briefly, Fredriksen, *Pagans' Apostle*, 21–31; on Jesus' eschatology, Allison, *Constructing Jesus*, 31–220.
16. The dry bones of "the whole house of Israel" bloom with flesh in Ezekiel 37.11; on all being raised to final judgment, Daniel 12.2–3. On these resurrection traditions more generally, Jon D. Levenson, *Resurrection and the Restoration of Israel.*
17. On Mark's coupling of Jesus' death and resurrection to the temple's destruction and, with that, to Jesus' second coming, *From Jesus to Christ*, 44–52, 177–87.
18. 1 Corinthians 15.12–14 and 20–23.
19. On the risen Christ as the "first fruits" of the general resurrection, 1 Corinthians 15.23–26, stressing the defeat of death; on the transformation of the living, 15.50–52. Earlier in this same letter, exhorting his assembly to sexual self-discipline, Paul gives his reason: the "appointed time has grown very short" and "the order of this world is passing away," 1 Corinthians 7.29, 31.
20. Jesus appoints "the twelve" in Mark 3.14. They serve as straight men to his elusive teachings, e.g., at 4.10 and 34. On purity and hand washing, Mark

7.3; as an audience for Jesus' questions about his own messianic identity, 8.27–30; as witnesses to the Transfiguration, 9.2–8; James and John and precedence, 10.35–45.

21. These special followers are invested with charismatic powers, Mark 3.13–15; 6.7; Matthew's expansion of their abilities, Matthew 7.22 and 10.1–42. On their restriction to a Jewish mission field, Matthew 10.5–7 and 15.24.
22. On the twelve, Luke 9.1–2; on the seventy, Luke 10.9, 17. On the disciples (and Jesus) immersing Jesus' followers, John 3.22–30 and 4.1; on the twelve as a special group, John 6.67–71; on hearers as disciples, John 20.24. The twelve gather for the last supper—a Passover meal in the Synoptics—in Mark 14.17–24 and parallels; cf. John's more elusive reference, 13.2–30.
23. Paul gives his list of witnesses, which he "received" (presumably from those who were members of the movement before him), in 1 Corinthians 15.3–7. Mark identifies this core group both as "apostles" and as "disciples," Mark 6.7, 33.
24. Matthew relates the twelve disciples to (the eschatological in-gathering of) the twelve tribes at Matthew 19.28. Paul alludes to the same idea of the eschatological redemption of the plenum of Israel in Romans 11.26; see further on this idea Fredriksen, *Pagans' Apostle*, 314, s.v. "Israel"; on the ways that this idea harks back to the soaring eschatology of Isaiah, Ross Wagner, *Heralds of the Good News*. Finally, on pairs of the seventy as Jesus' "warm-up" groups, Luke 10.1; Martha receives wandering members of the movement in her house, Luke 10.38–42.
25. For the crowd at the triumphal entry as Jesus' followers, see Luke 19.37–38.
26. Luke names villages close to Jerusalem, Emmaus, Luke 24.13, and Bethany, 24.50. The community rejoices in the temple, Luke 24.53, and remains in Jerusalem, Acts 1.4. Paul goes to Jerusalem to confer with Peter, and also sees James, within three years of receiving his call to be an apostle, Galatians 1.15–17; he returns "after fourteen years"—thus, close to midcentury?—according to Galatians 2.1–10. This second meeting, despite the problems occasioned by the relative chronologies of the two texts, is often seen as the same meeting described in Acts 15, the so-called Apostolic Council.
27. Paul in Romans 11.26 cites Isaiah 59.20 on redemption of Israel beginning from "Zion." Acts 1.8, though diminishing the eschatological notes sounded by Paul, likewise emphasizes that redemption begins from Jerusalem; cf. Isaiah 2.2–4.

28. On this idea, the fundamental study by James Scott, *Paul and the Nations.* See further Fredriksen, *Pagans' Apostle,* 26–31 and 159–66.
29. Isaiah 66.18–20.
30. Luke 19.11.
31. On speaking "in tongues," 1 Corinthians 12.10, 13.1.
32. For charismatic speech becoming foreign languages, Acts 2.4–8; cf. 1.8.
33. Acts 2.17–21; cf. Joel 2.28–32.
34. Acts 1.3, 7–8. On not knowing time of end, because it comes like "a thief in the night," Paul and the gospels might be repeating a tradition that goes back to Jesus himself; 1 Thessalonians 5.2; cf. Matthew 24.43–44 and Luke 12.39–40; Fredriksen, *Jesus of Nazareth,* 78–89.
35. 1 Corinthians 16.22; and Acts 1.6, on the restoration of Israel's kingdom.
36. Acts 1.14; 2.1, 43–47; cf. 4.32–37; on the jump in membership, cf. Acts 1.15 and 2.41.
37. See Galatians 2.10, the concluding agreement of Paul's meeting in Jerusalem. He exhorts the Corinthian gentiles to contribute in 1 Corinthians 16.1; cf. 2 Corinthians 8.1–9.15, for his much longer pitch. On this contribution as a type of temple service, Romans 15.14–32, and specifically on "the holy" recipients there, 15.25–26.
38. The risen Jesus' speech at Emmaus, Luke 24.25–27.
39. Thus Joel 2.28–32, at Acts 2.17–21. "David," Psalm 16.8–11 and Psalm 110.1, authorizes Acts 2.25–29, 34; (Greek) Isaiah 57.19, Acts 2.39. Acts 2.23 reinforces these events by conjuring "the definite plan and foreknowledge of God."
40. Stephen's sweeping speech occurs in Acts 7.2–53. Luke describes Paul in Thessalonika at Acts 17.3 (emphasis mine).
41. 1 Corinthians 1.23.

4. BEGINNING FROM JERUSALEM

1. Isaiah calls Cyrus the Persian king "messiah" in Isaiah 45.1. John J. Collins reviews the diversity of messianic figures present in the Scrolls in *The Scepter and the Star;* see also, with Adela Yarbro Collins, *King and Messiah as Son of God.* For the many different interpretations—and applications—of this term, see esp. Novenson, *Grammar of Messianism.* For the messiahs of Aaron and of David in the Scrolls, Jan Willem van Henten, "The Hasmonean Period."
2. Even within the specific subcategory of "Davidic messiah," Matthew Novenson points out, there was scope for diversity. "Paul has a Davidic

messiah who dies and rises from the dead (Romans 1.3–4). 4 *Ezra* has a Davidic messiah who dies but does not rise from the dead (4 *Ezra* 7.28–29). The Qumran *Community Rule* has a Davidic messiah who is an accessory to a priestly messiah (1 *Qumran Scrolls* IX, 11). The epistle to the Hebrews has a Davidic messiah who is himself a priestly messiah (Hebrews 7.11–17). *Bavli Sanhedrin* even has a Davidic messiah who judges cases by a divinely inspired sense of smell (*b. Sanh.* 93b). All of these texts represent defensible ancient interpretations of certain biblical house of David texts, but they do not remotely constitute a single model of the "Davidic messiah"; "The Messiah ben Abraham in Galatians: A Response to Joel Willitts," 165.

3. See, for example, Psalms 17.8 and 51.1; also 2 Kings 23.25.
4. For example, Exodus 4.22; Deuteronomy 14.1; Psalm 82.6; Jeremiah 3.19, 31.20; Hosea 11.4; repeated by Paul at Romans 9.4.
5. Psalm 2.7 celebrates the "begetting" of the Davidic king upon his coronation/anointing; cf. Psalm 89.20, 26. Paul in Romans 1.3–4 and 15.12 celebrates the Davidic messiahship/"divine" sonship of Jesus; see Fredriksen, *Pagans' Apostle*, 131–51.
6. Thus Jeremiah 33.17, on the eternity of David's royal line.
7. On this difference of emphasis between lineage and function, or messiahs "born" and "made," Novenson, *Grammar of Messianism*, 65–113.
8. Morton Smith, "What Is Implied by the Variety of Messianic Figures?" 68; see too, on "messiahs present and absent," Novenson, *Grammar of Messianism*, 114–60.
9. See Isaiah 11.1–16, on the shoot from Jesse; Jeremiah 33.14, on the Davidic branch; Psalms of Solomon 17–18, on the eschatological Davidic ruler.
10. See the classic essay of John Gager, *Kingdom and Community: The Social World of Early Christianity*, esp. 20–49, for the ways that such reinterpretation lessens the "cognitive dissonance" that results from the evident disconfirmation of a fervently held millenarian belief.
11. Jesus, like his co-religionists, referred to and prayed to his god as "Father." For a long moment, NT scholars, taking their cue from Joachim Jeremias, made many Christological claims about Jesus' "special" intimacy with God as evinced by his use of the Hebrew term "Abba." Such claims were tidily demolished by James Barr, "Abba Isn't 'Daddy.'"
12. Fredriksen, *From Jesus to Christ*, 98–101.
13. Matthew begins his story with a genealogy that runs from Abraham, through David, to Joseph (Matthew 1.1–16), whom the angel addresses as "Son of David" (1.20). Both Joseph and Mary, a virgin (on this point

Matthew quotes Isaiah 7.14 LXX), evidently live in Bethlehem, which they flee upon learning of Herod's hostility (2.13). Hiding out in Egypt until the angel informs them of Herod's death, they avoid Bethlehem because Judea is ruled by Archelaus, Herod's son (2.22), and settle instead in Nazareth (2.23).

14. Luke offers a genealogy that runs from Joseph, through David, back to Adam (Luke 3.23–38): unsurprisingly, it does not coincide with that composed by Matthew. On Nazareth as Joseph and Mary's hometown, 2.4; on the time frame as indicating events in 6 C.E., the census (but only of Judea, not of the Galilee) under Quirinius, 2.2. Jesus is born in Bethlehem, the city of Joseph's distant ancestor David, whence the holy family returns to Nazareth (2.4, 39). Luke makes no mention of Herod, who would have been dead for a decade by the time of the Judean tax census. For a one-volume close commentary on these mutually exclusive evangelical birth narratives, see Raymond E. Brown, *The Birth of the Messiah*.

15. See Vermes's efforts to reconstruct a plausible historical context for the evolution of the virgin birth stories, *Jesus the Jew*, 213–22. For a more recent effort at reconstructing this context, Loren T. Stuckenbruck, "Conflicting Stories: The Spirit Origin of Jesus' Birth." The Davidic lineage traced through Joseph represents a different, and in a sense a competing, "Davidizing" strategy.

16. The original passage appears at Isaiah 7.1–16. Hebrew has a perfectly good word for "virgin": *beteulah*. The Hebrew of Isaiah's text, however, gives *'aalmah*, "young girl." It was the Septuagint translators who for some reason chose to use *parthenos*, "virgin," in their Greek text, even though Greek has a perfectly good word for "young girl," *neanis*.

17. For this reason, I am leery of the current vogue in "memory studies" in recent work on the historical Jesus. A "memory" implies the existence of something that indeed happened in the past, which is then passed on ("remembered"). Memory studies and borrowings from cognitive science seem a slippery way of sanctioning with an aura of (questionable) historicity some bit of tradition whose originary context most likely falls well after circa 30 C.E., the more-or-less consensus date of Jesus' execution. For a kinder description of these efforts, Allison, *Constructing Jesus*, 1–30.

18. Romans 1.3–4. I assume that Paul's convictions about Jesus' eschatological role—which we have seen detailed already in 1 Corinthians 15—immediately entailed Paul's presupposing Jesus' Davidic lineage. Paul's

Greek text contains no possessive pronoun ("his," Greek: *autou*) modifying "resurrection," and no preposition ("from," Greek: *ek*) modifying "the dead." The correct English rendering can thus only be "declared son of God in power by the spirit of holiness by *the* resurrection *of* the dead"—an event, Paul was convinced, that was shortly to occur. For the full argument, with texts, see Fredriksen, *Pagans' Apostle*, 133–45 and notes.

19. On Jesus' messianic defeat of cosmic powers and the establishment of the Kingdom, 1 Corinthians 15.21–28; on the specifically Davidic quality of the returning Christ's eschatological actions in this passage of 1 Corinthians, Novenson, *Christ among the Messiahs*, 146.
20. The returning Christ destroys the cosmic rulers and powers in 1 Corinthians 15.24–25; the eschatological trumpet sounds, summoning the dead, in v. 52. Christ's overwhelming martial power is evoked also in Philippians 3.21. The historical Jesus of Nazareth may have taught an ethic of passive resistance, but the eschatological warrior Christ returns armed and invincible.
21. Christ rules over the eschatological plenum of Israel in Romans 11.12 (Israel's "full inclusion") and in 11.26 ("all Israel" will be among the saved). Paul quotes Isaiah 11.4 and 10 LXX, about the Davidic messiah ruling over gentile nations, in Romans 15.12.
22. Mark 12.35–37, on the relative status of David and of the final messiah; Mark 14.61–62, on the revelation of that messiah's eschatological enthronement at God's right hand which, Jesus says at his trial, the high priest would live to see.
23. Thus, c. 200 C.E., Tertullian of Carthage will insist on Mary's own Davidic lineage, *On the Flesh of Christ*, 21.1–7.
24. Acts 2.14–36.
25. Acts 2.38, inculpating Peter's listeners.
26. Acts 2.41 gives the size of the attending crowd.
27. On Pilate's having decided to release Jesus, Acts 3.13; on the foretold suffering of the messiah, 3.18; on the distant Second Coming, 3.21; on "the Jews" repenting for the death of the messiah, 3.26.

    First Thessalonians, Paul's earliest letter (from the late 40s?), seems to support this sweeping inculpation of Jerusalem's Jews. In 2.14–16, this passage of the letter praises this gentile community for their stalwartness in the face of (undefined) persecutions from their own countrymen, "for you suffered the same things . . . as [did the Judean assemblies] from the Jews, who killed both the Lord Jesus and the prophets, and drove us out, and displease God and oppose all men by hindering us from speaking to the nations so that they may be saved—so as always to fill up the measure of their sins. But God's wrath has come upon them at last!"

For good reason, these verses have been seen as a later interpolation into Paul's letter. See especially the classic article by Birger Pearson, "1 Thessalonians" and, for a recent counterargument, Markus Bockmuehl, "1 Thessalonians." Theories of interpolation are rightly a court of last appeal, but in this case, for the reasons Pearson gives, I am persuaded. No manuscript tradition of this letter goes back before the second century, by which point—as both Matthew's gospel and Justin Martyr's *Dialogue with Trypho* confirm—the theme of intergenerational Jewish guilt (slayers of prophets; Christ-killers) is well established. And the finality of God's wrath, invoked here in the past perfect tense ("has come," v. 16) coheres effortlessly with the temple's destruction in 70. Bockmuehl casts about for other historical events in the 40s than Paul might have had in mind. His efforts are fatally weakened, in my view, by his making Paul's appearance in Corinth before Gallio the lynchpin of his argument: he relies, in other words, on Acts 18.12 to date Paul's letter to Thessalonika. On the problems inherent with this procedure, see Gregory Tatum, *New Chapters in the Life of Paul.*

28. See Fredriksen, *Pagans' Apostle*, 17–31, which briefly reviews this form of theodicy.
29. Jesus' lament occurs in Luke 19.41–44. Richard Pervo's massive commentary on Acts presupposes that Luke had access both to Paul's letters and to Josephus. If that's true, then the evangelist did not read either source carefully, since he makes a mess both of Pauline chronology in his story about Paul's apostolic call, and of Josephus' chronology around the prophetic figures of Theudas and the Egyptian. Cf., for example, Acts 5.36–37, garbling the time periods of Theudas and of Judah the Galilean, and Josephus, *AJ* 20. I agree with Pervo's dating of Acts to the early second century; but I base my opinion more on Luke's expressing later ideas and presupposing later social formations (councils of elders; organized groups of widows; the word *Christianoi*, attested only in other early second-century texts).
30. The priests ask the apostles to stop preaching from the temple court, Acts 4.1–18; the apostles decline their request, 4.19–32. Later, the priests discipline the apostles, and then let them go, 5.12–34.
31. On the charge against Stephen as tendered by false witnesses, Acts 6.13–14. On Luke's (incoherent) city-wide persecution of everyone in the

movement except for the original apostles, Acts 8.1; my emphasis. Paul's later travails with the priests occur in Acts 22.30; 23.14; 25.2, all set in the late 50s C.E., under the procuratorships of Festus, then of Albinus.

32. Luke presents a coordinated mission in Acts 8.14, 24 and 11.1–2, 22. The so-called Apostolic Council in Acts 15 also highlights this theme. Paul confers with the apostles back in Jerusalem, Galatians 1.18–19; 2.1–10.

33. On Antioch as the beginning of outreach to gentiles, Acts 11.20. We meet Saul/Paul in Acts 8.1, and he starts out from Jerusalem to Damascus in 9.2.

34. For a survey of patterns of ancient Christian apocalyptic hopes, Paula Fredriksen, "Apocalypse and Redemption in Early Christianity: From John of Patmos to Augustine of Hippo." For the period from antiquity through the Middle Ages, Richard Landes, "Lest the Millennium Be Fulfilled: Apocalyptic Expectations and the Pattern of Western Chronography, 100–800 CE." Landes extends his analysis into the twentieth century in *Heaven on Earth: The Varieties of Millennial Experience.*

35. Leon Festinger, Henry W. Riecken, and Stanley Schachter, *When Prophecy Fails: A Social and Psychological Study of a Modern Group That Predicted the Destruction of the World.* On American millenarian movements, and their thriving even after the foreseen date of the End has passed, see Stephen O'Leary, *Arguing the Apocalypse: Toward a Theory of Millennial Rhetoric* (on the Millerites, who went on to flourish as the Seventh Day Adventist church); on the mentality of Endtime movements more generally, Paul Boyer, *When Time Shall Be No More*; also Landes, *Heaven on Earth.* John Gager pioneered the application of theories of social psychology to the early Jesus movement in *Kingdom and Community.* For the ways that the Qumran group's sense of "apocalyptic" time was preserved by deadening cognitive dissonance through creative reinterpretation of prophecy, Jonathan Ben-Dov, "Apocalyptic Temporality: The Force of the Here and Now," esp. pp. 298–99.

36. Gager, *Kingdom and Community*, 21. His point is that, by modifying its prophecies, Christianity (or better, plural: various forms of Christianity) succeed, but not as millenarian movements.

37. Romans 1, on the moral chaos caused by idolatry; Romans 2–7, on the ways that Jewish law could not help gentiles to reform; Romans 8, on the ways that adoption through Christ has saved gentiles by offering them a path to righteousness apart from Jewish law. For this interpretation of Romans see Stanley K. Stowers, *A Rereading of Romans: Justice, Jews, and Gentiles*; Runar Thorsteinsson, *Paul's Interlocutor in Romans 2:*

Function and Identity in the Context of Ancient Epistolography; Fredriksen, *Pagans' Apostle*, 141–66; and the essays collected in Rafael Rodriguez and Matthew Thiessen, eds., *The So-Called Jew in Paul's Letter to the Romans.*

38. The delay of the Kingdom allowing for more time for the gentile mission, Romans 11.13–26; on Paul's travel plans to reach Spain, 15.19. He still, obviously, foresees a delay.
39. Romans 11.26, quoting Isaiah 59.20–21.
40. On this traditional sequencing of eschatological redemption—Israel first, pagans/gentiles second—see Sanders, *Jesus and Judaism*, 212–21; Paula Fredriksen, "Judaism, the Circumcision of Gentiles, and Apocalyptic Hope: Another Look at Galatians 1 and 2," at pp. 559–64.
41. That the crucifixion should function as a summons to repentance is how, I think, Jesus' death was originally conceptualized as being "for sin, in accordance with the scriptures"; 1 Corinthians 15.3.
42. On sending out the apostles, Matthew 10.5–42; cf. Luke 9.1–6.
43. "You will not have gone through all the towns of Israel"; Matthew 10.23.
44. "When I sent you out with no purse or bag or sandals, did you lack anything?" asks Luke's Jesus. "But now, let him who has a purse take it, and likewise a bag. And let him who has no knife sell his mantle and buy one"; Luke 22.35–38, my translation of *machaira* as "knife."
45. For a narrative description of Jews in pagan places (the ancient city) and pagans in Jewish places (synagogues and Jerusalem's temple), Fredriksen, *Pagans' Apostle*, 32–60. Synagogue inscriptions and various literary sources attesting to pagan benefactions to Jewish communities are conveniently gathered and translated in Irina Levinskaya, *The Book of Acts in Its First Century Setting*. Philo mentions the "interfaith" feast celebrating the translation of the scriptures into Greek in *Life of Moses* 2.41. Finally, on the (pagan) city of Apamea's coin depicting Noah's ark, Pieter van der Horst, "The Jews of Ancient Phrygia," 141.
46. Fredriksen, *Pagans' Apostle*, 85–93, on the dangers of alienating pagan gods.
47. Albert Schweitzer speculated that Jesus' "eschatological universalism forbids a mission among the Gentiles" because, according to the biblical prophetic paradigm, Israel is redeemed first, the nations thereafter. *The Mysticism of Paul the Apostle*, 178–83.
48. On the Christ movement's surprised—and surprising—generation of "eschatological gentiles" in advance of the Eschaton, Fredriksen, *Pagans' Apostle*, 73–93.

5. THE ENDS OF THE AGES

1. Acts introduces the murderously violent, persecuting Saul/Paul in 8.1 and 9.1–2. Paul himself mentions his own past as a persecutor in Galatians 1.13, 1 Corinthians 15.9, and Philippians 3.7. What he meant by "persecute" is different, as we shall see, from what Acts presents.
2. Josephus on violating the laws of charitable giving, *AJ* 4.238. On the offender's choice to submit to such a penalty, Anthony Ernest Harvey, "Forty Strokes Save One: Social Aspects of Judaizing and Apostasy," 79–86.
3. E. P. Sanders, *Paul, the Law, and the Jewish People*, 192, italics in the original; for his whole discussion, 186–92.
4. The god of Israel fights with the Egyptian gods, Exodus 12.12; God is the greatest god, Psalm 86.8; and all the other gods bow down to him, Psalm 97.7; so too Jeremiah 10.6. For more on the god-congested universe of ancient "monotheism," Fredriksen, *Pagans' Apostle*, 10–13, 38–42; also Fredriksen, "How Jewish Is God? Divine Ethnicity in Paul's Theology." See also Emma Wasserman, "Gentile Gods at the Eschaton: A Reconsideration of Paul's 'Principalities and Powers' in 1 Corinthians 15." For Paul's allusions to foreign gods (and their social agency), see too James D. G. Dunn, *The Theology of Paul the Apostle*, 33–38, 104–10.
5. Philo refers to the bodies in the heavenly firmament as "visible gods" in his commentary on Genesis, *On the Creation of the World*, 7.27. On the nations' gods as *daimonia*, Psalm 95.5 (Greek), alluded to by Paul in 1 Corinthians 10.20.
6. On the ways that diaspora Jews accommodated their pagan neighbors both human and divine, Fredriksen, *Pagans' Apostle*, 32–49; on pagan god-fearing or "Judaizing" (the voluntary assumption of some Jewish practices), 49–60.
7. Josephus narrates his youthful experiments with different "schools" of Jewishness in *Vita* 7–12. For ways of conceptualizing the Jewish adherence to the gospel message *not* as "conversion," see especially Brent Nongbri, "The Concept of Religion and the Study of the Apostle Paul," 1–26.
8. Paul complains about interference from the "god of this age," in 2 Corinthians 4.4. The former gods of his Galatian ex-pagans are merely "elemental spirits," cosmic lightweights, Galatians 4.8–9. On pagan gods as "demons," little deities, 1 Corinthians 10.20–21—though, as he says to his assembly there, everyone knows that they exist, 1 Corinthians 8.5–6 ("many gods and many lords"). These lower deities are "destroyed" in 1

Corinthians 15.24; they are rehabilitated to worship the true god once Christ returns to conquer them, Philippians 2.10–11; in Romans 8, they groan while awaiting redemption.

9. Psalm 97.7. See also Wasserman, "Gentile Gods."
10. This "law-freeness" relates only to the issue of circumcision. In terms of its demand that pagans forsake their native gods and their sacrifices before divine images ("idol worship"), the gospel quite specifically insisted on its gentiles honoring the first two of the Ten Commandments: no other gods, and no images. And the apostles' own commitment to their own Jewish ancestral customs was completely independent of pagan "policy." See Paula Fredriksen, "Why Should a 'Law-Free' Gospel Mean a 'Law-Free' Apostle?"
11. Paul sums up Romans 15.10 with this verse from Isaiah 11.10. For the ways that Isaiah's prophecies structure Paul's letter, see esp. Wagner, *Heralds of the Good News*.
12. Philip's adventures are related in Acts 8.26–40.
13. The story of Cornelius appears in Acts 10, briefly reprised in 11.5–17. It's confusingly presented—Peter baptizes Cornelius; he doesn't "rise and eat" him—but this vignette does a nice job of expressing a certain hesitancy that may well have accompanied the movement's initial incorporation of gentiles. For an illuminating consideration of Acts 10, see Matthew Thiessen, *Contesting Conversion*, esp. 124–31.
14. These debates over criteria of admission for gentiles occur in Acts 11.2 and 15.1–5; their charismatic acts resolve the issue, 15.8.
15. Paul's lush intra-apostolic trash talk may be found at Galatians 2.4, 12–13; Philippians 3.2; and 2 Corinthians 5.13–14.
16. Paul relates his version of the argument with Peter in Antioch at Galatians 2.11–14. Oceans of ink have been spilled over the interpretation of this passage and the situation of community meals implied there. For my best guess, see *Pagans' Apostle*, 94–105.
17. As Schweitzer noted long ago, "The fact that even the second [Christian] generation does not know what to make of his [Paul's] teaching suggests the conjecture that he built his system upon a conviction which ruled only in the first generation. But what was it that disappeared out of the first Christian generation? What but the expectation of the immediate dawn of the messianic kingdom of Jesus?" *Mysticism of Paul*, 39.
18. The later deutero-Pauline epistles, for example, 1 and 2 Timothy and Titus, do present such ordered and organized communities.
19. On "Hellenists" and "Hebrews," Acts 6.1–6; on the Jerusalem "persecution" as the springboard for the diaspora mission, 11.20.

20. This Greek synagogue inscription, found in Jerusalem near the Temple Mount, reads: "Theodotos the son of Vettenus, priest and ruler of the synagogue, son of a ruler of the synagogue, son's son of a ruler of the synagogue, built the synagogue for the reading of the Law and for the teaching of the commandments; also the strangers' lodging and the chambers and the conveniences of waters for an inn for them that need it from abroad, of which [synagogue] his fathers and the elders and Simonides did lay the foundation." The text and translation of this inscription is available in Anders Runesson, Donald D. Binder, and Birger Olsson, eds., *The Ancient Synagogue from Its Origins to 200 C.E.: A Source Book*, no. 26, 52–54. Greek-speaking Jews on pilgrimage from abroad, in other words, could avail themselves of the synagogue's amenities, as well as hear "instruction" in the Law and the commandments, presumably in their vernacular Greek.
21. Galatians 1.17–18, for Paul's wanderings between receiving his revelation and finally going to Jerusalem to speak with Peter.
22. For a wonderfully clear orientation in this tangle of religio-political divine-human relations, see Michael Peppard, *The Son of God in the Roman World: Divine Sonship in Its Social and Political Contexts.* Mediterranean intercity diplomacy was conducted by determining genealogies that traced back to shared divine-human couplings, on which the elegant essay by Christopher P. Jones, *Kinship Diplomacy in the Ancient World.*
23. On Augustus's subvention of these sacrifices in Jerusalem's temple, see Philo, *Embassy to Gaius*, 317.
24. Ibid., 188.
25. *AJ* 18.264, 271.
26. The story about Gaius and Petronius—one of Josephus' great cliff-hangers—is told in *BJ* 2.203 and in *AJ* 18.305–7.
27. *Embassy to Gaius*, 214–17, on the danger of a general Jewish revolt.
28. Daniel 9.27; 11.31; 12.11.
29. On "one like a son of man," Daniel 7.13–14. The archangel Michael appears in order to win battles at 12.1; resurrection and judgment soon follow, 12.2. On the words sealed until the end of time, 12.9, cf. v. 4, emphasis mine.
30. A resonance sounds between Daniel's imagery and Paul's language in 1 Thessalonians 4.15–17. "Those who have fallen asleep . . . [will rise when] the Lord will descend from heaven with a cry of command, with the archangel's call"—the archangel Michael, Daniel 12.1?—"and the sound of the trumpet of God." At that point, both the living and the dead, says

Paul, "will be caught up together in the clouds to meet the Lord in the air" (v. 17). Daniel 7.13–14 famously speaks of "one like a son of man" before God's throne, "with the clouds of heaven," who was given universal dominion. Paul nowhere uses the phrase "son of man" for Jesus; but the clouds, the archangel, the resurrection, and the eschatological dominion that feature in 1 Thessalonians 4 for the returning Jesus seem to me to echo these same themes from Daniel. And this letter was composed only a few years after the incident with Caligula. These are observations, not an argument. Still valuable are the remarks of Donald H. Juel, *Messianic Exegesis: Christological Interpretation of the Old Testament in Early Christianity*, 151–70.

31. On the desolating sacrilege where it should not be, Mark 13.14. Josephus reports the Roman sacrifices on the Temple Mount in *BJ* 6.316. In two essays, N. H. Taylor also speculated that Caligula's efforts made their mark on the Christ-assembly in Jerusalem, and on Mark, "Palestinian Christianity and the Caligula Crisis," parts I and II; but since he assumes these followers to be antitemple, he construes Caligula's effect quite differently from the way that I do here.
32. Mark 13.1–4.
33. Mark 13.5–10, the last verse specifically on the mission to the Diaspora that will necessarily precede the End.
34. On the coming son of man (that is, the triumphant returning Jesus), Mark 13.26–27, cf. 8.38; on "this generation" not passing away before Jesus returns—a period bridging the generation of 30 C.E. and of 70 C.E.—Mark 13.30; on waiting and watching, 13.37. See too Fredriksen, *Jesus of Nazareth*, 78–89.
35. Acts 12.1–4.
36. Luke narrates Peter's escape and the execution of his guards in Acts 12.6–19. Agrippa's death occurs shortly thereafter, 12.20–23. (Josephus offers a similar tale, *AJ* 19.343–52). Nothing like an explanation complicates Luke's story: We are left to guess why and how James and Peter strayed into Agrippa's crosshairs. Royal agency, and James's manner of execution—beheaded by a Jewish king, a fate similar to John the Baptizer's under Antipas—suggests that the problem was political, not religious as such. (Antipas, recall, had been anxious about the possibility of John's inciting sedition.) Had James's offense been religious, we would expect Luke to say what that was; we would expect the Sanhedrin to be somehow involved; and we would expect James's manner of execution, like Stephen's, to be by stoning. Peter's unexplained arrest and miraculous escape simply account

for his leaving the city, whence he goes, vaguely, "to another place" (Acts 12.17). Chapter 12 of Acts at least gets us on a timeline: these things occurred before and close to Agrippa's death in 44 C.E.

37. Following Jesus' prediction of the temple's utter destruction, Peter, James, John, and Andrew ask, "When will this be, and what will be the sign when these things are all to be accomplished?," Mark 13.4.
38. Compare Mark 13.14 with Luke's parallel, 21.20.
39. Josephus relates this material in *AJ* 17.273, 278–82, and, for Athrognes, 17.271–72.
40. *AJ* 17.278.
41. On John of Gishala, *BJ* 4.390, cf 4.389: John acted like a "tyrant"; Menachem, *BJ* 2.434, 441–42; cf. 4.510; Simon bar Giora, *BJ* 4.510, cf. 7.154–55. See too Novenson's sharp analysis of these passages, *Grammar of Messianism*, 141–42.
42. This is Novenson's excellent observation. I quote him here: "By using readily intelligible Greek terms for what insurrectionists do ('grasping for the kingship,' 'wearing the diadem'), Josephus makes their activities more clear, not less so, for his Roman patrons. . . . [H]e effectively translates the rebels' native revolutionary rhetoric ('stars,' 'scepters,' 'messiahs') into gentile vernacular ('diadems,' 'kings,' 'tyrants'). *That is, he translates messiah language into a Roman idiom.*" *Grammar of Messianism*, 145; emphasis mine.
43. On the "ambiguous" messianic oracle, *BJ* 6.312–13.
44. Romans 15.12, citing Isaiah 11.10.
45. Tacitus, *Histories* 5.13, 2; Suetonius, *Vespasian* 4.5; texts and translations, with notes, in Stern, *Greek and Latin Authors on Jews and Judaism*, nos. 281 and 312.
46. Novenson's observation, *Grammar of Messianism*, 144.
47. On Theudas, *AJ* 20.97–98; on the unnamed charismatic figures, *BJ* 2.259; cf. *AJ* 20.168; on the Egyptian prophet, *BJ* 2.261–63; *AJ* 20.170. Luke's chronology is confused, Acts 5.36–37, Theudas and Judah the Galilean; 21.38, the Egyptian.
48. On Theudas, cf. Exodus 14.16ff. and Joshua 3.13–14; on the Egyptian, cf. Joshua 6.20.
49. Josephus on John the Baptizer, *AJ* 18.116–19.
50. On Paul's return to Jerusalem, Acts 21.11, 18.
51. Acts 21.21, the (false) accusations against Paul; 28.14, Paul arrives in Rome. In 24.5, Tertullus refers to the community back in Jerusalem as "Nazarenes."

52. Josephus tells of James's death—and of its consequences for Ananus—in *AJ* 20.199–201.
53. Paul refers to bringing the collection to Jerusalem in Romans 15.25.
54. Paul invokes Isaiah 59.20, the "Redeemer will come from Zion," in Romans 11.26; earlier, he had recalled for his community in Corinth that the "ends of the ages" had already come upon them, 1 Corinthians 10.11.
55. Josephus describes Eleazar's actions in *BJ* 2.409–10.
56. Josephus begins his description of the siege of Jotapata in *BJ* 3.141; the walls are breached, though resistance continues, *BJ* 3.251–52; Josephus, captured, prophesies Vespasian's imperial ascent, *BJ* 3.399–408.
57. On the lugubrious prophet Jesus, *BJ* 6.300–309; on Josephus' efforts to coax the city to surrender, *BJ* 6.96–99.
58. Josephus relates the story of the refuge on the colonnade, *BJ* 6.283–86.

EPILOGUE

1. For a recent assessment about traditions that locate the deaths of Peter and of Paul in Rome, see Brent Shaw, "The Myth of the Neronian Persecution," 93–94.
2. Antiquity produced a rich assortment of apocryphal gospels and acts of various apostles. Paul in particular becomes teamed with an unforgettable female sidekick, Thekla. These "adventures of the apostles" are available in English translation in Hennecke and Schneemelcher, *New Testament Apocrypha*.

   Modern scholarship on the first generation has been no less fecund. Of recent work, outstanding is James Dunn's history, *Beginning from Jerusalem*. Weighing in at over 1,340 pages, Dunn's book is literally a monument to the scholarly abhorrence of a vacuum. To my knowledge, his is the lengthiest single study. Stuffed full of interesting information, gleanings from other ancient sources, and collegial engagement with the huge polyglot secondary literature, *Beginning from Jerusalem* is a marvelous assemblage of learning; but essentially, Dunn retells the story offered by Luke. The present study, by contrast, looks to reconstruct the stages that led up to—and are suppressed beneath—Luke's narrative.
3. All current work on the historical Jesus situates Jesus within a first-century Jewish context. Many then account for his mission and, ultimately, his crucifixion, by claiming that Jesus found something wrong with contemporary Jewish practices (be these purity laws, temple sacrifices, Sabbath observances, kosher food laws, or whatever—all those ancestral

practices, in other words, that define "ancient Judaism"). For an incisive (and wry) analysis of NT scholars' construction of a "Jewish, but not *too* Jewish Jesus," the work of James G. Crossley, esp. "A 'Very Jewish' Jesus: Perpetuating the Myth of Superiority," and his opening chapter in *Jesus and the Chaos of History*; further, and enriched by the intertext of *Life of Brian*, see his "Meaning of Monty Python's Jesus."

The so-called "New Perspective on Paul" suffers from this same complex of insistence (on Paul's deep Jewishness) and denial (but not *that* Jewish). Paul was *very* Jewish; he just didn't like Torah observance, circumcision, kashrut, or ethnic boundary markers very much. For analysis of this scholarly school, see Mark Chancey's new introduction to the fortieth anniversary edition of E. P. Sanders's epochal *Paul and Palestinian Judaism*. Finally, for the inclusion of gentiles in God's Kingdom as a traditional aspect of Jewish eschatological expectations, Terence L. Donaldson, *Judaism and the Gentiles: Jewish Patterns of Universalism (to 135 CE)*; reading Romans as Paul's manifesto of this view, Krister Stendahl, *Final Account: Paul's Letter to the Romans*.

4. E. P. Sanders has articulated this idea of "common Judaism" in his many publications, most compellingly in *Judaism: Practice and Belief*. Assenting, Martin Goodman explores the rhythms of practical diversity and enduring identity in *A History of Judaism*.
5. On the ways that Paul in particular witnesses to this "Davidization," see esp. Novenson, *Christ among the Messiahs*; for the gospel writers as well as Paul, Fredriksen, "'Are You A Virgin?' Biblical Exegesis and the Invention of Tradition." On the kerygmatic freight carried by Mark's use of "son of man," Fredriksen, *From Jesus to Christ*, 44–52.

Scholarship on the phrase "son of man" cycles like a fever through work on the New Testament. Awkward in Greek but good Aramaic, it has a claim to serving as Jesus of Nazareth's own third-person self-designation, a periphrastic "I," on which see esp. Vermes, *Jesus the Jew*, 160–91. The phrase, alas, appears nowhere in Paul (much to my regret: had Paul used it in 1 Thessalonians 4, I could have made a stronger case for Caligula's effect on early Christology). In Mark, "son of man" carries a lot of narrative freight, driving Jesus' two-cycle advent as Suffering Son (in the run-up to the crucifixion) and Victorious Son (at the Parousia). The phrase also appears in John's gospel, and in the material shared by Matthew and Luke that is not in Mark (the so-called "Q" source). Its multiple attestation suggests that the phrase entered tradition early, perhaps with Jesus himself. But all of our *evidence* for all of these sources (including the elusive Q) falls well after 40, the year of Caligula's death. Indeed, except for Paul's letters, all our evidence comes from the period after 70.

In brief: The amount of secondary scholarship on "the son of man" is simply staggering. For a heroically concise bird's-eye survey of this scholarly terrain and of the questions perennially shaping it (though only up to the year 2010!), see Allison, *Constructing Jesus*, 293–304, especially the (very) fine print in his notes.

6. Romans 13.8–10 invokes the second table of the Ten Commandments; 1 Corinthians 7.19 and Galatians 5.14 urge observance of Law. Paul pronounces the Law as holy and the commandments as good in Romans 7.12, and praises the giving of the law and the enactment of its cult in Jerusalem in Romans 9.4–5. For the ways that Paul shares this emphasis on the Ten Commandments with John the Baptizer and with Jesus, see Fredriksen, *Sin*, 6–49 and notes. A movement to construe Paul within, as opposed to "against," Judaism is now a plainly visible part of the scholarly landscape: see Fredriksen, *Pagans' Apostle*, and the works cited *infra* 176 for just a sampling; also the gathering of Mark Nanos's many articles in the several volumes of *Reading Paul within Judaism*.
7. Philo, *Life of Moses* 1.158, with reference to Exodus 20.21; Origen on David and Paul as *dii*, *Commentary on Romans* II.10, 18. On the elasticity of ancient divinity, see further Fredriksen, *Pagans' Apostle*, 144–45 and 241 n. 29; on the theological ramifications of this ancient cosmic architecture, ibid., 39–41.
8. See Philippians 2.6–7; the superhuman knees of lower divinities bend in 2.10. On Jesus as a divine mediator, 1 Corinthians 8.6; as a human being (*anthrōpos*), though "from heaven," 1 Corinthians 15.46. Further on this interpretation of Philippians, Fredriksen, *Pagans' Apostle*, 133–45. On the continuing divinity of Christian emperors and their cults, which perdured long after Constantine, esp. Douglas Boin, "Late Antique *Divi* and Imperial Priests in the Late Fourth and Early Fifth Centuries."
9. Galatians 2.11–14 confusingly relates their dispute; for one attempt to untangle it, *Pagans' Apostle*, 94–110.
10. Reviled as "false brothers" by Paul in Galatians 2.4, and as "mutilators" in Philippians 3.2. Paul describes his and James's "fellowship" on this issue—namely, that gentiles-in-Christ need not be circumcised—in Galatians 2.7–10. The men from James who roil table fellowship in Antioch (2.11–13) seem concerned about food (whether the menu or the venue), not about circumcision. On the Jewish mission to circumcise gentiles as a

midcentury innovation internal to the Jesus movement, Fredriksen, "Judaism, the Circumcision of Gentiles, and Apocalyptic Hope"; and *Pagans' Apostle*, 100–108; further, Matthew Thiessen, *Paul and the Gentile Problem*.

11. On God's irrevocable promises, Romans 11.29; on the "fullness of the gentiles" (that is, all seventy nations) and "all Israel" (the eschatologically reassembled twelve tribes), 11.25–26; see too 15.8–12, where the nations rejoice with God's people. Wagner explores these great themes from Isaiah in *Heralds*; much more briefly, Fredriksen, *Pagans' Apostle*, 159–64 and notes.

12. Eusebius (early fourth century) relates this tradition in *Church History* 3.5, 2–3; so also Epiphanius, *Panarion* 29.7, 7–8. For a scholarly assessment and historical *mise-en-scène*, see William Horbury, "Beginnings of Christianity in the Holy Land;" see also Jonathan Bourgel, "The Jewish Christians' Move from Jerusalem as a Pragmatic Choice."

13. Jerome, *Letter* 75.4, 13, addressed to Augustine (in the Augustinian notation). Faustus's complaint is preserved in Augustine, *Against Faustus*, 19.3.

The term "Jewish-Christian" has been the subject, recently, of much critical scholarly reflection, though attention focuses not on the first generation of Jesus-followers, but on the later period of late antiquity. See especially Matt Jackson McCabe, *Jewish Christianity Reconsidered*; James Carleton Paget, *Jews, Christians, and Jewish Christians in Antiquity*; and Annette Yoshiko Reed, *Jewish Christianity and the History of Judaism*.

Finally, and to the more haunting question: Why and how does anti-Judaism become so constitutive of later, gentile Christian identity? For the formative Roman period, Paula Fredriksen, *Augustine and the Jews: A Christian Defense of Jews and Judaism*, 41–102 and 213–375. For the three-thousand-year history of the ways that these dynamics still define the modern West—"Judaism" as "a category, a set of ideas and attributes with which non-Jews can make sense of and criticize their world" (p. 3)—David Nirenberg's panoramic and morally lucid study, *Anti-Judaism: The Western Tradition*.

BIBLIOGRAPHY

PRIMARY SOURCES

JEWISH AND EARLY CHRISTIAN TEXTS

I cite biblical texts (both OT and NT) and Apocrypha according to the Oxford Annotated RSV or NRSV; otherwise, where noted, I translate the texts myself.

The Jewish Annotated New Testament, 2nd ed., ed. Marc Brettler and Amy-Jill Levine (New York: Oxford University Press, 2017), offers the NRSV translation together with a rich assortment of commentary and short, informative essays on the Jewish matrix of the Jesus movement as it is represented in the New Testament.

The Greek text of Jewish scriptures is conveniently available in *The Septuagint* (Grand Rapids, MI: Zondervan, 1970). For the Greek and the Latin of the NT texts, *Novum Testamentum Graece et Latine*, ed. Eberhard Nestle and Kurt Aland (Stuttgart: Deutsche Bibelgesellschaft, 1984).

The Old Testament Pseudepigrapha, 2 vols., ed. James H. Charlesworth (New York: Doubleday, 1985), conveniently offers English translations: of *Enoch* in 1: 5–89, and of *Jubilees*, in 2: 35–42.

For texts from Qumran, see *The Dead Sea Scrolls in English*, trans. Geza Vermes, 3rd ed. (Harmondsworth: Penguin Books, 1987). A universe of texts, translations, and academic essays on this ancient library is now available through the website of the Orion Center at the Hebrew University, Jerusalem.

Philo of Alexandria's works are collected, translated, and well indexed in the Loeb Classical Library, 10 vols., and 2 supplementary vols. (Cambridge, MA: Harvard University Press, 1929–36). Josephus, likewise: Loeb Classical Library, 10 vols. (Cambridge, MA: Harvard University Press, 1927–65).

Two convenient and very well-organized compendia of Jewish inscriptions translated into English are available in *Jews among the Greeks and Romans: A Diasporan Sourcebook*, ed. and trans. Margaret Williams (Baltimore: Johns Hopkins University Press, 1998); and in Irina Levinskaya, *The Book of Acts in Its Diaspora Setting* (Grand Rapids, MI: Eerdmans, 1996).

For classical writers Pliny the Elder, Suetonius, and Tacitus, who comment on Judea in the early Roman period, see *Greek and Latin Authors on Jews and Judaism*, 3 vols., ed. and trans. Menachem Stern (Jerusalem: Dorot Press, 1986).

LATER ANCIENT CHRISTIAN TEXTS

Augustine. *Against Faustus*. Trans. Roland J. Teske. Hyde Park, NY: New City Press, 2007.

——. *City of God*. Trans. Henry Bettenson. New York: Penguin Books, 1972.

——. *Eighty-Three Different Questions*. Trans. David Mosher. Fathers of the Church 70. Washington, DC: Catholic University Press of America, 1982.

——. *Propositions from the Epistle to the Romans* and *Unfinished Commentary on the Epistle to the Romans*. Ed. and trans. Paula Fredriksen. Chico, CA: Scholars Press, 1982.

Eusebius. *The History of the Church from Christ to Constantine*. Trans. G. A. Williamson. Rev. and ed. Andrew Louth. New York: Penguin Books, 1989.

New Testament Apocrypha. Ed. and trans. E. Hennecke and W. Schneemelcher. 2 vols. Philadelphia: Westminster Press, 1963–64. This collection contains the apocryphal "adventures of the apostles" and other important later Christian stories (such as the perils of St. Thekla).

Origen. *Commentaire sur l'Épître aux Romains*. 4 vols. Ed. C. H. Bammel. Trans. Luc Brésard. Sources chrétiennes. Paris: Les Éditions du Cerf, 2009–12.

——. *Commentary on the Epistle to the Romans*. 2 vols. Trans. Thomas P. Scheck. Washington, DC: Catholic University of America Press, 2001–2.

Tertullian. *On the Flesh of Christ.* Ed. and trans. as *Tertullian's Treatise on the Incarnation,* by Ernest Evans. London: SPCK, 1956.

SELECT SECONDARY BIBLIOGRAPHY

For a full bibliography of the works informing the current volume, I refer the reader to my *Paul: The Pagans' Apostle,* 255–80. Cited below are those scholarly discussions that were especially useful in framing *When Christians Were Jews.*

Allison, Dale. *Constructing Jesus.* Grand Rapids, MI: Baker Academic, 2010.

———. *Jesus of Nazareth: Millenarian Prophet.* Minneapolis: Fortress Press, 1998.

Barr, James. "Abba Isn't 'Daddy.'" *Journal of Theological Studies* 39 (1988): 28–47.

Barrett, C. K. *Jesus and the Gospel Tradition.* London: SPCK, 1967.

Becker, Adam H., and Annette Y. Reed, eds. *The Ways That Never Parted.* Tübingen: Mohr Siebeck, 2003.

Ben-Dov, Jonathan. "Apocalyptic Temporality: The Force of the Here and Now." *Hebrew Bible and Ancient Israel* 5 (2016): 289–303.

Bermejo-Rubio, Fernando. "Between Gethsemane and Golgotha; or, Who Arrested the Galilean(s)? Challenging a Deep-Rooted Assumption in New Testament Research." *Annali di Storia dell'Esegesi* 33.2 (2016): 311–39.

———. "(Why) Was Jesus the Galilean Crucified Alone? Solving a False Conundrum." *Journal of New Testament Studies* 36.2 (2013): 127–54.

Bockmuehl, Markus. "1 Thessalonians 2:14–16 and the Church in Jerusalem." *Tyndale Bulletin* 52 (2001): 1–31.

Boin, Douglas. "Late Antique *Divi* and Imperial Priests in the Late Fourth and Early Fifth Centuries." In *Pagans and Christians in Late Antique Rome,* ed. M. R. Salzman, M. Sághy, and R. L. Testa, 136–61. New York: Cambridge University Press, 2015.

Bond, Helen K. *Caiaphas: Friend of Rome and Judge of Jesus?* Louisville: Westminster John Knox Press, 2004.

———. *Pontius Pilate in History and Interpretation.* Cambridge: Cambridge University Press, 2004.

Bourgel, Jonathan. "The Jewish Christians' Move from Jerusalem as a Pragmatic Choice." In *Studies in Rabbinic Judaism and Early Christianity,* ed. Dan Jaffé, 107–38. Leiden: Brill, 2010.

Boyer, Paul. *When Time Shall Be No More.* Cambridge, MA: Harvard University Press, 1992.

Brandon, S. G. F. *Jesus and the Zealots*. New York: Charles Scribner's Sons, 1967.

Brown, Peter. *The Body and Society*. New York: Columbia University Press, 1988.

Brown, Raymond E. *The Birth of the Messiah*. New Haven: Yale University Press, 2007.

——. *The Death of the Messiah*. 2 vols. Garden City, NY: Doubleday, 1994.

Carleton Paget, James. *Jews, Christians, and Jewish Christians in Antiquity*. Tübingen: Mohr Siebeck, 2010.

Collins, John J. *The Apocalyptic Imagination*. 2nd ed. Grand Rapids, MI: Eerdmans, 1998.

——. *The Scepter and the Star: The Messiahs of the Dead Sea Scrolls and Other Ancient Literature*. New York: Doubleday, 1995.

Collins, John J., and Adela Yarbro Collins. *King and Messiah as Son of God*. Grand Rapids, MI: Eerdmans, 2008.

Crossan, John Dominic. *Who Killed Jesus? Exposing the Roots of Anti-Semitism in the Gospel Story of the Death of Jesus*. San Francisco: HarperCollins, 1998.

Crossley, James G. *Jesus and the Chaos of History*. Oxford: Oxford University Press, 2015.

——. "The Meaning of Monty Python's Jesus." In *Jesus and Brian: Exploring the Historical Jesus and His Times via Monty Python's* Life of Brian, ed. Joan E. Taylor, 69–81. London: Bloomsbury T&T Clark, 2015.

——. "A 'Very Jewish' Jesus: Perpetuating the Myth of Superiority." *Journal for the Study of the Historical Jesus* 11 (2013): 109–29.

Donaldson, Terence. *Judaism and the Gentiles: Jewish Patterns of Universalism (to 135 CE)*. Waco, TX: Baylor University Press, 2007.

Dunn, James D. G. *Beginning from Jerusalem*. Grand Rapids: Eerdmans, 2009.

——. *The Theology of Paul the Apostle*. Grand Rapids, MI: Eerdmans, 1998.

Festinger, Leon, Henry W. Riecken, and Stanley Schachter. *A Theory of Cognitive Dissonance*. Stanford, CA: Stanford University Press, 1957.

——. *When Prophecy Fails: A Social and Psychological Study of a Modern Group that Predicted the Destruction of the World*. New York: Harper & Row, 1956.

Flusser, David. *Judaism and the Origins of Christianity*. Jerusalem: Magnes Press, 1988.

Fonrobert, Charlotte Elisheva. "The *Didascalia Apostolorum:* A Mishnah for the Disciples of Jesus." *Journal of Early Christian Studies* 9.4 (2001): 483–509.

Fredriksen, Paula. "Apocalypse and Redemption in Early Christianity: From John of Patmos to Augustine of Hippo." *Vigiliae Christianae* 45 (1991): 151–83.

———. "'Are You A Virgin?' Biblical Exegesis and the Invention of Tradition." In *Jesus and Brian: Exploring the Historical Jesus and His Times via Monty Python's* Life of Brian, ed. Joan E. Taylor, 151–65. London: Bloomsbury T&T Clark, 2015.

———. "Arms and the Man: A Response to Dale Martin's 'Jesus in Jerusalem: Armed and Not Dangerous.'" *Journal for the Study of the New Testament* 37.3 (2015): 312–25.

———. *Augustine and the Jews: A Christian Defense of Jews and Judaism.* New Haven: Yale University Press, 2010.

———. "Beyond the Body/Soul Dichotomy: Augustine on Paul against the Manichees and the Pelagians." *Recherches Augustiniennes* 23 (1988): 87–114.

———. *From Jesus to Christ: The Origins of the New Testament Images of Jesus.* 2nd ed. New Haven: Yale University Press, 2000.

———. "How Jewish Is God? Divine Ethnicity in Paul's Theology." *Journal of Biblical Literature* 137.1 (2018): 193–212.

———. *Jesus of Nazareth, King of the Jews: A Jewish Life and the Emergence of Christianity.* New York: Alfred A. Knopf, 1999.

———. "Judaism, the Circumcision of Gentiles, and Apocalyptic Hope: Another Look at Galatians 1 and 2." *Journal of Theological Studies* 42 (1991): 532–64.

———. "Markan Chronology, the Scene at the Temple, and the Death of Jesus." In *New Views of First-Century Jewish and Christian Self-Definition: Essays in Honor of E. P. Sanders,* ed. Mark Chancey, Susannah Heschel, and Fabian E. Udoh, 246–82. Notre Dame, ID: University of Notre Dame Press, 2008.

———. *Paul: The Pagans' Apostle.* New Haven: Yale University Press, 2017.

———. *Sin: The Early History of an Idea.* Princeton, NJ: Princeton University Press, 2012.

———. "What You See Is What You Get: Context and Content in Current Research on the Historical Jesus." *Theology Today* 52 (1995): 75–97.

———. "Why Should a 'Law-Free' Mission Mean a 'Law-Free' Apostle?" *Journal of Biblical Literature* 134 (2015): 637–50.

Gager, John. *Kingdom and Community: The Social World of Early Christianity.* Englewood Cliffs, NJ: Prentice-Hall, 1975.

Goodman, Martin. *A History of Judaism.* Princeton, NJ: Princeton University Press, 2018.

———. *Rome and Jerusalem: A Clash of Ancient Civilizations.* New York: Vintage Books, 2008.

Gregory, Andrew. "*Acts and Christian Beginnings:* A Review Essay." *Journal for the Study of the New Testament* 39 (2016): 97–115.

Harrill, J. Albert. *Paul the Apostle: His Life and Legacy in Their Roman Context.* Cambridge: Cambridge University Press, 2012.

Harvey, Anthony Ernest. "Forty Strokes Save One: Social Aspects of Judaizing and Apostasy." In *Alternative Approaches to New Testament Study*, ed. Anthony Ernest Harvey, 79–86. London: SPCK, 1985.

Hengel, Martin. *Acts and the History of Earliest Christianity.* Philadelphia: Fortress Press, 1979.

———. *Between Jesus and Paul.* Philadelphia: Fortress Press, 1983.

Hengel, Martin, and Anna Maria Schwemer. *Paul between Damascus and Antioch: The Unknown Years.* London: SCM Press, 1997.

Horbury, William. "Beginnings of Christianity in the Holy Land." In *Christians and Christianity in the Holy Land*, ed. Ora Limor and Guy G. Stroumsa, 7–89. Turnhout: Brepols, 2006.

Irshai, Oded. "Dating the Eschaton: Jewish and Christian Apocalyptic Calculations in Late Antiquity." In *Apocalyptic Time*, ed. A. Baumgarten, 113–53. Leiden: Brill, 2000.

Jones, Christopher P. *Kinship Diplomacy in the Ancient World.* Cambridge, MA: Harvard University Press, 1999.

Juel, Donald H. *Messianic Exegesis: Christological Interpretation of the Old Testament in Early Christianity.* Philadelphia: Fortress Press, 1988.

Kermode, Frank. *The Genesis of Secrecy: On the Interpretation of Narrative.* Cambridge, MA: Harvard University Press, 1979.

Landes, Richard. *Heaven on Earth: The Varieties of Millennial Experience.* New York: Oxford University Press, 2011.

———. "Lest the Millennium Be Fulfilled: Apocalyptic Expectations and the Pattern of Western Chronography 100–800 CE." In *The Use and Abuse of Eschatology in the Middle Ages*, ed. Werner Verbeke, Daniel Verhelst, and Andries Welkenhuysen, 137–211. Louvain: Leuven University Press, 1988.

Levenson, Jon D. *Resurrection and the Restoration of Israel.* New Haven: Yale University Press, 2006.

Levinskaya, Irina. *The Book of Acts in Its First Century Setting.* Vol. 5, *Diaspora Setting.* Grand Rapids, MI: Eerdmans, 1996.

Lincicum, David. "F. C. Baur's Place in the Study of Jewish Christianity." In *The Rediscovery of Jewish Christianity: From Toland to Baur*, ed. F. Stanley Jones, 137–66. Atlanta: Society of Biblical Literature, 2012.

Ma, John. "Relire les *Institutions des Séleucides* de Bikerman." In *Rome, a City and Its Empire in Perspective: The Impact of the Roman World through Fergus Millar's Research*, 59–84. Leiden: Brill, 2012.

Martin, Dale. *The Corinthian Body*. New Haven: Yale University Press, 1995.

——. "Jesus in Jerusalem: Armed but Not Dangerous." *Journal for the Study of the New Testament* 34.1 (2014): 3–24.

Mason, Steve. *Josephus and the New Testament*. 2nd ed. Grand Rapids, MI: Baker Academic Publishing, 2003.

McCabe, Matt Jackson. *Jewish Christianity Reconsidered*. Minneapolis: Fortress Press, 2007.

Meeks, Wayne. "The Stranger from Heaven in Johannine Sectarianism." *Journal of Biblical Literature* 91 (1972): 44–72.

Meier, John P. *Law and Love*. Vol. 4 of A *Marginal Jew*. New Haven: Yale University Press, 2009.

——. *Mentor, Message, and Miracles*. Vol. 2 of A *Marginal Jew*. New Haven: Yale University Press, 1994.

Mimouni, Simon Claude. *Jacques le Juste, frère de Jésus de Nazareth*. Montrouge: Bayard, 2015.

Morgan, Teresa. *Roman Faith and Christian Faith:* Pistis *and* Fides *in the Early Roman Empire and Early Churches*. Oxford: Oxford University Press, 2015.

Myllykoski, Matti. "James the Just in History and Tradition: Perspectives of Past and Present Scholarship (Part I)." *Currents in Biblical Research* 5.1 (2006): 73–122.

——. "James the Just in History and Tradition: Perspectives of Past and Present Scholarship (Part II)." *Currents in Biblical Research* 6.1 (2007): 11–98.

Nanos, Mark D. *Reading Corinthians and Philippians within Judaism*. Vol. 4 of *Collected Essays of Mark D. Nanos*. Eugene, OR: Cascade, 2017.

——. *Reading Galatians within Judaism*. Vol. 3 of *Collected Essays of Mark D. Nanos*. Eugene, OR: Cascade, 2018.

——. *Reading Paul within Judaism*. Vol. 1 of *Collected Essays of Mark D. Nanos*. Eugene, OR: Cascade, 2017.

——. *Reading Romans within Judaism*. Vol. 2 of *Collected Essays of Mark D. Nanos*. Eugene, OR: Cascade, 2018.

Nirenberg, David. *Anti-Judaism: The Western Tradition*. New York: W. W. Norton, 2013.

Nongbri, Brent. "The Concept of Religion and the Study of the Apostle Paul." *Journal of the Jesus Movement in Its Jewish Setting* 2 (2015): 1–26.

Novenson, Matthew. *Christ among the Messiahs*. New York: Oxford University Press, 2012.

——. *The Grammar of Messianism: An Ancient Jewish Political Idiom and Its Users*. New York: Oxford University Press, 2017.

——. "The Messiah ben Abraham in Galatians: A Response to Joel Willitts." *Journal for the Study of Paul and His Letters* 2 (2012): 163–69.

O'Leary, Stephen. *Arguing the Apocalypse: Toward a Theory of Millennial Rhetoric*. New York: Oxford University Press, 1994.

Pearson, Birger A. "1 Thessalonians 2:13–16: A Deutero-Pauline Interpolation." *Harvard Theological Review* 64 (1971): 79–94.

Peppard, Michael. *The Son of God in the Roman World: Divine Sonship in Its Social and Political Contexts*. New York: Oxford University Press, 2011.

Pervo, Richard I. *Acts*. Hermeneia Commentaries. Minneapolis: Fortress Press, 2009.

Rebillard, Éric. "Missionaries, Pious Merchants, Freelance Religious Experts, and the Spread of Christianity." In *Subjects of Empire*. Cambridge: Cambridge University Press, forthcoming 2018.

Reed, Annette Yoshiko. *Jewish Christianity and the History of Judaism*. Tübingen: Mohr Siebeck, 2017.

Richardson, Peter. *Building Jewish in the Roman East*. Waco, TX: Baylor University Press, 2004.

——. *Herod: King of the Jews and Friend of the Romans*. Columbia, SC: University of South Carolina Press, 1996.

Rodriguez, Rafael, and Matthew Thiessen, eds. *The So-Called Jew in Paul's Letter to the Romans*. Minneapolis, MN: Fortress Press, 2016.

Runesson, Anders, Donald D. Binder, and Birger Olsson, eds. *The Ancient Synagogue from Its Origins to 200 C.E.: A Source Book*. Leiden: Brill, 2008.

Sanders, E. P. *The Historical Figure of Jesus*. London: Allen Lane, Penguin Books, 1993.

——. *Jesus and Judaism*. London: SCM, 1985.

——. "Jewish Association with Gentiles and Galatians 2:11–14." In *The Conversation Continues: Studies in Paul & John in Honor of J. Louis Martyn*, ed. Robert T. Fortna and Beverly R. Gaventa, 170–88. Nashville, TN: Abingdon Press, 1990.

———. *Jewish Law from Jesus to the Mishnah: Five Studies*. London: SCM, 1990.

———. *Judaism: Practice and Belief, 63 BCE–66 CE*. Philadelphia: Trinity Press International, 1992.

———. *Paul: The Apostle's Life, Letters and Thought*. Minneapolis: Fortress Press, 2015.

———. *Paul: A Very Short Introduction*. Oxford: Oxford University Press, 1991.

———. *Paul and Palestinian Judaism: A Comparison of Patterns of Religion*. 2nd ed. Minneapolis: Fortress Press, 2017.

———. *Paul, the Law, and the Jewish People*. Philadelphia: Fortress Press, 1983.

Schweitzer, Albert. *The Mysticism of Paul the Apostle*. Trans. William Montgomery, with an introduction by Jaroslav Pelikan. Baltimore: Johns Hopkins University Press, 1998. First published New York: Henry Holt, 1931.

———. *The Quest of the Historical Jesus*. Ed. John Bowden. Trans. William Montgomery. Minneapolis: Fortress Press, 2001. Originally published as *Geschichte der Leben-Jesu-Forschung*. Tübingen: J. C. B. Mohr, 1906.

Scott, James M. *Paul and the Nations: The Old Testament and Jewish Background of Paul's Mission to the Nations with Special Reference to the Destination of Galations*. WUNT 1, 84. Tübingen: Mohr Siebeck, 1995.

Shaw, Brent. "The Myth of the Neronian Persecution." *Journal of Roman Studies* 105 (2015): 73–100.

Skarsaune, Oscar, and Reidar Hvalvik, ed. *Jewish Believers in Jesus*. Peabody, MA: Hendrickson Publishers, 2007.

Smith, Moody D. *John among the Gospels*. 2nd ed. Columbia: University of South Carolina Press, 2001.

Smith, Morton. "What Is Implied by the Variety of Messianic Figures?" *Journal of Biblical Literature* 78 (1959): 66–72.

Stendahl, Krister. *Final Account: Paul's Letter to the Romans*. Minneapolis: Fortress Press, 1995.

Stowers, Stanley K. A *Rereading of Romans: Justice, Jews, and Gentiles*. New Haven: Yale University Press, 1994.

Stuckenbruck, Loren T. "Conlicting Stories: The Spirit Origins of Jesus' Birth." In *The Myth of the Rebellious Angels. Studies in Second Temple Judaism and New Testament Texts*, 142–60. Grand Rapids, MI: William B. Eerdmans Publishing Company, 2017.

Tatum, Gregory. *New Chapters in the Life of Paul: The Relative Chronology of His Career*. Washington, DC: Catholic Biblical Association of America, 2006.

Taylor, N. H. "Palestinian Christianity and the Caligula Crisis. Part 1, Social and Historical Reconstruction." *Journal for the Study of the New Testament* 61 (1996): 101–24.

———. "Palestinian Christianity and the Caligula Crisis. Part 2, The Markan Eschatological Discourse." *Journal for the Study of the New Testament* 62 (1996): 13–41.

Thiessen, Matthew. *Contesting Conversion*. New York: Oxford University Press, 2011.

———. *Paul and the Gentile Problem*. New York: Oxford University Press, 2016.

Thorsteinsson, Runar. *Paul's Interlocutor in Romans 2: Function and Identity in the Context of Ancient Epistolography*. Coniectanea Biblica New Testament Series 40. Stockholm: Almqvist and Wiksell, 2003.

van der Horst, Pieter. "The Jews of Ancient Phrygia." In *Studies in Ancient Judaism and Early Christianity*, 134–42. Leiden: Brill, 2014.

van Henten, Jan Willem. "The Hasmonean Period." In *Redemption and Resistance: The Messianic Hopes of Jews and Christians in Antiquity*, ed. M. Bockmuehl and J. Carleton Paget, 15–28. London: T&T Clark, 2009.

Vermes, Geza. *Jesus the Jew*. Philadelphia: Fortress Press, 1973.

———. *The True Herod*. London: Bloomsbury, 2014.

Wagner, J. Ross. *Heralds of the Good News: Isaiah and Paul "In Concert" in the Letter to the Romans*. Supplements to Novum Testamentum 101. Leiden: Brill, 2002.

Wasserman, Emma. *Apocalypse as Holy War: Divine Politics and Polemics in the Letters of Paul*. New Haven: Yale University Press, 2018.

———. "Gentile Gods at the Eschaton: A Reconsideration of Paul's 'Principalities and Powers' in 1 Corinthians 15." *Journal of Biblical Literature* 136.3 (2017): 727–46.

Wedderburn, J. M. *A History of the First Christians*. London: T&T Clark, 2004.

Weiss, Johannes. *Jesus' Proclamation of the Kingdom*. Philadelphia: Fortress Press, 1971. Original publication, Göttingen, 1892.

Winter, Paul. *On the Trial of Jesus*. Rev. ed., ed. T. A. Burkill and G. Vermes. Berlin: De Gruyter, 1974.

Zetterholm, Karin Hedner. "Jesus-Oriented Visions of Judaism in Antiquity." *Jewish Studies in the Nordic Countries Today: Scripta Instituti Donneriani Aboensis* 27 (2016): 37–60.

Zetterholm, Magnus, ed. *The Messiah in Early Judaism and Christianity*. Minneapolis: Fortress Press, 2007.

Names and Places

Ancient Documents and Authors

OLD TESTAMENT

NEW TESTAMENT

JEWISH TEXTS

Subjects